UP AND RUNNING

Adventures of Software Entrepreneurs

Charles "Ed" Sherman

Editor: Monet Thomson
Text design: Thomas Clark
Cover design: D.A. Gray
Illustrations: Lilo Kilstein
Photography: Gary Kildall by Andree Abecassis Photography
 Larry Dingus and Carolynn Shannon Jenkins by Sybil Shannon
 Mitchell Kapor by Fay Foto Service, Inc.
 Larry Byrnes and Larry Wilber by Naomi Lasdon
 Helen Warn by Roger Brooks Architectural Photographer
 Charles, Debbie and Glenn Teslar by Saaye Photo Studio

ASHTON·TATE ■

TABLE OF CONTENTS

TABLE OF CONTENTS

DEDICATION

to adventurers

The dictionary says "adventure" is the undertaking of risks. The great mythological adventures—such as those of Jason, Sinbad, or Ahab—express the spiritual essence of pitting oneself against fate on a quest beyond the frontiers. Even in ancient days the term "adventure" was understood to include a pioneering commercial enterprise like the adventures of Marco Polo or any of the other great international traders, businessmen and plunderers who entrepreneurialized their frontiers to lay the foundation for the modern world, such as it is. Their descendants in spirit would include the likes of Cecil Rhodes, J.P. Morgan, the Rockefellers, the DuPonts, Kellogg, Henry Ford, and Thomas Watson.

Herein lie the tales of our current crop of questers, the microcompu-ter software adventurers, represented by the founders of Microsoft, Digital Research, Lotus, VisiCorp, Softsel and more than two dozen other entrepreneurs who tell their own tales in these pages. This book is dedicated to them all, and to all of those that they represent, for shaping one of the grandest adventures of our times.

Here's hoping that you will have a small adventure of your own as you explore their experiences. This book is dedicated to you, too, for without *you* where would *they* be?

PREFACE

In 1979, Tom West's group at Data General got the prototype of the powerful new Eagle minicomputer up and running, and later his story became the subject of Tracy Kidder's prize-winning book, *Soul Of A New Machine*. But 1979 is also when the microcomputer industry really got up and running, bringing computer power to the people and the promise of a great new renaissance. And 1979 is the year that the mind of the new machine—the software—finally matured and got up and running as an industry.

In the world of the big mainframes and minicomputers, one of those pricey, hand-tailored programs is up and running when it finally works without bugs; but a mass-produced, off-the-rack microcomputer program is not up and running as a product until it has a publishing company that is also up and running and capable of carrying it onto the mass market. The publishing company is the final stage through which a microcomputer program reaches its ultimate expression; it is the carrier of whatever wonders the microcomputer revolution will bring. The software entrepreneur is the person who creates those companies.

Originally, this was going to be a how-to-do-it book about how to become a software entrepreneur. When we set out on the research trail, the questions we asked were: (1) "What is the microcomputer software industry like?" and (2) "What does it take to be a successful software entrepreneur?" However, as happens on any good adventure, we found far more than we went looking for and a different book was written.

It took a Buddha to find the meaning of the world by contemplating a single pebble. Although possessed of a lesser degree of wisdom and insight, we were contemplating a somewhat larger subject and found a world of different messages and meanings in the software industry. Like Buddha's pebble, or the world, the software industry has mirrored surfaces, so that what is seen depends on who's looking and from what angle. Therefore, instead of presenting analysis telling you what we think it all means, we chose to present the fascinating stories of the software entrepreneurs in their own words. You can find your own meaning and draw your own conclusions. Most of what follows, from Chapter Three on, is pretty much what we were told by the founders of the greatest new industry on earth.

Chapter One

SOFTWARE MUSHROOMS

$\mathbf{F}$ ive miles above northern New Mexico, a passenger jet raced the sun for the western horizon, through the air that was clear with the pale crispness of late November. Most of the passengers on the plane were strangers, but they were all headed for exactly the same place: Las Vegas. It was one day before the opening of the fifth annual Fall COMDEX, the world's largest computer trade show, the fastest growing trade show of any kind on earth.

COMDEX/Fall '83 was no ordinary trade show—it had become a virtual Mecca for the microcomputer industry. For any company intent upon being in the micro business on a national scale, an annual pilgrimage was very nearly required. That's where the dealers would be and where big deals would be made. In fact, not showing up in style could raise questions and eyebrows. All of the convention city's 50,000 rooms—barely enough to hold the COMDEX crowd—had been booked for months in advance, so anyone headed for Las Vegas at this time was certain to be going there for the same reason. For ten days, Las Vegas and COMDEX would be synonymous.

The passengers were animated and buzzing like kids on a field trip. For most of them, COMDEX had already started. The public is not invited to COMDEX, only people in the trade, so everyone on that plane knew they were part of an "in" group, and they roamed the aisle, meeting and greeting one another with an easy familiarity based on common interests: computers and business. No, make that business and computers.

This was a relatively young and very convivial group, casually dressed and relaxed. There were a lot of women, apparently in important corporate positions. Small huddles of people gathered up and down the aisleway; some were chatting with members of their own group, but most were making new contacts. Above the hum of the jet engines, you could sometimes catch fragments of conversation. Almost all of it was shop talk, sometimes about chips, circuits, and new technologies, but usually the topic was business. Business gossip, to be completely accurate:

"Did you hear? IBM is working on their own operating system for the PC. It's supposed to be compatible with MS-DOS, but keyed into their big computer plans. Jeez, if that's true, they'll be pulling their hair out at Microsoft, won't they? But, you know, if you believe half of what you hear about IBM, you'd go nuts, so who knows?"

"Bet you haven't heard that Adam Osborne is already starting another new company. Supposed to be a secret, some kind of software thing. My boss—she's that blonde over there—she wants to know where Osborne gets his nerve, but I want to know how a guy that's crashed one company, how does he get venture capital to start another one right off the bat like that?"

"Howdy. Y'all in hardware? Oh, publishin.' Well, how about that Lotus company? Nine months from start-up, and y' know what? They got sales over $16 million. Per quarter! And they jus' picked up $36 million fer goin' public. All's I can say is, I am truly, deeply impressed! And on top a that, it's not such a bad program, either."

Besides gossip, there was some pre-show deal-making. "Listen," one lady was telling this paunchy dude, "we're going to set up training seminars just for retailers like you, okay? Now, if you wanted to send one or two people from each of your stores, we could run a special workshop, okay?

SOFTWARE MUSHROOMS

They'll learn the product cold in one or two days, okay? It's good for your company, too; helps build a group feeling." She was patting his arm, and he was nodding thoughtfully every time she said "okay?"

Miles below the plane an anonymous city slid by, another vast landscape of crackerboxes and cubical skyscrapers that could stimulate nothing but concern. What will represent our age to the future? What is this culture leaving that compares with the great buildings, sculptures, and artworks of the past? The buzz of excitement on the airplane answered: ideas, that's what—great structures of thought.

Every achievement starts as an idea, but the greatest constructions of our age are almost purely mental. In cosmological science, for example, our concept of the creation, workings, and ultimate evolution of the physical universe is sweeping, profound, and beautiful. From atomic particles to black holes through higher math and physics, the whole construct is pure thought—thoughts that could not have been conceived without software. The calculations are run by software, the computer-enhanced images of quasars and galaxies are the product of software, and the paychecks are written with software. The major discoveries of this era would not have been possible without software.

In less than one generation, software has already become indispensable and ubiquitous. Moon shots? Not possible without software. National defense? Inconceivable without software. Or consider the vast communications network that welds our world together with a global nervous system run by software. If our Earth has a future without a global disaster in it, that future will only be possible with software in a starring role.

But greatness isn't found just in major achievements—sometimes it comes in millions of little ones. In the last few years, software has come down out of the institutions to become a tool for the ordinary citizen, and that may be the most revolutionary news of all. Contrary to Orwell's vision for 1984, computing power is now in the hands of the people, a powerful tool for dealing with Big Brother. Now we can set our little computers to generating the paperwork required by the governments' big ones and get back to productive work.

4

Is there a town in North America so small and so remote that it doesn't have some kind of computer activity in it? Even in remote Bamfield, B.C. (population 200)—accessible only by water or by driving for hours on dirt roads—there are at least two Kaypros, as well as clutches of children who jabber excitedly about the Apple at school. From giant institutions to rustic cabins, for work or for fun, software has become inextricably interwoven into every facet of everyones' lives.

Robert Lydon, *Personal Computing* **magazine**

Even professionals who work with software for years on a daily basis lose none of their sense of awe for its inherent power and potential. Bob Lydon, for example, is editor and publisher of *Personal Computing* magazine, one of the biggies with about 500,000 paid circulation. About six weeks before COMDEX he delivered the keynote address at another trade show, the National Software Show in San Francisco. His fifty-minute talk was addressed to people in the software trade, and while it ranged far and wide, parts of it expressed his views on the role of software as the driving force in the microcomputer industry.

"A computer is a solution in search of a problem, not a box of electronic parts. It can solve any problem that can be expressed in mathematical terms, yet it stirs the imagination and encourages creativity. A computer system is an imagination machine. It can do anything, but it is the software that makes it do 'something'—something useful, something entertaining, something someone wants to do. Software makes reality out of the imagination machine.

"Software is the single most important factor in the success of the microcomputer revolution. It is software that fuels the enormous growth of sales and changes the computer from a technical curiosity into a usable tool.

"This imagination machine that you've helped to create with your software does more than just save time for the user, or make him more efficient. One of the very real benefits of personal computing is that it's something that many of us feel good about doing. It actually brings personal satisfaction, and in some cases happiness. No, it won't replace sex, and satisfaction is not a benefit, unfortunately, that you can list along with the specs on your package or include in your ads, but it is one that many people experience. This personal aspect of computing is one of the things that makes being a part of our industry rewarding. We are providing individuals with personal satisfaction.

"How can you market the possibility of this experience to the person that doesn't yet give a damn about computing? Unfortunately, you can't, not directly. We still have a very difficult time telling the man on the street what computing is all about, what it can do for him. This industry hasn't been able to translate the features of our products into the benefits that the consumer can relate to, and that's a major impediment to the growth of our industry. But by making our products easier to use, and by developing new applications and giving the user maximum benefits for the dollar, we will greatly expand the number of people who try computing.

"We're now in our heyday, and we're playing for very big stakes. The (microcomputer) software market is big, all right—it's about $2 billion today, and it will grow to $7-10 billion in the next few years, yet it's not limitless. This is a very complex market with many fragments and subtleties, and you've got to be very smart to succeed in this business. The bottom line is simply that the software industry must represent real value to the user.

"We're the software engine that's driving the entire personal computing revolution. It's a major challenge, and definitely a responsibility."

SOFTWARE MUSHROOMS

Even with the sun nearly set, passengers on the COMDEX plane had a clear view across four states, an Olympian perspective that until modern days was available only to gods and spirits. One could hardly find a better place than high up in the clouds from which to contemplate an overview of the software industry.

From the big view you could easily see, for example, that microcomputer software was the fastest growing, most creative and exciting segment of the entire computer world. The big mainframe computers first hit the streets in the early 1950s, which means that traditional software firms have had a twenty-five year head start. Nonetheless, microcomputer software companies have already come into their own and are attracting most of the new action. Consider these facts:

● In terms of 1982 revenue, five of the top twenty-five software firms peddle microcomputer software exclusively, and many of the major traditional firms are moving into the market aggressively, mostly through acquisitions. The five are, in order: MicroPro, VisiCorp, Softsel, Digital Research, Microsoft.
● Of all software companies, the three fastest growing in 1982 were exclusively in the microcomputer market. Of the ten fastest growing software firms, five peddle microcomputer software exclusively and at least two of the others are heavily involved in it. The five leaders are, in order: Softsel, MicroPro, Ashton-Tate, Digital Research, and Microsoft.
● Microcomputer software accounted for at least 10% of all software sold in 1982 and that market share (worth about $1 billion) will grow to 25 to 35% by 1987.
● The leading microcomputer software companies grew at an astonishing average rate of 209% in 1982. Softsel hit 353%.
● Even while their revenues have grown remarkably, the leading four microcomputer software companies have lost market share, dropping from an aggregate of about 28% to 22% between 1981 and 1982. This shows that the market is expanding very rapidly, but at the same time the number of major companies is also growing.

The market for microcomputer software is made up of many different segments, some of which are still undeveloped and unsettled.

CHAPTER ONE

SOFTWARE MUSHROOMS

7

Microcomputer Market Estimates

Category	1982	1987
	($ in millions)	
Productivity	$335	$2,000
Business	191	915
Systems	146	817
Entertainment	115	821
Education	60	353
	=====	=======
Total	$944	$5,425

The three largest market segments—systems software, business software, and productivity tools—are also the ones that have been around the longest. They have been the heart of the industry, and so far they are the most representative. Systems software consists of those programs that run the computer, and so of necessity this was the first major software industry. As soon as possible, entrepreneurs produced programs that would be useful to people in business—things like accounting and financial modelling—and programs that would make people more productive. Productivity tools do things like word processing, spreadsheet calculating, data management, and so on. Because at least 75% of all micros are used in business and productivity settings, this body of software has played the major role in the development of the industry to date.

Educational software is still a mere embryo of what will become a full-grown giant, its ultimate features as yet undetermined. The home computer market has never really gotten off the ground. The computer games (entertainment) market is tricky to analyze as it runs on a different set of rules and would be more appropriately considered part of the entertainment industry, being closer to records and movies than anything else. These are all important and lucrative segments of the software market, but all of the entrepreneurs and companies examined in this book come from the more settled and developed fields that are in better focus and easier to get a handle on.

Two things are immediately impressive about the software industry—its hefty size for its young age and its explosive rate of growth. Just take a look at the figures. But don't be surprised if the figures you read don't always agree from place to place—they are all estimates derived from a variety of sources. In a secretive industry, accurate figures are hard to come by, and the numbers given usually depend upon who's speaking, when, and to whom. Even with these limitations, the figures tell a profound story.

Microcomputer Software Sales

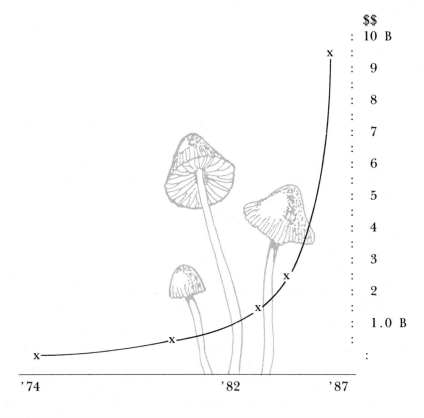

CHAPTER ONE

SOFTWARE MUSHROOMS

Software was barely in existence only one generation ago, yet in business terms its sales have exploded to $11.2 billion in 1982, and that figure is expected to rise to $27.5 billion in 1985. *Micro*computer software sales were about $1 billion in 1982 (some have estimated as much as $2 billion), and are expected to leap to $7 or 10 billion by 1987. The market share of microcomputer software will, therefore, increase from 10% to 33% in five years.

When charted, this kind of growth makes something like an asymptotic curve. *Asymptotic* is a mathematical term brought vividly to life by David Tranter, my old college chum in the math department. He rode his motorbike over one day and showed up in a rage about being attacked by "a god-damned asymptotic dog." In non-math terms *asymptotic* refers to any curve that approaches slow and flat along the horizontal, then rises sharply to run almost vertically. That may offend purists, but that's how it is used here.

This kind of curve describes many events in nature apart from the dog that attacked David—anything that has an explosive growth cycle; for example, fermentation (the geometric multiplying of yeast) in a vat of home-brew, or the action in California following the Gold Rush. It will also accurately describe the rise of the technological society in general and software in particular.

Some scholars muse that technology is more or less equivalent to speed or acceleration and that the rise of technology has been for the most part the story of increasingly rapid interactions and events. It is a more-faster world churning along on the high end of some asymptotic curve. If that's correct, then the microcomputer phenomenon fits right in. After all, the whole purpose of computers and software has been to increase the speed with which things can be done: the point of productivity software is to get more work done faster; educational software is supposed to hurry the process of learning; the point of computer games is to shoot targets down or get through a maze faster.

If technology is speed and if we are a technological society, then it is most fitting to find software riding high on the froth. Is it any wonder that

10

software—being dedicated to speed, productivity, information, and communications—should be at the leading edge of a massive society in ferment? And, now that marketing has become the dominant influence in the software industry, it even gives off a certain amount of gas as a by-product. Naturally, submerging yourself in it can be quite intoxicating.

There is a yeasty effervescence that permeates the microcomputer industry, a creative excitement that puts it in sharp contrast to all those other industries and businesses where people consider their jobs to be a burden, and where they seem to live for the five o'clock bell, weekends, and holidays. Most people seem to feel bored or oppressed by their work. In the highly acclaimed book *Working*, Studs Terkel compiled hundreds of interviews with people from all walks, most of whom claimed that their lives were made miserable by the oppressive, limiting and confining nature of their jobs. Too bad he didn't know about the software industry: in a national survey of computer professionals in six different job categories, 94% were not considering leaving the field, 81% were not planning to change areas within the field, and only 6% expressed any job dissatisfaction at all.

People in software tend to be involved in a personal way. They work long and hard and thrive on it. For them, their jobs are an opportunity to be part of something creative and satisfying, something bigger than themselves, a way of life. That's what they say, anyway. They also say that they usually can't wait to get to work. If you drop in on weekends or holidays at your average software enterprise, you'll find a lot of the staff present. And the best thing of all is the absence of that incessant struggle between "workers" and "management" that infects too many other industries. What a waste. In most software enterprises the entire staff functions more like a team, a family, or a community. They pull together toward common goals.

Another characteristic of software people is that they tend to do everything in a flat-out rush. They are also fiercely competitive, which makes them hurry even more to get things done before someone beats them to the punch. Software technology is advancing at a gallop, the infant industry is in a state of frothing ferment, and borrowed money costs by the

SOFTWARE MUSHROOMS

hour. This explains why software products are sometimes announced far ahead of delivery or rushed to market before being completely tested.

You often read or hear that software sales are mushrooming. Mushrooms are another life form that display asymptotic growth characteristics. All year there's nothing there, then suddenly a crop of fungal fruit thrusts out of the ground, rising fast like . . . well, like software sales. But the similarity doesn't stop there.

Mushrooms are actually the fruits of a large underground body called mycelium. This is a gossamer mat of microscopic fibers, a network of hairs that insinuates itself throughout a large area in the soil. When conditions are exactly right, the mycelium rushes material and supplies to focal points to form reproductive organs, and the spore-bearing bodies are quickly assembled, then thrust up and out where it is their job to procreate.

In a similar way, software permeates major areas of society, its unseen fibers and tendrils quietly, invisibly, penetrating every facet and layer of our lives. Periodically, the software industry marshals the resources of its vast invisible networks to quickly build up a procreative spore-bearing body called the trade show. These specialized organs (the trade shows) may be any size from small to gigantic, but they always emerge seemingly out of nothing, clamor actively for three to five days performing acts of stimulation and procreation, then disappear as quickly as they came. The trade show is truly a software mushroom.

The software mushroom has become a very important species. There are so many micro shows and expos now that a whole new industry has sprung up just to accommodate them, and many of the major national drayage and parcel express corporations have set up separate divisions just to service micro events. But one show stands out above all the rest. The largest, most notorious, and gaudiest of all the software mushrooms—and the one most representative of the microcomputer industry—is COMDEX/ Fall. It appears annually, late in November, and has grown each year to the point that it now engulfs most of Las Vegas, the city of lights, action, glitter and speed. As mushrooms go, COMDEX most closely resembles an *Amanita muscaria*—the exotic Magic Mushroom.

12

— ● —

The plane veered toward a large glow on the dark horizon: COMDEX and Las Vegas, pulsing with scintillating gigiwatts, a giant electromagnet. It was time to start coming down out of the clouds and get ready to grapple with street-level realities. Soon the plane landed in the bright lights, depositing at last its load of passengers, just one small fraction of the 90,000 COMDEX participants that were making their way through the vast microcomputer network to take part in the annual fertility rite.

There couldn't possibly be any city more appropriate than Las Vegas to house the microcomputer industry's most prestigious and representative annual event. Las Vegas is a fantasy island in the middle of nowhere. It can exist in such a desolate landscape only because of the power of entrepreneurial energy and the attraction of action. Money and action, that's the fundamental commodity of Las Vegas, its *raison d'etre*.

The passengers walked the corridors of the airport, ears ringing with the clangor of the slot-machines, eyes dazzled by the glittering lights. The highway to the hotel was a similar cacophony of light and sound, its wide boulevard made into a tunnel by towering banks of incandescent glare, and the hallways through the hotels and casinos were more of the same assault on the senses, a subliminal appeal to base instincts.

When at last the passengers walked onto the floors of COMDEX, there was hardly any difference—just more noise, razzle and dazzle. The whir of slot machines was replaced by the whir of disk drives, and at COMDEX money doesn't clang, it rustles. There were gamblers on both sides of the COMDEX doors, but there was a big difference between the glazed zombies that lined up in rows at the one-armed bandits and the alert, creative wheelers and dealers lining the midways at COMDEX. You could see it in the way they moved. You could see it in their eyes.

CHAPTER ONE

Chapter Two
(Appendix A)

UNDERSTANDING THE MICRO MARKETPLACE

Being a microcomputer software entrepreneur is like playing a computer arcade game where the challenge is to steer safely through a rapidly moving obstacle course: you have to be alert and have quick reflexes just to stay in the game. The software business is no longer a bandwagon that you can just jump on—it is now a madly whirling carousel, and if you don't have a good sense of timing and an instinct for opportunity, you can get thrown.

To a large degree, the ever-changing features of today's market are the result of the way the micro industry has developed in its short but action-packed history. You have to know what's happened to have a hope of guessing what could be coming next—or to know what the entrepreneurs are talking about. There isn't room for the whole microcomputer horse opera, but here are some selected arias and highlights. If you know a lot about the micro world, you should consider this chapter to be your *Appendix A: Background* and you can browse, skim or skip through it.

14

A (VERY) BRIEF HISTORY OF THE MICROCOMPUTER

Before the Microcomputer—1945 to 1974

The very first computers emerged in the mid-1940s, the result of exciting and intense collaborations between university and industrial research, rushed along by the war effort and fueled by infusions of government funding. The first operational vacuum tube processor in the world was ENIAC at the University of Pennsylvania, intended for ballistics trajectory calculations. It was a calculating machine the size of a house but without any memory or storage capabilities. Meanwhile, Bell Labs developed the first transistor in 1947, a discovery that would eventually produce revolutionary results as transistors evolved into integrated circuits and then into micro-chips.

The first computer to get up and running as a commercial product was the UNIVAC-I, introduced in 1951 by Remington Rand, predecessor of Sperry Rand Corporation. This machine was made with vacuum tubes, but smaller ones than had hummed away in ENIAC and its kind. Although IBM had been in on earlier research, it was slow to enter the commercial market, but it caught up quickly in a way that has now become familiar. By 1956, IBM had captured 85% of the U.S. computer market and was firmly established as number one in most countries.

The giant computers, known as *mainframes,* are the creatures of governments and corporate giants. No one else can afford to buy one, or if given one, to operate it. They cost anywhere from several hundred thousand up to tens of millions. In the early 1960s, IBM introduced a relatively low-priced mainframe, the IBM-360 Model 30. The CPU (Central Processing Unit) alone was built into a water-cooled enclosure five feet by six feet, and had to be kept in a special air-conditioned room eighteen feet square, along with the control console, a keypunch desk, and a printer. It cost 280,000 of those fat 1960 dollars (just one would buy dinner), and you had to hire a staff of specialists to keep it running. That machine, by the way, was not nearly the computer that any desktop micro is today.

UNDERSTANDING THE MICRO MARKETPLACE

15

In 1964, the *mini*computer entered the marketplace in the form of the PDP-8 made by Digital Equipment Corporation (DEC). Minicomputers are smaller and cheaper than mainframes, costing several tens instead of several hundreds of thousands or millions of dollars. They still require expert care and handling, but they made it possible for *somewhat* smaller businesses and agencies to acquire computing power.

Computers were for the most part inaccessible—removed from the world of mere mortals by dense barriers of cost and thickets of technological intricacy. It was, moreover, the policy of all manufacturers to keep tight control over the software and peripherals used on their machines. The same company that manufactured the computer hardware would also own all the systems and applications software which they would lease to their customers. It was as if you could only tune in CBS programs if you owned a CBS-TV, or as if you could only drive a Ford on Ford's roads.

Before 1974, all computers were operated by an elite priesthood of computer professionals who tended to the intricacies of hardware and software. They were the only ones who could approach the machines or speak to them in the esoteric languages of Assembler or FORTRAN or COBOL. Great things were being accomplished in those digital temples, but that time was in many ways like the dark ages when only monks could read and write, a time when all knowledge was closely held and all diplomacy and research was conducted in dead languages, ancient Latin or Greek. Everything worked beautifully—for the monks.

This state of affairs was interrupted and the elitist patterns shattered by the introduction of the personal computer. In fact, Orwell's target year, 1984, can be better celebrated as the tenth anniversary of the personal computer, for it was late in 1974 that MITS of Albuquerque first announced their Altair computer kit for $397. From that point forward, computers have increasingly become available as tools of the people.

When the printing press brought literacy to the man on the street, it became one of the driving forces of the Renaissance and utterly changed the world. The computer and information revolution is heralded today as being even more pregnant with promise. Canadian author David Godfrey calls it

16

"Gutenberg Two" in a book by that name. He suggests that the changes brought about by printing presses were nothing compared to the changes that will be made by computers. You can see it happening already; compare the social impact of software when it was exclusively in the hands of professionals with the way software is steamrolling now that it is in the hands of millions of exuberant amateurs.

The Microcomputer—1971 to Present

After a brief period of incubation, the personal computer emerged as the single most exciting, creative, and fastest growing segment of the computer industry.

In 1971, there were only about 88,000 computers in the United States and perhaps double that number in the whole world. That's the year that Intel Corporation introduced one of their first microchips, a tiny silicon flake that contained the central workings of a computer. There was the 4004, then the 8008, and by 1973 Intel had evolved the 8080, the chip that would soon give rise to the first microcomputer and become the heart of a boom industry. By the end of 1983, there would be about 6 million personal computers.

In 1973, Gary Kildall, a part-time consultant for Intel, was working on a language, PL/M, that he wanted to adapt to the new microchips. For that project he began to develop an operating system that would allow the new chips to work with the (then new) floppy disk storage devices. The result was the Control Program for Microprocessors, or CP/M, which was only intended for Kildall's own work.

A chip and an operating program do not make a computer, not by a long shot, and they especially do not make a commercial product. It wasn't until very late in 1974, when MITS announced the Altair, a microcomputer kit designed around the 8080 microchip, that the world's first personal computer was born. It was featured on the cover of the January, 1975 issue of *Popular Electronics*.

UNDERSTANDING THE MICRO MARKETPLACE

17

Within days of the MITS announcement, Bill Gates, a 19-year-old Seattle lad at Harvard, holed himself up in his dormitory room with his old friend Paul Allen. After five weeks of feverish effort, they announced the release of Microsoft BASIC, the first microcomputer language, ready to run on the MITS Altair. In much less than a nutshell, this is how Microsoft became the first microcomputer software company in the world.

Late in 1975, Gary Kildall completed the development of CP/M and began to license it commercially. In 1976, Gary and his wife, Dorothy, founded Digital Research, Inc. in their bedroom.

Also in 1975, another 19-year-old, Steven Jobs, and friend Steven Wozniak, began tinkering with a different new chip, the Motorola 6502. They eventually built a little hobby microcomputer that they showed off at the Homebrew Computer Club in Palo Alto. A local store agreed to order fifty. And so, with an initial investment of $2500, which was all they had, the Apple computer company was born in a garage.

The MITS Altair was obviously a device for avid hobbyists, people who could wire the thing together and tinker with it until it worked and who could then write programs for it, for there was no software on the market. What market? In those days there wasn't any market for microcomputers or the few software products to be on. Hardly anyone had heard of microcomputers, and fewer had any idea of their applications. The Apple I was a bit more accessible to the public, because it at least came assembled, but again there was little software other than what you could write for yourself or scrounge up through the few hobby groups.

In 1977, another hobby-oriented electronics outfit, Tandy Corporation, entered its own microcomputer contender, the TRS-80 Model I. They hired Bill Gates to develop some software for their line, which gave Microsoft a big boost. Tandy opted, unlike Apple, to keep close control over their software, peripherals, and marketing, relying upon their huge network of wholly-owned Radio Shack stores to move merchandise. Meanwhile, Apple was having their first million-dollar year and was gearing up to do some serious mass marketing with the Apple II. Commodore, too, decided to enter the micro sweepstakes.

18

Major Microcomputer Events

1970

71   Intel's first chips, the 4004 and 8008

72

73   Kildall starts to write CP/M for his private use
Intel's 8080 chip introduced

74   **BIRTH OF THE PERSONAL COMPUTER**
MITS introduces the Altair microcomputer kit

75   Gates writes BASIC, founds Microsoft with Paul Allen
Kildall founds Digital Research, begins to license CP/M
Jobs & Wozniak design and build the first Apple computer
    and start Apple Computer Co. in their garage

76

77   Tandy introduces the TRS-80
Commodore introduces the PET
    Apple sales hit $1 million

78   Apple launches its first major marketing effort
    Microsoft sales hit $1 million

79   VisiCalc puts micros into business headlines
MicroPro introduces WordStar
First COMDEX/Fall in Las Vegas

1980

81   Ashton-Tate introduces dBASE II
IBM announces the IBM-PC in the fall

82   First IBM-PCs shipped
Lotus Corp. introduces Lotus 1-2-3 in October
    Apple sales $582 million
    Microcomputer software sales hit $1 billion

CHAPTER TWO

UNDERSTANDING THE MICRO MARKETPLACE

Microsoft sales $34 million
83 Osborne Computer Co. goes under
Atari and Texas Instruments back out of home computer market
Apple sales $1.1 million
Tandy sales $1.1 million
IBM-PC sales $1.5 million
1984 **TENTH ANNIVERSARY OF THE PERSONAL COMPUTER**
Apple Macintosh introduced
Integrated software, multi-tasking, windows, and mice
AT&T announces UNIX alliance with Digital Research
Human Edge introduces first expert system
Dayflo introduces an intelligent information system

By the end of 1978, Microsoft had developed FORTRAN for the microcomputer, and had licensed Microsoft BASIC to Apple and Tandy. Although a few of the early applications programs were just starting to appear—word processors, accounting packages, and data managers—the microcomputer had not yet evolved out of the hobbyist category.

After its introduction in 1975, CP/M's ready availability made it an attractive choice for new micro makers and it was quickly adopted by most of them, soon to number in the hundreds. This process was greatly facilitated by Tony Gold's Lifeboat Associates of New York, the first micro software clearinghouse. CP/M users were soon collectively more numerous than any other user group, and this is what first made the mass marketing of software attractive. By 1979, CP/M was emerging as the *de facto*, unelected industry standard operating system.

Late in 1979, MicroPro introduced its word processor, WordStar, and an increasing number of applications programs began to emerge. This was about the time that a company called Personal Software (now VisiCorp) introduced VisiCalc, a clever program developed by Software Arts that allowed the user to set up a spreadsheet of interconnected blocks of data in order to make bids, estimates and projections. It was an extremely

20

adaptable and useful "what if?" tool for business managers. VisiCalc gave a noticeable push to a trend already in the making, and became known as the product that moved microcomputers off of hobby benches and onto office desks. Because it was only available on the Apple II at first, Apple's sales got a big boost, and VisiCalc is credited as the first software product to sell hardware.

Fall COMDEX Exhibitions in Las Vegas

Year	No. Exhibitors	No. Attendees
1979	157	4000
80	354	9100
81	648	23,500
82	1106	50,000
1983	1400	80,000

It is difficult to put a date on something so ubiquitous, something that is more a natural force than an event, but around 1979/80 marketing emerged as a primal force in the microcomputer industry, and by 1982 it had an iron grip. Unlike the mainframes and minis, the microcomputer addressed a mass market, and was fast becoming treated as a consumer item. Microcomputer software is not like those custom-designed programs that cost a king's ransom and sell or lease to relatively few customers. Micro software sells straight off the shelf at a modest price to hundreds of thousands of anonymous buyers. Micro software has to be advertised to millions of users across North America and around the world, and that means reliance on marketing.

In 1981, Ashton-Tate introduced dBASE II, a *relatively* easy-to-learn data management language, suitable for home-made applications, and even more suitable for the rapid development of sophisticated custom applications. The product was wildly successful, and soon there was a subsidiary industry of support for dBASE II users.

UNDERSTANDING THE MICRO MARKETPLACE

21

In the fall of 1981, IBM created a great stir in the industry by announcing its entry into the field with the IBM-PC. By the time the IBM-PC hit the market in earnest in early 1982, it was suddenly a whole new ball game, and a new market bonanza was unleashed as entrepreneurs rushed to provide software and peripherals for the IBM-PC. Late in the year, Lotus Corporation announced a package of integrated business applications for the IBM-PC, and took their first step toward becoming the most recent and most spectacular software superstar. Their $5 million in venture startup capital was a jolting record for the industry.

In 1983, IBM-PC sales topped all others; micros began piling into the Fortune 1000 corporations and other levels of business; and the IBM look-alike industry was up and running, as were suppliers of peripherals and software for the new family of machines. The CP/M 8-bit market was still growing, but in spite of high sales figures the Osborne computer company went under. This shocking event was caused by internal mismanagement, but it proved that micro ventures were not exempt from the rules of business. Further tidal waves were stirred when it became known that Atari, Texas Instruments, and nearly everyone else were falling on their faces in the home computer market. High-tech investors and market watchers sobered up considerably.

New families of powerful and sophisticated software emerged in 1983, offering several applications integrated into one package, bigger and better data management, and better graphics. Early in the year, Apple announced the Lisa, a highly sophisticated, advanced, and pricey machine that is still waiting to take off. Tandy introduced the highly innovative Model 100 lap-sized computer. The 1983 Fall COMDEX overflowed the convention and hotel facilities of Las Vegas, and hit new records for size, attendance, and hype.

In 1984, Apple released the Macintosh computer, a refreshingly different concept which is the only hopeful alternative to the style of computing offered by the IBM-PC and all the other computers. More big news in this year was the entry of AT&T with a line of supermicros and an alliance with Digital Research to develop a library of languages, utilities,

22

and applications to run under the UNIX operating system. This year also saw the introduction of the first micro expert system by Human Edge, and the Dayflo system which takes information management into new realms. Dayflo came in with $10 million in venture capital, fully double the record set by Lotus last year. The market is packed tight with brilliant products and hot companies, all making so much clamor that the poor consumer is likely to be overwhelmed—as are some of the smaller software companies.

MAJOR MICRO FAMILIES

By 1980, the microcomputer market was booming and more than a little chaotic, due to the many makes of microcomputers that were not compatible with one another. Incompatibility means that it is difficult or impossible for the user of one machine to get a favorite program to run on a different machine, or even to transfer raw data from one machine to another. This is a headache for the confused consumers and even more so for software publishers who, of course, need to include as many users as possible in their markets. And programmers are forced to spend a great deal of time and energy modifying programs to get them to work on all those different computers.

Some incompatibilities are caused by different floppy disk formats, others by different screen controls, but the major cause of the incompatibility problem has to do with the different operating systems used by the various computers.

Operating Systems

Computer hardware is just a pile of dead parts until some coded instructions start ordering the electrons around inside it to make things happen. The coded instructions, or program, that runs the computer is called the *operating system*, and the programs that do useful work for people are called *applications programs*. An operating system is often called *DOS* for

Disk Operating System, so you get Apple-DOS, TRS-DOS (from Tandy Radio Shack), MS-DOS (from Microsoft), and so on.

The operating system is the government and the bureaucracy of the computer system. It speaks directly to the Central Processing Unit (CPU) in its own internal language. Everything that happens in the computer must go through the operating system. As with human forms of organization, there is almost no limit to the different ways the same operation can be organized, so there could be any number of different operating systems to work the same CPU chip. This is exactly the case with CP/M and TRS-DOS, for example, both of which order the operation of the Intel 8080 and Z-80 chips, but which are entirely incompatible with one another. Apple IIs and Commodores use the Motorola 6502 chip, which has a completely different internal structure (and therefore a different internal language), so their operating systems are even more drastically different from those that operate the Intel family of chips.

When an application is written so that it works with one particular operating system, then it will not easily run under any other without extensive revision of the program. This is the problem of *transportability*. If there were only one microcomputer operating system on the market, most programs would work on most computers. On the other hand, if every manufacturer wrote their own unique operating system, there would be very little transportability of programs between different computer brands, and the industry would be in even more chaos than it is now.

The Original Big Three Computer Families

By 1981 there were only three operating systems that dominated in MicroBabel. Apple and Radio Shack had their own proprietary operating systems, but the largest family was that wildly heterogeneous group of computers from literally hundreds of makers that ran under CP/M. Because of the large base of users, each of the three major computer families had attracted a significant body of applications software.

24

CP/M was different from the two proprietary systems, as it was available to be adapted for use by any manufacturer. Because the same operating system was installed on so many micros and used by so many people, CP/M was what first made the mass marketing of software possible. Soon there were thousands of CP/M applications software packages, and this wide variety of quality software reinforced the market position of CP/M. It is a telling fact that there was a big market for products that got CP/M onto Apples and TRS-80s, but no one tried to get CP/M machines to run TRS-80 or Apple programs.

Tandy's strength has always been their chain of thousands of wholly-owned and operated Radio Shack retail stores that sell the TRS-80 line exclusively. Apple's strength, apart from being in at the beginning, has always been that their machine is a hobbyist's delight, and that they encouraged other companies to make products and programs that would run with the Apple. This creative variety has made Apple a fun family to work and play in, and the creative variety of third party products and software has kept the Apple vital. Apple's graphics capabilities made it superior in the area of games and educational programs, and VisiCalc established them in the business arena, so for the best of all worlds (hobby, home, games, business) you had to choose an Apple II. However, with few exceptions, the best selection of hardware and productivity programs were available in the CP/M camp, so for serious business applications, CP/M computers were the first choice for years—until IBM and MS-DOS came along late in 1981.

Enter Big Blue: 16-Bit Chips, the IBM-PC, and MS-DOS

The first microchips, the ones in millions of Apples, TRS-80s, and CP/M machines, all have an 8-bit internal architecture. This means that the size of each character that the chip recognizes and manipulates has eight binary digits. This is much smaller and more limited than the CPUs on mainframe and minicomputers which use thirty-two or sixty-four bits per character. It means that the smaller chip has to work longer and harder to process the same amount of information. But the most important limitation is that the 8-bit chips can only address a maximum of 64K RAM (the computer's working memory space), which poses a definite obstacle for applications programmers.

The announcement of the new IBM-PC and its 16-bit Intel chip was seen as a green flag by all the program developers. Because 16-bit chips can manipulate far more RAM memory, into the megabyte range if necessary, it was suddenly possible to build programs that do more work faster. At last there was room to develop a better and more sophisticated user interface. And the name IBM guaranteed that there would be a big market for the new products.

The IBM-PC was a market blockbuster right from the second it was first announced, in spite of the fact that there was almost no software available for it for some time. Major inroads were suddenly made by micros into the corporate world, and even detractors said that IBM, by its mere presence, gave credibility and status to the microcomputer industry. More important, it provided stability and promised to put an end to the confusion of incompatibility.

The IBM-PC works under the PC-DOS operating system developed by Microsoft, which also sells a virtually identical operating system under the name MS-DOS. IBM originally came to Microsoft looking to buy BASIC and a CP/M operating system, and Microsoft naturally referred them to Digital Research for the operating system part of the deal. Inexplicably, IBM soon ended up back at Microsoft which had meanwhile bought up an existing 16-bit operating system, a CP/M look-alike, that was under development at Seattle Computer. Microsoft rebuilt the look-alike, but under extreme time pressure from IBM. That's how it happens that the current industry standard operating system that defines the way millions of people do their computing was partly the result of a series of flukes.

Digital Research, Inc. eventually released an operating system for the 16-bit chips; called CP/M-86. It is not compatible with the CP/M that works the 8-bit 8080 and Z-80 chips, now called CP/M-80 to distinguish it. Unfortunately for DRI, their late and uninspired entry was lost in the wave

26

of hyperbole generated around the IBM-PC. In late 1983, Digital Research released their highly competitive Concurrent DOS operating system which permits several different programs to run at the same time, provides multi-user capability, windowing, networking, and which will emulate MS-DOS to some extent. Microsoft is, of course, forging ahead with upgraded versions of MS-DOS and their new Microsoft Windows with which they hope to stay in the lead.

There are two critical points here: 1) any computer that can run MS-DOS can certainly run CPM-86 and Concurrent DOS, because they all operate the same 16-bit chip; and, 2) neither PC/MS-DOS, CP/M-86, nor Concurrent DOS will run CP/M-80 programs because they are designed for a different 8-bit chip. The choice is not between PC/MS-DOS and CP/M so much as between 16-bit and 8-bit machines. From the long view, it is likely that CP/M-80 and PC/MS-DOS are both just a wrinkle on the nose of computer history, but for now the 16-bit systems are leading the market.

However, in spite of predictions of an early demise, the 8-bit CP/M-80 systems are proving surprisingly tenacious. This is mostly because of a big price advantage and the fact that the smaller machines are completely satisfactory for a wide range of applications. If you can find a CP/M-80 program that does what you need, then whenever a bigger, better program comes out for the IBM-PC, this may leave you envious, but no worse off. Finally, there are already millions of CP/M-80 machines out there, and sales continue to be brisk, especially in the portables. The 8-bit systems are a huge and growing market that no software publishers in their right minds would dare ignore. The little devils may be with us for years to come.

Market watchers love to play "What if?" and their favorite one lately goes, "What if IBM comes out with their own proprietary operating system, different from and incompatible with MS-DOS?" One hears frequent rumors to this effect, and if this should happen, and if consumers continue to grab their forelocks and checkbooks every time they hear the name IBM, then this could do mortal damage to MS-DOS and change the name of the game.

CHAPTER TWO

UNDERSTANDING THE MICRO MARKETPLACE

27

In the microcomputer world, change *is* the name of the game. And every change creates a wide open window of opportunity for entrepreneurs.

UNIX Over the Horizon?

As microcomputer systems become progressively faster and more powerful, they will outgrow both CP/M and MS-DOS because neither one of those operating systems is ideal for large-size or multiple-user situations. Looming over the horizon is UNIX, an operating system from the world of mainframes and minis that has a dedicated and enthusiastic following among programmers. There is already an established and growing market in the bigger, high-end micros (called supermicros or minimicros) such as the Fortune, Zilog, Altos, and Victor, and they all use some version of UNIX already. There are extreme incompatibilities between the machines in the UNIX world, but the field is still young and undeveloped. Is this the wave of the future?

UNIX is a very big system that doesn't fit comfortably on today's micros, and worse, it is notoriously unfriendly to the point of being almost incomprehensible to the non-technical user. However, as many are quick to point out, UNIX has one very big thing going for it—there isn't anything else. And then there's the fact that the operating system is slowly beginning to disappear to the user. Micros grow ever larger and more powerful as the price of microchips continues to plunge, permitting program size to expand accordingly. As applications programs become bigger and more sophisticated, they operate the operating system for you. In programs like Lotus 1-2-3 and Dayflo (a new information system), the user almost never sees the operating system and couldn't care less which one it is.

Industry watchers have long thought that if AT&T, the owner of UNIX, were to decide to push it, then UNIX could easily become a major force in the industry. This seems to be underway now. In early 1984, AT&T began its descent into the marketplace by negotiating an alliance with Digital Research to develop languages and applications for UNIX, then they announced an entire line of 32-bit supermicros. Microsoft has long had

XENIX, a micro version of UNIX, and IBM has announced its own UNIX system, the PC-IX. On your mark, get set . . . .

The *Other* Microcomputer

The newest addition to the major micro families is Apple's Macintosh—a direct challenge to the IBM-PC and the only innovative way to do computing on the mass market. Over seven hundred software companies, including almost all the superstars, are already hard at work to bring out the latest and best versions of their various software products on the Macintosh, plus some new ones. There may be another software bonanza for those in a position to take advantage of the opportunity.

MAJOR MARKET SEGMENTS AND THE SOFTWARE SUPERSTARS

In the April 2, 1984 issue, *InfoWorld* magazine printed a list of the top twenty microcomputer software publishing companies and their 1983 revenues. The source was *SoftLetter*, an industry research outfit that derived the figures from the companies, company insiders, and industry analysts. According to them, the software superstars and their relative ranks are:

Software Superstars

		millions			millions
1	MicroPro International	$60	6	Ashton-Tate	$35
2	Microsoft	55	7	PeachTree Software	21.7
3	Lotus Development	53	8	Microfocus	15
4	Digital Research	45	9	Software Publishing	14
5	VisiCorp	43	10	Human Engineered Soft.	13

UNDERSTANDING THE MICRO MARKETPLACE

29

These are the companies that rose to the top of the heap and that dominate one or more sectors in the marketplace. These are the companies that software entrepreneurs watch, try to learn from, and emulate.

The software superstars occupy various parts of a market that is extremely diverse and fragmented, mostly along lines that are defined by the function of the software and to whom it is sold. This market divides conveniently into three major categories that correspond, more or less, to stages in the expanding usefulness of the microcomputer. These are:

- Systems software and languages
- General applications
- Vertical applications

When the microcomputer emerged in 1975, the first things that were needed were the essentials, the operating systems and languages to make it go. Microsoft began their superstar career by producing Microsoft BASIC, the first microcomputer language, and Digital Research, Inc. rose to dominate the industry on the strength of their widely accepted CP/M operating system.

The next category of software that evolved was the general applications programs, so-called because they do things that are useful to almost every computer user. The big five general applications are word processing, spreadsheets, data management, communications, and graphics. MicroPro grew into an industry giant with the resounding success of its word processor, WordStar, first shipped in 1980. In that same year, VisiCorp cut new trails into the world of business and met spectacular success with the first microcomputer spreadsheet program, VisiCalc. In 1981, Ashton-Tate blasted off with the first widely accepted data management program, dBASE II, and in 1983, Lotus rose like a comet with 1-2-3, its powerful package of integrated general applications programs for the IBM-PC.

The most recent category, one that is still emerging, is the *vertical* market software. *Generic* products are those that are useful to computer users at large, therefore the target market is almost everyone who wants to

30

be productive with a computer. This would include all systems, languages, and general applications programs. Some people use *horizontal* to mean the same thing as generic. *Vertical* products are those that are especially designed for and marketed to a very specific, narrowly-defined target market. Examples of vertical market products would include packages for medical office management, construction, insurance offices, real estate operations, and so on.

The vertical markets have only begun to flourish, and have not yet produced a star quality company. Meanwhile, makers of general software like Lotus 1-2-3 and Dayflo are all designing their products so that you can create *templates* or *overlays* that will quickly customize their generic products for very specific applications, thus making them attractive to vertical software developers and private consultants. Dayflo, for example, is an information system that can be customized by an independent developer to be immensely useful to, say, travel agents. The vertical markets are considered to be the best bet for new software entrepreneurs, because the highly-defined target audience makes marketing much cheaper than for generic products that are marketed in the highly competitive and expensive national arena.

DAVID AND GOLIATH IN THE MICRO WARS

As the market shakes itself out, many believe that there will eventually be only a handful of leaders at the top. Meanwhile, while the software superstars battle one another for market position and preeminence, they have to keep a wary eye on the true giants. IBM revenues in 1983 were about $1.5 billion just from its PC operation, which made IBM number one in the micro industry, yet that figure represented only about 4% of IBM's total gross of about $37 billion worldwide. AT&T is an even larger company, weighing in at about $50 billion. In contrast, Apple and Tandy each grossed about $1.2 billion, and the largest revenue earned by any independent software company was the $60 million reported by MicroPro.

UNDERSTANDING THE MICRO MARKETPLACE

31

There's an African saying that goes, "When the elephants fight, the smaller animals had better be nimble." This is good advice in the micro industry, where even small moves by giants like IBM and AT&T can drastically effect the fortunes of all the smaller companies. Microsoft's revenues soared when it formed a relationship with IBM to develop PC-DOS, although the romance began to seem more like a one-night stand when IBM picked another company to develop its PC-IX UNIX system.

Similarly, Digital Research got a big boost from its UNIX software alliance with AT&T. This will help even the odds between DRI and rival Microsoft in their ongoing micro wars. They say it is unrelated, but DRI announced an infusion of $22 million, the largest private investment on record in the industry. Gary Kildall says that it is "merely a normal business operation prior to going public," and that the money will go into their "war chest." War chest? Now who could they be at war with?

When IBM came in, the entire micro industry changed overnight, so naturally everyone is on tenterhooks wondering about the scope of AT&T's plans. AT&T is cast as the only company that can compete with IBM, but whatever they ultimately intend, AT&T is off to a slow start in the world of competition with the colorless and disorganized introduction of their line of 32-bit supermicros in April, 1984. Not that these are not wonderful machines, but they are nothing compared with AT&T's revolutionary potential in communications.

AT&T owns and operates a worldwide communications network, a major portion of the nervous system of the planet Earth. Once they are through reinventing the supermicro, they should begin to hook us all up with wonderful communications devices and tele-micros. That could be an earth-shattering escalation in the communications revolution, and worthy of a colossus like AT&T. This must be something they are planning to do—it needs to happen.

Stewart Alsop II, the editor of *InfoWorld* magazine, points out that AT&T has no experience with microcomputers and even less with competition, so we may be "blinded by sheer size." But anything that a company the size of IBM or AT&T does, effectively or not, can be counted upon to make tidal waves in the micro puddle.

Perhaps the most fascinating battle currently being waged is that of Apple against IBM. Apple's 1983 revenues of $1.2 billion were only 4% of IBM's, yet they plan to take them on in a direct confrontation by offering the world "the other computer." David has attacked Goliath, but we don't know yet whether Goliath has noticed.

Up to the end of 1983, all microcomputers were more or less similar in operation. That is, they all had an operating system involving cryptic commands to load programs, copy files, manage disks, and send data to modems and printers. Then each application program had to be learned. The IBM-PC may have become leader of the pack, but it is not innovative, and many believe it to be a damper on progress because it fixed the dominant standard at a relatively low level. Manufacturers spend their energies getting as close as possible to IBM instead of striking out in new directions. After all, who wants to fight IBM? Well, Apple does.

In January, 1984, Apple introduced the Macintosh in a brilliant marketing campaign. The Mac is the only truly innovative computer in the mass market, and the only one with any chance of loosening IBM's stranglehold on the industry. The Apple Mac is a very friendly little machine, but with extremely powerful 32-bit capabilities. It is so easy to use that you don't really need much of a manual—how it works is obvious. The Macintosh and its sales campaign are very good, as they must be, because Apple has put all its eggs in the Macintosh basket to bring us a choice, not an echo.

Long before the Mac was released, Apple stimulated crash Mac projects at leading software superstar companies like Microsoft, Lotus, Software Publishing, and hundreds of others. Lotus founder Mitch Kapor thinks the Mac is "really special." He says the way it works is much more natural, and that it will change the way people think and work. Many of the software entrepreneurs interviewed for this book were very excited about the Macintosh possibilities and were making plans to get in on what they anticipate will be another software boom.

CHAPTER TWO

UNDERSTANDING THE MICRO MARKETPLACE

33

Mike Murray, Apple Computer Inc.

The best man to speak in depth about what the Macintosh will mean in the software marketplace is Mike Murray, Apple's marketing manager for their 32-bit family. One of the micro industry's bright young men, Murray has been deeply involved with software product development for the Mac, and he is also the man who manages the best conceived, organized, and executed PR and sales campaign ever to be unleashed upon the microcomputer marketplace.

What impact do you think the Macintosh will have on software development, and what opportunities will it create?

MIKE MURRAY: Okay... (draws a curve). This is not a derby, it's a bell-shaped curve. Under this curve are twenty-five million knowledge workers. Those are the people that we think computers are for right now. It is not clear to us what a home computer is for, okay? but in terms of professionals and adults who want to use computers, we target these people called knowledge workers. A marketing person divides the group up and gives them names (draws on chart).

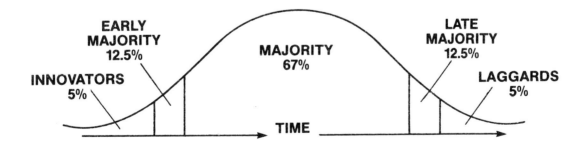

The Target Market: 25 Million Knowledge Workers

EARLY MAJORITY 12.5% • MAJORITY 67% • LATE MAJORITY 12.5% • INNOVATORS 5% • LAGGARDS 5% • TIME

34

Our research, that we confirm about every six months, shows us that to date all personal computers sold, ours and everyone else's, have only filled in the first area, the early innovators. There's only about 5% penetration, or 1.25 million units that have gone into this professional market so far. But the number of professional computer users is rapidly growing, and by the end of this year it will probably be at three or four million.

Now, it takes a typical person twenty to forty hours to learn how to use their personal computer, and then each time you move from one application to another it takes that much time again, like with word processing that you've just mastered spending twenty to forty hours. WordStar has a *400*-page manual! Then you have to spend the same amount of time learning the next program that you use. Why? Because they each have different commands to do pretty much the same operations. So you end up having to carry around a little pocket guide, and you get mixed up, or you can't remember what to do. That's the state of the situation they're in right now.

So these early innovators under our curve, no problem, they're the kind of people who learned how to drive cars first, they were the first people to fly, they were the pioneers in the old days who literally walked across the plains. They put up with a lot. But the people in the majority of the curve—no way in the world! They're the people who are going to wait for Interstate 80 to be paved and they'll drive across the plains.

In order for us and IBM and anybody else to get out into the majority part of the market curve where there are about twenty million people, we aren't going to do it with last year's technology. The Macintosh only takes about three or four hours to learn, and it's just this little thing that doesn't look complicated or threatening, even though it's really very powerful.

UNDERSTANDING THE
MICRO MARKETPLACE

35

Aren't the people in your target market, the knowledge workers, employed in major corporations that are addicted to IBM?
Oh, no. About 30% of the knowledge workers are in large corporations. The other 70% are in medium and small companies. There's really only a thousand companies in the Fortune 1000. Now, how many companies are *not* in the Fortune 1000? Several million in the United States.

Your point—I can't just walk around it—was that a lot of these large companies are predisposed toward IBM. However, we're seeing already that someone in Big-Blue Land goes and buys 5000 IBM-PCs for all their Grade 46 managers. Some manager shows up for work on Monday morning, and there's this PC sitting there with *three* 400-page manuals, two of them just to get going on the system before he can start learning the software. The guy gives it a try and pretty soon he decides to work on it later, and it ends up as a door stop. We're seeing that happening right now.

So what we have to do is go out there and cry on street corners, on soap boxes, you know, that there is something much better, that technology has *not* frozen, and that Apple is an innovative company that is not being different for the sake of being different. We've got something that will really help people to do real things.

Is there any plan to make Apple network with IBM-PCs so they can work compatibly?
We think that this summer or late this fall IBM and AT&T and whoever else wants to be a key player in real networking is going to play their cards, and we'll see what's going to happen. What we're going to provide is the ability to put clusters of products in departments and be able to work very efficiently, up to thirty-two devices all plugged together in your department. Now if you have an IBM mainframe somewhere, there will be the ability to hook up to that, or to any other kind of network.

Can a company have a mixture of IBMs and Macs working together on the same data?
You can do that right now. If you're talking about just moving raw data, that's possible. Microsoft stuff and Lotus stuff can move back and forth, but Mac's graphics won't move onto any of the other computers because they don't have the capability.

What about that single, lonely little disk drive? Having two drives is so much more convenient, so why did you only give us one?
When we get 512K memory on the Mac, some of the inconvenience goes away, or you can add a second drive externally any time. Our long-term design point of view is that when you have little clusters of equipment working together in a small business or department, that you would much rather have an external file server and four Macintoshes sharing it, and the cost per system is less; that's what we're working towards. The external file server can have twenty megabytes on it for about the same price as the extra disk drives on those four Macs, so you can get fifty times the memory. That's the trade-off, but it's a problem, I understand that. The ultimate design goal is to get this whole thing down to a notebook size, that's obviously where we're going.

What's it like creating software on the Macintosh as compared to those other machines. Is there any difference?
Oh, yes. On typical computers, you have the hardware, the disk operating system, and then the various applications programs that tie in, and each program has to have its own menu manager, math package, screen and keyboard operations, and so on. They might be okay, but the point is, they're all different. Now the Macintosh has this 32-bit hardware, and that comes with an operating system that includes the User Interface Toolbox, which has over 460 powerful software subroutines. There's Quickdraw with its super graphics capabilities, and the menu manager, the window manager, mouse

manager, icon managers, and so on. All of that's built in. We've standardized the user interface.

In the world of those other computers, the burden of responsibility for learning how to use the system and software is placed on the end user. That's where you get a lot of different user interfaces and 400-page manuals. But we're asking software developers to become pretty technical to understand our Apple Mac system. It takes a lot of effort and it requires a different type of thinking and orientation. The first application is really difficult to write, but after they've learned it, the next applications are a piece of cake. It really separates the men from the boys. If you really are a professional developer, the Mac is really neat, but if you're a hacker, you probably won't know what to do.

But didn't a lot of Apple II success came from a horde of amateurs developing funky but sometimes fascinating programs?
That's a myth, although I'm heretical in saying that. Yes, there are 16,000 applications, but if you do research you find that the typical Apple II user uses two-and-a-half applications, period.

But doesn't that mean there aren't going to be that many people that can develop small vertical applications on the Mac? You know, for their tennis pro shops or pig farms?
People will still do that on the Mac, but they won't be using the elegant user interface. You can write a plain application in BASIC or Pascal, or something. But the smart thing is for people to write templates to lay on top of Multiplan or Lotus 1-2-3.

We've been really pleased that since we introduced the Mac two months ago, we've had over seven hundred software developers contact us saying they want to do Macintosh applications. If 20% of them do it, if we get 140 great applications in the first year, that's really a lot. We're giving technical seminars around the country, and the response has been very enthusiastic. We have totally open

38

architecture and tell them how to do it all. The twenty best companies in the country have been putting 30-50% of their staff on Macintosh projects—their best people.

I see the software industry going through some fast changes, and I think a shakeout is coming very rapidly so there'll be just a few companies up on the top. If I were running a software company today, I would support people that create smaller applications that use my product. I would go to the little cottage developers, and I would be the one that provides the seminars that teaches them how to do Mac software, and I would become this master publisher of their Macintosh software. I have the expertise on knowing how to do it, and those little guys can't afford to go out and spend millions of dollars on advertising. Ultimately, the real gravy train is where I layer my proprietary program with every one of those little applications that can tie into my program and use the Macintosh User Interface through it, so they're all linked together and the data can flow back and forth. That to me is a $500 million company in a couple of years. No one seems to see that yet.

A point that I'd like to really hammer home is that I think in eighteen months we'll see some really new kinds of software showing up. We're just at the point of taking the crank off the front of the car with the Macintosh, but the Apple II and the IBM-PC—those are almost like horse-and-buggies. Mac is certainly the most different computer out there, and the Macintosh family of products will be the alternative to IBM.

This is a new beginning, and we're going to build on it, and in seven years, we'll have an incredibly robust product family, hopefully in four years. To measure us now is premature. This is just a beginning. The computer has to fit into people's lives. If we continually try to make the person fit into the computer's way, we're going to fail.

Chapter Three

IN THE BEGINNING: MICROSOFT

Even a hardened city person first entering the fifth Fall COMDEX would probably feel like Conan the Barbarian coming in from the wilderness. My god, the lights, the colors, the shiny new toys, and all those eager, smiling people with arms outstretched in greeting; every booth by its mere appearance is a promise of eternal wealth and joy if you would just step in and sample their wares, soft or hard. It was an assault on the senses. It was exciting. It was bewildering. It was the microcomputer industry in 3-D, Quadraphonic Feelavision; every four-color, full-page ad from every thick, glossy computer magazine, all brought to sudden life, thrashing and flashing, by some demon wizard in suede shoes.

To call most of those exhibits "booths" does not do them justice. The Intertec "booth" was an entire suite of designer-decorated offices, and the Great Plains Company built a big corral where you could try to rope one of their products to win it. Dayflo Software set up a small professional stage on the side of their exhibit where they put on a Broadway-quality musical every hour or so. A lot of booths were actually clever little buildings, put up for

40

just the five days of COMDEX. There were several high-rise booths with action on two levels, and one even had a small enclosed theater below with a go-go dancer on top of it. That was dumb, since most people looked up and never even saw whose booth it was. Signs and structures towered thirty to fifty feet over the midway; me, too! me, too! Here we are! And the midways stretched on, and on, and on.

There was a whole side-aisle occupied by companies from Great Britain, a pavilion full of Koreans, an enclave of Canadians, Japanese all over the place, Germans, Australians—companies from around the world. There were Saudis roaming the floor, but they weren't selling, they were buying. No companies from Borneo, but they may have had a suite at one of the hotels. A lot of smaller companies set up hospitality suites without actually having a booth on the floor—it's cheaper, and a good way to do a certain kind of business.

It's one thing to tell you that there were over 1400 exhibitors there, occupying over 6000 booth spaces, all lined up on eleven miles of aisles, but it is quite another thing to try to take it all in. COMDEX dwarfs an ordinary mortal. You would need a full day just to walk through very quickly, so to get the most out of it you had to study the catalogue, make charts and lists, and devise a strategy. Doing the Fall COMDEX requires organizational ability and purposeful execution of tactics. Maybe it's a test.

COMDEX boss, Sheldon Adelson, said that 25% of the exhibitors were software companies. Good! That narrowed the field right down to only 350 booths to visit. Fortunately, it turned out that there were really only six different programs at COMDEX: there were seventy five database programs, sixty spreadsheet products, over a hundred word processors, even more accounting applications, piles of graphics products, and lots of systems software. Best but fewest of all were the unique and innovative programs. Take a sampling from those groups and you could probably learn something.

How could anyone ever make sense of an industry this big, this fast, this turbulent? More to the point, how could anyone get a business launched in such raging currents? Even more immediately to the point, how could all of this be squeezed into a book that makes sense?

The answer was finally revealed in the form of two ancient precepts. First: it can't be done, so don't sweat it. Second: start at the beginning.

In the beginning there was was Bill Gates. With Paul Allen created he Microsoft, and Microsoft created BASIC, and seven summers later created they the Word, and they did prosper.

BILL GATES OF MICROSOFT

After IBM, which is more a force of nature than a company, probably the strongest single influence in the micro marketplace today is Bill Gates, founder and Chairman of the Board of Microsoft. Microsoft was the world's first microcomputer software company, and they are now the foremost independent software developer on earth; foremost in breadth of field, foremost in influence, and foremost in that universally recognized measure, revenues. Throughout the years they have demonstrated over and over again that they have a talent for technological innovation, and that they can recognize opportunities and seize them.

The Microsoft product line now ranges through the entire spectrum of software products: programming languages and tools like BASIC, FORTRAN, COBOL, Pascal, and a C Compiler; operating systems like MS-DOS and XENIX; applications software like MultiPlan and Microsoft Word; and even some games. They have also introduced several hardware devices, special boards designed to enhance the operation of software on the Apple and the IBM micros. In 1983, approximately 40% of all microcomputers shipped carried Microsoft software.

Microsoft's future strategy includes a major thrust into retail software sales in general. In particular, they are big supporters of the Apple Macintosh and will market a family of high class productivity software for the Mac which they expect will provide a significant part of their revenue growth.

The Growth of Microsoft

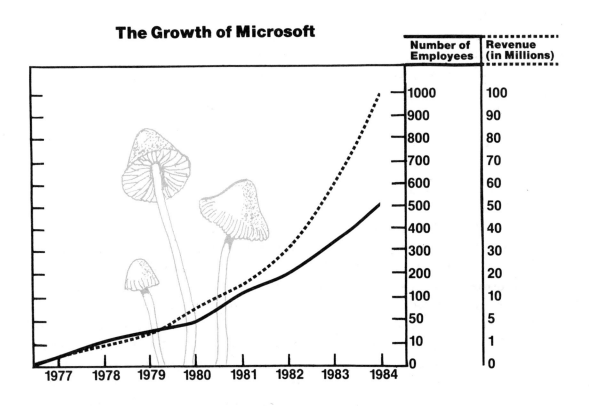

	Number of Employees	Revenue (in Millions)
	1000	100
	900	90
	800	80
	700	70
	600	60
	500	50
	400	40
	300	30
	200	20
	100	10
	50	5
	10	1
	0	0

1977   1978   1979   1980   1981   1982   1983   1984

Microsoft quickly overflowed its newly-built facilities, so they had to grow into another nearby building. The building that houses Bill Gates and most of the company leaders is modernly attractive, but organized in a strictly efficient and functional way. The place is a giant think tank, with hundreds of little offices, cubicles really, strung along endless corridors, all wired together through a central computer system. This mental gymnasium was highly charged and stimulating, no doubt because of the creative work going on, but all the same there was nothing warm or chummy about the place, and there wasn't much in the way of a comfortable, communal place to meet, relax and gossip. However, for a dedicated programmer it might be the closest thing to heaven.

CHAPTER THREE

IN THE BEGINNING: MICROSOFT

43

Bill Gates is a very mental person, as you might guess. He taught himself to program when he was thirteen, and that was well before programming was generally available to the public. He is the *wunderkind* of the software world, a veritable *enfant terrible*, which is what E.T. really stands for. Stories about him have been told and retold so frequently that he is becoming a part of our folklore, a mythological hero, and he's not even thirty yet.

Despite his position, his brilliance, stature, wealth and power, Bill Gates is a disarmingly casual guy, both in dress and manner. And in a way that's hard to describe, he seems almost vulnerable. Bill is quite slender, and his height is deceptive because he sits in a deep slouch most of the time. Even when he stands he hunches constantly, as if the pressures of being who, what, and where he is are weighing upon him.

Bill Gates and his friend Paul Allen are proof for the argument that great entrepreneurs are born, not made. When Bill was still at high school in Seattle in the early 1970s, he and Paul cooked up some high-tech adventures, like the time they started a company called Traff-O-Data to analyze traffic data, or when they consulted for industrial giant TRW and successfully designed a computerized electricity grid for the Bonneville Power Administration. The entrepreneurial spirit burned hot in their veins, and when the first Intel chip, the 8008, came out in 1971, these lads went right out and got an NSF grant to study parallel microprocessors in Artificial Intelligence applications.

Paul Allen quit Washington State University after two years to join Honeywell as an assistant programmer, and from there he watched the emergence of the first microprocessors. Bill wrote minicomputer software and attended Harvard. From time to time they kicked around different ideas for a hardware or software company, but when MITS announced their Altair personal microcomputer kit in December, 1974, they were galvanized into immediate action. Bill holed up in his dorm room where he and Paul wrote a BASIC language for the 8080 microprocessor in five weeks. They turned right around and sold it to MITS, and Microsoft was up and running.

Well, maybe not running, exactly. Gates stayed at Harvard for another year, then left in 1976 to join Allen at MITS. There, the two worked to develop and promote the Altair, moonlighting to build up Microsoft. BASIC was refined and sold to other customers, such as GE, NCR, and Citibank. In 1977, Microsoft got a big boost from a contract with Tandy Radio Shack to develop software for their new TRS-80 micro. That's the year they quit MITS and moved to Seattle to spend full time on Microsoft and the year they released FORTRAN.

Also in 1977, Gates met Kazuhiko (Kay) Nishi, a young Japanese micro magazine editor and entrepreneur who is now Microsoft's V.P. of New Technologies. They hit it off big, and Kay became Microsoft's Japanese connection, a cornucopia of contacts and action. Far more important, however, is the fact that he and Bill have a spark, a creative catalysis. Their biggest coup came in 1982 when they designed, programmed, and organized the manufacturing resources for a lap-sized portable computer. They sold the idea to Tandy, who soon brought out the innovative and highly successful Model 100.

In 1978, Microsoft introduced COBOL for micros and licensed their BASIC to Tandy and Apple. In 1979 they developed BASIC for the 16-bit chip, and decided to develop applications and end user software.

July of 1980 was memorable. That's when IBM began secret talks with Microsoft about a personal computer. This was a special honor, because IBM had never before contracted with an outside firm for development work. IBM had picked what it considered to be the best mind in the business. Gates referred IBM to Digital Research for an operating system, but after DRI fumbled, Microsoft ended up developing the operating system as well as the programming tools and languages for IBM's new 16-bit personal computer. When the IBM-PC soared, it took Microsoft up with it.

If you are number one, everybody shoots at you, so Microsoft will continually face challenges. Digital Research is launching competitive languages and operating systems in order to win back their position in the market. That battle may be fought over multi-user and multi-tasking

CHAPTER THREE

IN THE BEGINNING: MICROSOFT

features—the ability for several users to run on the same system, and the ability to run more than one program simultaneously. Microsoft countered with Windows, a program that will allow the user to run several programs at the same time, to work with them on the same screen if desired and to share data between them. Also in the ring for a grudge match is VisiCorp, recently eclipsed by Microsoft's superior spreadsheet program, MultiPlan.

IBM has put out its own version of UNIX, different from Microsoft's XENIX, and there are always rumors that IBM will some day soon move to a different operating system of its own. AT&T has ganged up with DRI to work on UNIX System V, DRI has put out Concurrent DOS 3.1, and VisiCorp has put out VisiOn. To stay on top, Microsoft will just have to keep putting out.

Until mid-1982, Bill Gates ran Microsoft almost by himself, but to meet the major challenges that loom ahead, Microsoft assembled an impressive management team that is now headed by Jon Shirley, who left his position as V.P. of Computer Marketing for Tandy Corporation in 1983 to become President of Microsoft. Gates is now Executive V.P. and Chairman of the Board.

William H. Gates, Microsoft Corporation

Many other companies have become dominated by their marketing departments, so they are called "market-driven." But because Bill Gates and many of his managers are technical people, Microsoft stands out as an ideal example of a company that is technology-driven. This does not mean that they are not capable marketers; quite the contrary. When Microsoft Word was introduced in the fall of 1983, they spent $3.5 million on promotion and pulled the spectacular stunt of putting a demonstration disk in hundreds of thousands of *PC World* magazines, together with a dozen or so full pages of instructions.

46

Now that is a marketing trick that drastically raises the stakes for any competitor who wants to come in.

Listening to Bill Gates talk is extremely interesting. This is one man who has been in the industry since the beginning, who now sits at the top, and who has a great deal to say about how things will go.

Given the conditions in the industry today, if you had a talented, bright friend who was interested in starting a software company, what advice would you give?

BILL GATES: (Laughs) I've talked to hundreds and hundreds of people who've said that. I would say, why don't you start a car company and then after you've done that, come and talk? Why don't you start an airplane company? I don't know, depending upon what part of the business you want to come into, it's a very different thing now than when we started.

To expect somebody to just start out with all the skills and be able to get up to critical mass in terms of the money they'll need, and the attention they'll need, and stuff like that, I think is extremely naive.

I'd tell the person, go to work. Find a software company that is really a software company—not just has a couple of big hits that they are living off of, but really has a methodology for developing software products, for refining what those products should be. Go to work for that company, and learn whatever it is. And then, after you've really learned the industry and how things go on, then maybe go out and do your own company.

There are some areas where you can do your own company. If you want to develop really good games and educational stuff, and get somebody to publish them, there is plenty of opportunity. You'd better be a really, really good artist, and really creative in terms of how you do stuff, like the guy who wrote our Flight Simulator. There's opportunities for that type of stuff.

CHAPTER THREE

Vertical market things are good. If you look at travel agents, architects, even the big ones, lawyers, doctors, stuff like that. I don't think some kid out of school is going to do that. I think it will be a marriage between somebody who understands the excitement of personal computers and how to take advantage of them, and somebody who knows how to market and distribute to lawyers, probably somebody who's been a lawyer. If you get those two skills together, either in one person or in a company, I think there's incredible opportunity. I think that is one of the most untapped areas right now.

Let's go back a bit. What were things like when you started Microsoft? Did you intend to become an industry leader?

There were no other microcomputer software companies. We had a concept of what we wanted to do as a software company back then. The early stage was easy; we wanted to make all the software that was available on minicomputers available on micros.

We had actually designed a personal computer based on the 8080, and we thought real seriously about doing a hardware company. Then I said to Paul, no, let's just do a software company. It seemed kind of too early, because at this time nobody was using micros, I mean absolutely not. Nobody recognized that they had that much power. They were being used in calculators. So the idea of doing software at that stage was kind of weird in a way, because there were no customers.

We talked about how we could make all the software that was available on minicomputers available on micros. So we looked at what each of the minicomputer companies had done. We got their catalogues and we said, "Okay, these are the compilers, these are the development tools, okay, how many years would it take us to make the equivalent of that stuff available on the 8080?"

We were doing some work with artificial intelligence on an NSF grant, but that money had run out. Then we got the *Popular Electronics*

48

(January, 1975) where the Altair was on the cover. That was the thing where we said okay, let's do the software company idea. We were kind of tired of just waiting for things to happen. This was something concrete. They were actually offering kits in the magazine. We talked about a lot of things, but that was when we decided, okay, we would do software, and as people recognized the importance of micros, and as people used them more and more, we would be there with software. Particularly with the BASIC, the first thing to do is the BASIC.

When we started, there was no industry, there were no other software companies. We just had a vision that there would be a software industry. I had always wanted to do a software company. I'm a pure software person. I have no ability to do hardware like Paul. I had always wanted to do a software company, but prior to the microcomputer industry, where were the software companies? There was Cullinet—I knew how much they spent on marketing, what their profit was, I knew how ADP worked, I knew how Computer Sciences worked. I hadn't studied those companies just because I said, "Oh, I want to make a microcomputer do neat things." No, we actually thought about the concept of a software company.

All the software companies to that point were simply selling stuff onto IBM mainframes, and those companies were very marketing intensive. Initially they had a founder who did a good developmental product, but their long term asset was their marketing. They had guys paid $100,000 a year to go off and sell to IBM mainframes. And all the software I had written before Microsoft, I had written for minis or mainframes. It was systems software, where either I would have to put together an end user sales force to try to sell it, or I could sell it to the manufacturer of the machine.

I had gone through a lot of things, like where I had gone to DEC, and every time I took them a piece of software they would give me a nice helicopter ride, and they would say, "You've got to come to work here. We'll pay you a bunch of money, and that's what you ought to do." The amount of money they offered me for this stuff had been super low, because they knew there was nobody else I could take it to. They wouldn't take me seriously until I said, "Oh, no. I'm going to get my own sales force." But their installed base wasn't as big as IBM's, and so even if I had wanted to do it, it would have been very, very hard.

So there was no position to start a software company, and the idea of the microcomputer really changed the rules. Once you get a microcomputer, then you get many, many hardware companies all using the same instruction set (the microchip's internal language). The initial business model is that you are sort of an extension of (the hardware manufacturer's) engineering department, where they're taking engineering dollars, and instead of writing their own BASIC, they come out and buy your BASIC. The first year and a half of the business, that was strictly it—going to NCR, Radio Shack, Data Products, a lot of funny people, and selling them the BASIC for use on their micro machines.

We didn't say to ourselves that we wanted to be a leader, because it was was very unclear at the time who our competitors would be. First of all, it was a very small market, and we were trying to expand the market by telling people how great micros were. Second, the in-house development groups were trying to do their own thing. In fact, Apple did their own BASIC, Radio Shack did their own BASIC, those were eventually cancelled, and they took our things. But right at first, it was everybody's tendency to do the stuff themselves.

Remember how small things were back then? What was Ed Roberts' (MITS) ambition? I was always amazed when he said he wanted to have a $10 million a year company. I thought that's such a small number, this is ridiculous. It was nothing. I didn't drop out of school to get involved in a $10 million a year company. Our company is about ten times the size of what MITS was at its absolute peak.

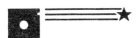

50

Okay, what *did* you drop out of school for?

To have an involvement in putting a microcomputer on every desk and in everybody's home, some day, somehow. We kind of laughed at ourselves, because we said if we really had such good vision—which we did, and we believed it with our hearts and souls—if we were financial wizards, we would have invested in Intel, in terms of money. But we wanted to do it. We wanted to actually write the code, and write the pieces. The thing that raised our competitive instinct the most, was not, okay, some guy is making a lot of money or something like that, but someone else is really pushing towards that goal, and making things easier to use, more than we are, and we are kind of being left behind—that's what really gets us to say, god, we got to do better, we got to think up more ideas, we got to try harder, move faster.

A lot of people have nostalgia for the days before the industry got to be all big business and hyped up. Do you share that?

Sure! I don't think you have time for me to go through my nostalgia. Most of the people you talk to in the business now had nothing to do with the industry when it was small. They didn't go to the World Altair computer convention. They never built an Altair computer. There were a few people, like Gary Kildall (Digital Research) or Seymour Rubinstein (MicroPro), they came in about a year-and-a-half after we did. There was a phase in the industry between about '77 and '79 where everybody knew everybody. I mean, I knew all the guys. I knew Millard over at Imsai, Ed Roberts at Altair. The manufacturers were kind of rude to each other because they were kind of competitors. But the software guys—Jim Warren was running the (West Coast) Computer Faire, everybody was friends with him, Gary was a nice guy who kind of had an operating system, Seymour worked at Imsai, and then he did his own software company. The West Coast Computer Faire was sort of a gathering point where we would be. Ted Nelson would come out, and we would talk to each other about what was going on.

The whole thing was not, "What is our relative position in the industry?" so much as it was, "God, we know something that nobody else does. Gee, isn't this the world's greatest thing and how can we make it happen faster?" Ted Nelson talked about things like—and it turns out to be pretty naive in retrospect—how we are going to crumble IBM with all this stuff we're doing, and we really understand how and where it's going to be. But I think he captured some of the spirit of those days.

That was so much fun! The very first computer convention, the World Altair computer convention, we had no idea that people would come. Dave Bunnell who later started *PC* magazine, and then started *PC World* magazine, was the marketing guy back at MITS. He said let's just have a convention. We knew most of the people around the country because we had gotten a big, blue GM van, we called it the "MITS Mobile," and had driven it around the country with a couple of Altairs.

Everywhere we'd go, we would do a little bit of advertising before we went in. We would go and do a seminar on the Altair—this was when the Altair was the *only* machine. This was like the end of '75. Every time we left one of these cities, we would say, "Okay, we want to pick somebody here to form the local users' group." That's how the Home Brew Club got started, that's how the Boston Computer Society got started. They were good groups, and in a way there's less user's groups now than there were then, because those were hard core. For a while they really prospered.

We had this crazy conference in Kansas City where we were going to standardize everything. We were going to standardize cassette tape formats, and so the guy from Sphere Computer flew in, the guy from South Tech came in. Those were the two big competitors. Imsai and Sol came a little bit after that, and Imsai turned out to be the best competitor to MITS, although you know both of them died out.

52

There was Polymorphic, there was Digital Group, Les Solomon came in from *Popular Electronics*, and Wayne Green came.

That's all gone now, isn't it? In order to be creative now don't you have to be a member of a major corporation or something?
There's still the insider's group. It's a different group. It's not quite as free-form as it was. It's a very conscious thing now, where you plan in advance who you are going to talk to, about some sort of alliance, or joint venture or things like that. There's this Rosen conference that a lot of people go to. Ben Rosen was one of the original industry insiders and he was a guy who understood how this crazy micro world and financial world were going to come together at some point, and he gave people advice. He was nice to a lot of people. He was nice to Jobs (Apple) and me and Jonathan Rotenberg and Dan Fylstra, a lot of people were his friends. He started getting the micro people to come to his conferences and mix with those sort of people.

There is still kind of an insider's group which is Fylstra (VisiCorp), Mitch Kapor (Lotus). We were good friends with Mitch, he was our best friend at VisiCorp when he worked there. He was a product manager, he tested all their stuff. Everybody who has a company knows everybody. But it's not the free form thing. If some stranger walked into the group and had some idea, it's not that open.

Do you think that the way marketing dominates the industry now is a bad thing?
Oh, no. It's a natural thing. There is no single crummy product that's been marketed so well that it's been successful. The fact is that it's the combination. You can kind of multiply your technical strength by your marketing strength and get your net effectiveness factor.

CHAPTER THREE

But can't you out-market a good product with one not so good?
Yeah, but it's so hard to agree on what's good and what's bad in this industry. The metric you end up using is success, and you can't separate out the marketing from the product quality part. In systems software, or productivity software, marketing is really big. We've embraced that. We enjoy the fact that we can put a bunch of disks in magazines, and we can run a lot of ads. So we have to adapt to that environment.

It is a different environment now. I mean, back then, just having things done was enough. There were so many things to do, that it was very rare for two people on the software side to do the same thing.

Why do people think VisiCalc is the program that took the microcomputer off the hobby desk and put it on the business desk?
People love simple explanations, like "Apple invented the personal computer." I don't know who those other eighteen companies were that I was working with before Apple was even founded, but, you know, that was simple. So people think Steve Jobs invented the personal computer, and VisiCorp invented applications. Yeah, VisiCalc was the most successful, but before VisiCalc there were about a dozen word processors, about three different types of spreadsheet programs, like Desk Top Plan. VisiCorp found it and went and bought it up, and decided that they would have those two categories. In fact, there were a couple of spreadsheet-like things down on micros, and tons of them on minis. There were word processors where you could add up columns of numbers. Some things even had little formulas. But VisiCalc was relatively unique, and it was by far the most successful of all those early things.

Had Apple hit a plateau in sales before VisiCalc?
No way! They were just going into the transition from non-disk systems to disk systems. They were doing just fine. People had started

to write entertainment software for them. I remember back in those days people were saying that they thought 10% of Apple's sales were due to VisiCalc. Nowadays people are saying, oh, god, I wonder if *all* of Apple's sales are due to VisiCalc.

No, the original penetration numbers for VisiCalc in the first couple of years were actually pretty low. It's only in the last twelve months that spreadsheets have such incredible penetration. That started to fall back off again on the Apple II because it's being positioned more and more as a lower cost machine, where a spreadsheet is less relevant. It's more of a training machine, a home machine. Apple always manages to fit in between the home and the business market.

Is it inevitable that from now on, IBM will call all the shots?
No. It is not inevitable. Right now it might feel like IBM controls everything, but this is a very innovative industry where there's a need for new things all the time. Part of IBM's cleverness is because they've got the plug-in slots, and they like third party software. A lot of the good innovative stuff that goes on works to their benefit because it plugs into the PC one way or the other, and that's the first thing that people plug it into.

The idea of tapping into innovation with slots, and like in the third party software industry, Apple sort of led the way with that, but IBM learned how to do it. Even so, if IBM doesn't really come up with some great products and other people do, and believe me there are a lot of people trying, IBM's position will be eroded. I think there is plenty of opportunity.

After all, there are independent retail operations that will be glad to take a better product, where better means a lot these days in terms of training, support, advertising, and real end user benefit. It doesn't just mean you move bits faster on the bus (internal data lines), which could have been the definition three or four years ago. But if company X has a really good product, and IBM has a really good product, then IBM wins, because they do have that position.

You imply that it takes more to make a better product than it used to. What are the elements now of a successful product?
Good tutorial, good brand name that sits on it, really wide distribution, runs on a bunch of machines, translated into a bunch of different languages—there are a lot of pieces that go into a success. Of the amount of work to introduce a new product, the actual development of the code, although it is certainly the most magical piece, is less than half of the work. If you take the manual, the tutorial, the intro kit, all the pieces that go into it, that's easily as many man-months as coding.

Is it difficult to decide when to stop writing a program and call it a product?
Sure. In today's marketplace, you don't want to introduce something and then three months later say now it's good, and later say now it really works and it's really good. Because of the noise level out there, even Microsoft has to come out with a big bang. So you've got to have it really perfect. Then the time pressure is really incredible. VisiCorp's got their thing out, Lotus is going to be out in June, Ashton-Tate might even improve their thing, and Jesus! Let's get it out! Let's get it out! And you read the magazines, see what's selling. You know, let's get our name up there.

Someone has to decide things, but that's the management of the software company, getting the tools right, and getting the right people, and then giving people good feedback, and making decisions like what is the spec? When are we going to freeze the spec? And making the tradeoff of, okay, we have a better idea, but are we going to jerk this thing around or are we just going to go for it?

There is so much to do that you've got to freeze the spec. You've got to document it, you've got the tutorial, you've got to do the testing, there is typesetting, there is ad copy. All these things where if you decide to change the product, you're not going to introduce it for four-and-a-half months. And we are efficient. We have our own in-house typesetting machine, and we can prioritize stuff. People work very long hours, but even so, if you decide to change a feature, that's got to be four months until the marketplace sees the thing.

That's one of the positions that I am in. For some of the products, I am the one who says, "Okay, let's sell it," or "No, let's wait."

Do you think it's important to make a micro so that it's obvious how you use it, the way a typewriter or a car is?
Being obvious to use is an obvious goal. Everyone has that goal. And making machines fast, that's good. Cheap? I think that's great, too. Cheap, easy to use, fast: they're all good. And everybody in the industry, every day they come into work, all day long and even into the night, that's exactly what they are trying to do.

Speaking of working into the night, the high-tech industries are said to be progressive in the way they treat their employees. Is Microsoft?
In this company it's not so much where there's this paternalistic entity that is going to take care of you no matter what. But if you are really energetic, and think things through, no matter how old you are, you can have a real effect.

Can employees share in the profits or buy stock?
A recent *Fortune* article accurately stated that over a third of the employees have options in the company, and that many people here have done quite well through their ownership of the company. It helps people feel a part of things, but there's even more than that on a day-to-day basis. It's really nice. We have a lot of different projects,

and we believe in small project teams. Our typical project development team is three or four people. Of those teams, usually only one of those people will be somebody who has proven experience in doing that thing before. The other ones will be pushed beyond their limit.

The average age here is quite low, and that's because this energetic, fresh approach to things in general has somehow led to having young people. Even though some of our more energetic people and best people aren't so young.

In terms of making big decisions, it's not like we decided to put factories down. We are creating an electrical property. We create software. That's not something where you get a lot of committees together and you meet about stuff. There's three or four people who developed the Word, three or four people who develop the Plan, three or four people who did the (Tandy) Model 100 (software), three or four people who did the MS-DOS. It's up to them.

Do people who develop products get any interest or royalty?
No way. No, come on! We're not a bunch of traders, where we say, "Hey, I wanna work on this thing because I get 2%, 3%, no, no, no, I won't come in on the weekend, can you give me another 10%, gimme another 4%?" This is not some financial market. We didn't decide to be stock brokers or people like that. We are professional engineers, who work for one company that's trying to achieve one goal. Not where this guy is competing with that guy, and he didn't get any development resources so his royalty isn't as big.

I'm sure as companies have grown there have been many theories in management, many things they have had to learn. But the idea of anything that doesn't reinforce the idea of "you all work together and we all have common goals," is really crazy.

What about giving programmers name recognition on a package they designed?

Most people come here and they work. Within the company there's some old hands, people like Charles Simonyi, who was at Xerox Park and did a high percentage of really good software there, and there's kind of a sense of recognition. It's a sense of, okay, everyone agrees that a few people here really know what they are doing. Everybody really admires them, and you aspire towards that same ability. You get to critical mass, where you have enough really good programmers that other people want to come here and prove themselves, and they can learn a lot from it. So within the company, certainly, there's recognition.

But doing that externally is a little weird. Trying to get the end user just to remember the name of the company alone is hard enough.

Also, our projects aren't one-man projects at all. If you want to do an integrated family of productivity tools, there is no way you can do that with less than twenty or thirty people. We go to universities, and we spend a lot of time creating, and we get the best people we can, and we leverage them with the best tools we can. You've got to have them all working in concert. It may come out as individual projects, but it has to be user-interfaced, the data exchange, all that stuff has to be architected as a group.

Some people think the industry is short term in its thinking. Does Microsoft have any long term goals?

Well, yeah. We have a development methodology which is part of a three year program to get to meet certain concrete efficiency levels in terms of developing new products. It's our goal to understand the development methodology best, and be the most efficient producers.

Getting your turnaround cycles down has incredible benefits in terms of being able to test, being able to jump on new hardware, being able to take feedback from end users and then change the product. It takes a year to get something done, by the time you're done. If somebody tells you it's crummy, you're not going to say "We'll start over."

The company was founded on the proposition that someday everybody is going to have a microcomputer on their desk, and everybody is going to have a microcomputer in their home. We're not market forecast people. We can't tell you when and at what price, and what company, and things like that. But we believe that there is real value in the microcomputer, and slowly but surely, we will make it effective enough, and easy enough to use, and it will evolve enough that everyone will want one.

What about the other companies? What are they accomplishing?
There is a lot of difference between the software companies right now. A huge difference. Just in terms of how serious they are about development methodology. Some of them are really more marketing companies. Some of them have lost their initial flavor. They've lost the young excitement, and they're just an organization. Which ones do I mean? I would say MicroPro has lost that and now there are all these sales guys with consumer backgrounds that run the stuff.

There's a big difference between being a good developer, like Wayne Ratliff at Ashton-Tate, and actually hiring and supervising good developers—we try harder than others at this. We still have a lot to learn, a long ways to go, but there's a lot of difference between the companies on those things. Scheduling software projects, deciding what the tools should be, getting the people to work together, and so on.

Who do you think is a good software developer?
Lotus. They develop software well, they do. They have a jewel, and I know what their next two things are and they're also quite good. Partly, they do it by focusing in. Software Publishing also keeps things small, simple, but it's a good development organization. VisiCorp?

They're trying, the results won't prove it, but they're trying, they have a couple of good things. It's a challenge when you grow big.

Look. The big winners of yester-year are MicroPro, Digital Research, Microsoft, and VisiCorp. Now there's new companies like Lotus, though Mitch is kind of an old guy, and Software Publishing is relatively new. Fred Gibbons is an ex-HP (Hewlett-Packard) guy, very young-spirited, pretty experienced, a good manager.

There's an old saying that you have to be careful of what you dream, because it might come true. Any surprises for you in what it was like to become big?
Starting a software company, and having a software company, there is a big difference between those things. A big difference in terms of what sort of skills you need. I mean, you're not leveraging your own ability to execute things, you are leveraging your ability to organize things, and choose the right people to do stuff, and get everybody enthused, and move in the same direction. That's a natural transition that we went through somewhere between '77 and '80. Sort of an ongoing process of what our various roles would be—which of us would continue to be just individual contributors, and which of us would be sort of managers. You never know, the people you work with initially, they're all very smart people, they were all very enthusiastic, but it turns out their interests and abilities long term are quite different, as is their willingness to grow into positions. So some people surprise you one way or the other.

Sure! There are some incredible surprises.

What's the title of your book again? Oh, that'll be interesting.

CHAPTER THREE

Chapter Four

GARY KILDALL AND DIGITAL RESEARCH

You couldn't go anywhere at the 1983 Fall COMDEX without tripping across evidence of either Microsoft or Digital Research or both. Those two companies are interwoven throughout almost every aspect of the microcomputer industry. In fact, it seemed as if the only booths that didn't have some product from one company or the other were selling things like binders or anti-static spray. And although COMDEX was spread across 1.25 million square feet of floor space in five Las Vegas sites, the Microsoft and Digital Research booths both sat in the East Hall barely four aisles apart, like two stellar bodies in a binary system, circling one another in an eternal struggle of tidal forces.

When Gary Kildall was at the University of Washington working on advanced degrees in computer science, Bill Gates was an anonymous little kid in the same city. However, Bill Gates was first off the mark in the embryonic microcomputer industry when he started Microsoft with the first popular micro language in 1975. Then Gary Kildall started Digital Research in 1976 with the first generic operating system, CP/M. Both men were

founders of the industry; both products set industry standards. Meanwhile, Gary was working on the PL/I language, which he brought out later, and Bill later came out with an operating system, MS-DOS, that he cooked up in a deal with IBM that sort of pulled the rug out from under Gary. People in the industry love to gossip about whether Bill Gates and Gary Kildall are still friends after that deal. Bill Gates told me that he still liked Gary Kildall, but thought that Gary had cooled considerably toward him, and Gary told me that he still respected Bill a lot and didn't blame him a bit for anything. Hi-ho!

It is very difficult, maybe futile, to try to decide whether Microsoft or Digital Research is the most important software company in the industry right now, but it is even harder to keep from teasing at the comparison. Both companies lead the micro industry at the most fundamental level—systems and languages. Both companies are driven by technology first, marketing second. Both are led by technical innovators who have put their stamp on the industry from the very earliest days, and in profound ways. Both are allied with real heavies like IBM or AT&T. Truly, these two companies stand as twin peaks on the same mountain.

THE DIGITAL RESEARCH STORY

Gary Kildall, 42, is Chairman of the Board, Chief Executive Officer and primarily responsible for the technical developments at DRI. The business aspects are managed by President John Rowley, who brought in a high degree of professional management experience and who has led the company to other products, markets and countries. Digital Research hired 250 people in 1983, bringing staff to about 400, and they were earning over $45 million in annual revenues by year's end. Their tentacles spread from the 63,000 square-foot head offices in Monterey, California to branch offices in Palo Alto, Los Angeles, Boston, Chicago, London, Tokyo, Dallas, New York, Paris, and Frankfurt. Not bad for a company that Gary and his wife Dorothy started in their bedroom in 1976.

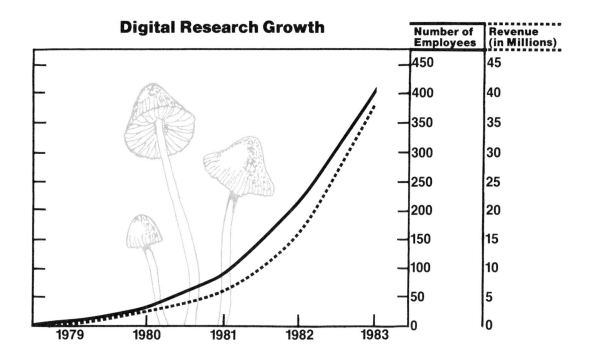

Digital Research Growth

	Number of Employees	Revenue (in Millions)
	450	45
	400	40
	350	35
	300	30
	250	25
	200	20
	150	15
	100	10
	50	5
	0	0

1979   1980   1981   1982   1983

DRI has only recently begun to look at consumer and educational markets. Before 1981, they concentrated on selling systems and languages through what they call "strategic alliances" in the industrial and commercial sectors. That is, in fact, one of their major strengths, for in addition to their immense base of 1100 or so hardware manufacturers (OEMs), they also have excellent relationships around the world with silicon chip makers, especially Intel. They recently forged a new relationship with IBM and will transport their entire language library to the IBM 3270-PC.

DRI is especially proud of their alliance with AT&T. Among other things, they will help develop software for the UNIX System V and the new Intel 286 chip, and work with AT&T to establish UNIX as a standard. President John Rowley says only "tiny parts" of the AT&T/DRI agreement are public right now. When asked if AT&T was planning to release any

hardware, Kildall said "I can't comment on that." Then I said, "Gee, you'd think that with AT&T sitting on that international communications network, and with their experience, that they'd have some plan to hook the whole world up with some kind of telephone-micro," and Gary said, "There's nothing public on that, yet." People could really get to fantasizing over that "yet."

Gary Kildall's most creative new project is to harness a micro with a videodisk player. It will combine digital and video information, and can be used for archival storage of such things as electronic encyclopedias, or for books that combine text and images (he suggested one on Van Gogh), or for games with astonishing visual content. He believes that random access videodisk technology will be one of the more important technologies and will have far-reaching impact in the future.

It could be just a coincidence, but after DRI lost the IBM connection to Microsoft, their actions became extremely competitive: they quickly expanded their very impressive product line of operating systems, languages, development tools, graphics, and local area networking software. DRI published a BASIC language that competes with Microsoft BASIC, and they even brought out a CP/M circuit board for Apple II computers, the Gold Card, that competes directly with Microsoft's SoftCard.

Other languages in DRI's product line include C, PL/I, FORTRAN, COBOL, and Pascal. Their goal is to develop "a technology that permits it to move, *en masse*, that entire catalogue of languages to new hardware environments." That means that products developed in any of their languages can be transported with relative ease across a wide range of computers and operating systems. Good news, and good luck! DRI is also entering the field of educational software with their Dr. Logo language, and they will enter the consumer home computing market as soon as anyone, anywhere, figures out what that market is all about. Their first effort in that direction is the long-overdue Personal CP/M and the Visual Interface Processor, intended to make CP/M easy to use for an ordinary person.

Struggling to get back into the 16-bit computer market created by IBM and co-opted by Microsoft's MS-DOS, DRI has come out with the excellent

GARY KILDALL
AND DIGITAL RESEARCH

new Concurrent DOS 3.1 operating system, that bridges PC-DOS and CP/M, offers concurrent execution of several programs, multi-user capability, windowing, and networking capabilities. Microsoft still dominates, but they are scrambling to keep their technology abreast of the competition.

Gary Kildall, Digital Research, Inc.

Gary Kildall is long, lean, and soft spoken. He dresses casually in jeans and western boots, and has a penchant for fine cars. He drove up for our 8 a.m. appointment in a gorgeous old Rolls, but said that he only drove it because his Porsche (about which he spoke fondly) was in for repairs. Despite his position and all the demands on his limited time, Gary Kildall is still a warm, comfortable and easy-going man. Strangely enough, he seems a bit shy.

Let's start at the beginning—how did CP/M come to be?

GARY KILDALL: Well, I was working with Intel on the 4004 chip in 1972, and then their next chip was the 8008, an 8-bit processor. I did the PL/M language for them, the Programming Language for Microprocessors. In fact that's where the name CP/M eventually came from. And of course the name PL/M sort of came from PL/I, so the genealogy of CP/M is really through the names PL/I, PL/M, and then CP/M—Control Program for Microprocessors.

I developed CP/M so I could get PL/M running on a small machine, a micro. Floppy disks were just coming out and I got one from Shugart, but I couldn't get a controller for a long time, so I spent about a year working on CP/M under simulation on a minicomputer, a PDP-10. This was about 1973. I got it up and running in about 1974.

I understand that in those days you had severe limitations in terms of machine size?
Yeah. A large memory machine would be 16K. It was really important to get the thing down to size, so CP/M itself was very small. It was written in PL/M. At that time I wouldn't really tell anybody that because there was sort of an implication that if you wrote in a high level language, there was inefficiency involved. So I'd just tell people it was written in assembly language, and that was okay.

Then, I guess about 1975, I was working as a consultant for Signetics on a PL/M-like language. I spent close to eight or nine months on that project, and didn't do much with CP/M. Then in late '75 I went back into the CP/M project, and I finished all the utilities, like the editors and the assemblers, and de-buggers, and copy utilities and all that. So those were all done in late '75.

Did you notice the Altair when it came out in early 1975?
Oh, yes, I knew about the Altair. I was at Intel consulting when they did the deal with Altair, and everybody was really totally amazed that they could come out with a whole box for $500. Especially since the processor seemed to be selling for $360. It turned out Intel had done a deal with them to get the price down. The Altair was cheesy. The design was not good, and also it was sort of a hobbyist machine. It wasn't really built to have a disk on it, although someone put one on later.

What were you trying to accomplish by writing CP/M?
Well, it was for my own use, initially. That was the idea. I wanted to get that compiler running and resident on it so I could go on and do my own work. It really wasn't spec'ed out for any other use except for PL/M support.

You know, the first versions of it, I wasn't really worried about protection or anything like that because I was using it myself. Then I licensed the first version of it to Omron of America, a big relay and hardware manufacturer. They were building a terminal system at the time. I was working at Intel and they came and asked Intel something about disk-based systems, and Intel turned around and directed them to me. The initial license for that was about $10,000 for the software license, unlimited, and another $15,000 for the hardware design.

Then the next big license was to Imsai, who had just developed a floppy disk system. The first deal was a royalty of $30 per copy I think, then it went to an unlimited license, later. But the thing that Imsai did, is they went out there and produced a piece of hardware with a floppy disk drive on it, and they sold a whole bunch of them to be a small business system and they didn't have any software at all. That was early in 1976.

Were you doing everything by yourself?
Well, my wife, Dorothy (McEwan), was doing it as well. What she did was she got the business license and things like that. Not the technical things. She was just administering it.

I was working with Signetics, as a consultant, and Jim Warren was involved with *Dr. Dobbs' Journal* at the time, and he suggested that I sell CP/M on an individual, per copy basis. We talked about it for a while, and put an ad in *Dr. Dobbs,'* or one of those magazines, and started getting some pretty good response. That was about the same time as we were doing the Imsai deal.

From 1976 to 1979, there was some competition for CP/M—quite a number of look-alikes that were CP/M clones. There was one called ZP/M. And there was another called CDOS, of course, the Cromemco disk operating system that was a CP/M clone. There were probably about four, five, or six of those that kind of popped up.

Do you know why yours connected and others did not?
I think part of it was due to the fact that we had really good utility programs with it, like the de-bugging system, and things of that sort that really helped out. DDT (the Dynamic Debugging Tool) may seem

pretty primitive now, but it was a very powerful tool then. Those kind of extra utilities I think really helped considerably. The other thing I think that was important was that we were a business that people could call on. We were there, and available. We set up in our bedroom and Dorothy helped keep it together. I wasn't consulting at the time, I was just sort of teaching and that was only half time.

When did it really start clicking?
I guess it was in 1979, because we started getting some additional products in, going a little beyond CP/M, things like the PL/I program. The thing that was a real transition for us, I think, was probably when we were about a $5 million company, and I realized the need to have a lot of help in terms of just the structure. This was probably in 1981. That was when I went out and got some venture capital.

I presume you didn't have any trouble getting capital?
We didn't have any trouble, no. There wasn't any problem with that. The venture capital people did a tremendous job in helping me out, getting people, and getting the organization set up.

Who was doing the product development?
I was doing most of it. A lot of it. I was doing PL/I at the time, and I also did versions of CP/M up through 2.2. We started hiring people to do development; I would say that probably happened about 1979 to 1980. That's when we got a little more serious. By 1980 we had something like twenty-five people. But the biggest problem we had in terms of development of new programs was the fact that I had that PL/I project for so long. It was two years. During that time the only other thing I did was work on CP/M 2.2. I took a break of three months and did that, then got back on PL/I. If I had not been working on PL/I so long, I would have been able to do some other things probably that were more productive. But it turns out that it's

the biggest selling language we have now. I was really surprised. It's because of the connection with IBM.

I guess the success of Digital Research was a case of the world beating a path to your door?

I think that was true for a lot of software people at that time, because software was scarce. But it certainly isn't true anymore. It's a much different business, it's changed tremendously in the last couple of years. I think it's a positive change, actually. It makes you more aware of customers, and what their needs are. You are much more aware of writing software that is going to sell. You are developing channels for the sale of software before the software is developed. Nowadays, what we do is we work with IBM, AT&T, and the big companies, all the big OEMs, to make sure that the products are going to have a channel for distribution.

Unfortunately, in this crowded market, there are a lot of good programs that people will never hear about. Have you given any thought to that?

Oh, yes, sure. It really is a distribution problem, and people are trying to solve that. The biggest problem is that merchants don't want to maintain inventory. It's not too bad to maintain inventory on books, because they are not very expensive, but inventory for software—well, software hasn't reached that point. Electronic distribution is what people are going to try and do, but it's not clear how to do that at this point. There are some things we are working on now. We are involved in videodisks, interactive videodisk storage technology and spin-offs. We're talking about that market being developed over the next year, like the first part of 1985, and that has a potential for being fairly good for software distribution also.

70

What was Digital Research's corporate strategy immediately before the IBM-PC thing came up?

We were definitely an OEM system software business. We were just out there selling CP/M as best as we could, to as many OEMs as we could, selling to a very broad base. We had PL/I going, things like the symbolic de-bugger, the text processor, and the macro assembler, and we had all the system utilities. I think the basic idea was to try and grow with the industry. We didn't want to go down below the growth of the industry, and we didn't want to go faster. We were just trying to pick up on what was going on as the OEM base grew, and make sure that we were out there talking to the OEMs as best we could, trying to keep things going that way.

What really happened between you and IBM? How did you miss that connection?

There's a standard story that I am sure you've heard about Digital Research screwing up a relationship with IBM. There are probably about four or five stories around the industry about what was happening.

The basic thing that happened is that IBM saw the Apple market was growing fairly rapidly, so they built an Apple clone. I mean, it's not the same processor, the same memory size or things like that, but it was built on the same philosophy as an Apple II. Small (low density) disk drives, a memory-mapped video, color graphics, things like that. So it was really built to go into that market that the Apple II was developing. What they did is the thing that IBM always does, and it's a good strategy. They go out there and they say, what are the successes in the industry that we're trying to get into? And they basically will do the same thing, but do it one better.

So they saw that the successes in the industry were the Apple, VisiCalc, Microsoft BASIC, CP/M, and the Pascal P system—those are the ones I can think of offhand. So they said, well, we'll go out and get those, and we'll get Apple by just building an Apple II-like system, and we'll get CP/M, Microsoft BASIC, the P system, and VisiCalc.

But they had the misconception that Microsoft was selling CP/M. In fact, they told me that later. They thought CP/M was a Microsoft product. It may have been because Microsoft was selling the Apple II SoftCard with BASIC and CP/M bundled. So they went to Microsoft and said, "We want to buy BASIC and CP/M." Microsoft said, "Fine, we'll sell you BASIC, but we can't sell you CP/M because we don't own it." IBM called us from Microsoft, and said they were going to be down the next day. I said, "Fine, we'll see you, and take care of you," and things like that.

I had business appointments set up that next day in San Jose with OEMs, but that was okay because we had a legal department at that point that Dorothy was running, so it was no big deal. But when they came down, they laid a non-disclosure on Dorothy and she had never seen anything like it before. IBM's non-disclosure, I don't know if you've ever seen anything like that, but it's amazing. IBM has been sued so many times, so their non-disclosures basically say that they can have all ideas that they are presented with. Unconditionally. I mean, that's what it says, and they admit that. But IBM doesn't go out and rip off software; they'll buy a piece of software from you if it looks like you own it. So what you have to do is, you have to have a basic trust before you even do business with them.

Well, Dorothy had never seen such a thing before, so she said she couldn't sign it and she put in a call to Gerry Davis, a lawyer, downtown here. He came and looked at it, and worked on some changes for wording and things like that. So they were basically working on this, the non-disclosure agreement, and I came back about three o'clock in the afternoon.

I met with them, and I said, "Well, just sign the damn thing." I mean, it was no big deal, you know, because I had dealt with IBM before Digital Research, so I said, "Well, just sign the damn thing and get on with it," and that was all taken care of. Now, we were

72

going on vacation the next day, and we happened to be on the same plane with the IBM people. We talked about it for a while, and we decided on the plane, we said, "Well, hey, that's great, let's go do business, and we'll be back in two weeks, so we'll get in contact with you and we'll just finish the deal."

So as soon as I got back, I called IBM and said, "Let's get on with the thing." And the guy that had come out here and negotiated, he said he was no longer in that group. He had been moved someplace else, and he said, "Well, we'll get back to you." Okay, fine, I waited a few days and I called back a few times, and I got kind of a dead end, it was like the line was just cut off, and there was just no response.

But why? I don't get it.
My feeling was, probably what happened was that, I mean, Bill Gates saw an opportunity there, and said look, you know... There was a time period there when I wasn't in contact with them, I was on vacation, we were on a cruise in the Caribbean. And Bill saw Seattle-DOS, that was a CP/M clone, but for the 8086. So Bill saw it, and said, "Hey, you know, I can buy that, and sell it to IBM as a CP/M thing."

So you think he talked them into something while you were on vacation?
Yeah. I mean, it was a reasonable thing to do. I mean, I'd probably do the same thing. It wasn't the non-disclosure thing or any breakdown in communications. We agreed on the plane with IBM that there was no problem; we were going to do business. When we left that plane trip, we were going to do business. But when we got back, the business just went into the bag. And I don't know what happened at IBM, and I don't know what happened at Microsoft, and it's not a really big deal. But the point of it is, I think Bill saw an opportunity, and like any good businessman, he took advantage of it.

CHAPTER FOUR

So what happened is that we didn't hear from them, like, the line went dead. There was nothing I could do with them. They were very closed down. They came back later and when I found out the PC was going to have a CP/M-like system, I talked to them and I said, "Look, it isn't CP/M. You know, you can't sell it as CP/M. CP/M is not generic, it's something we own. The title, the name, and everything else is something we own." What they had there was something that was basically very, very similar to CP/M, internally and externally. So I said, "You know, what you really need to do is license the real thing." They agreed that seemed reasonable to them, but because of timing, delays, and also because of the pricing that went on it, the $240 versus the $40 price tag ... The pricing is totally set by IBM, we had no control over that.

I don't think that there was anything that anybody did in that situation that was not a reasonable business thing to do, from the standpoint of Digital Research, Microsoft, or IBM. It was just a matter of business dynamics, that's all. And so what happened with us was that we ended up having to sharpen up our pencils a lot more, work real hard. So there are products like Concurrent CP/M, PC-Mode, and things like that, that just would not be around today if we hadn't had to get busy.

You reacted like you'd had a big kick in the ass, and got really competitive.
Which is great. I think it was really good for us. There was never any anguish. The thing that was really funny about it is that we were never selling into the Apple market, so we didn't have Apple-oriented products. We didn't have a BASIC for example.

Do you still consider the IBM-PC machine to be an evolved Apple?
Yes, definitely. It's clearly one step above the Apple, but the concept of the architecture is very Apple-like. For example, the Apple II hardware will never fundamentally change in its design, in its

architecture, because of the fact that there's so much software that's really in there working at the bit level, where the memory map is, and diddling bits and pixels and things like that. And the same thing is true for the IBM-PC. It won't be able to change. We're going to see an IBM-PC in essentially the same form for a long time, several years. Quite a few years. Because the software is so intimately tied to the hardware, and there is no software interface. There's no generalized graphics, for example. So let's say that graphics resolution doubles in the next three years. There is going to be an awful lot of software that will never change towards better resolution because it's tied to the IBM standard.

I think that tailoring it after the Apple II in concept is somewhat of a mistake, because with some thought they could have done better with the graphics interface. It could have been done in a device-independent way. That's the only place where I think there's a real problem. The graphics is what was evolving very rapidly at that time, and the IBM put somewhat of a damper on things. It says, here's what graphics are going to be for a while.

Aren't those low density disk drives a problem?
Yeah, well the XT is the only machine that makes any sense at all. The two small disk drives are, again, Apple II style, but I think most people that do any serious work will get the IBM-PC XT.

After the sudden and massive swing to MS-DOS, what kinds of steps did you take to get back into a competitive stance?
I think there are a couple of things. One, we were not hit anywhere near as hard as the press or the general population thinks we were. Our OEM sales were running strong. See, there's the conception and there's the reality of the situation. PC-DOS is the thing that's selling very well. It's not MS-DOS. PC-DOS sells real well, and that's the thing that passed us up.

CHAPTER FOUR

GARY KILDALL
AND DIGITAL RESEARCH

The thing is, if you take a look at revenues generated out of operating systems between Microsoft and Digital Research, we generate quite a bit more. They have about 200 OEMs, and we have about 1200. So in terms of numbers, we're okay. But it's the IBM PC-DOS that we see as the competition. So what we did is we came up with the Concurrent CP/M idea, and that's selling really well to the Fortune 1000. And the PC-Mode, where we support PC-DOS files, that's very successful.

Do you have any plan for going into applications in a big way?
Not in a big way. We set up the consumer division, and that's where we have consumer-oriented products. We are doing some applications-oriented things there.

Was that move the result of the competitive burst you put on after IBM and Microsoft made their move?
Well, no. See, we had developed a really good OEM business, and we knew how to deal with OEMs, how to write contracts, and how to do OEM things in general. Then we wanted to develop some retail channels and end-user awareness. Because one of the things that happens with the competitive situation is that if the end users are not aware of your products, or of your name, then the PR can generally be pretty bad.

What are your plans for the next market wave?
We're doing things with AT&T. I don't remember exactly how we got involved with that. That came out of the commercial division, and people in the commercial division have been nurturing that whole relationship for some time, and it finally happened. We're dealing with them on applications, and languages, of course. We'll set up the CP/M library for UNIX, to run on anything that runs UNIX. I can't say a whole lot about it, unfortunately, at this point because most of that stuff is not public.

Does this mean that you think UNIX will be the new market standard?
It will be another standard. It's not going to be anything that replaces existing standards. I don't think it's unreasonable to have a couple of different standards, because there are different purposes. For example, Concurrent CP/M is real good for doing real-time work, where UNIX isn't.

What kinds of markets will UNIX take over?
Well, I think they are going to be probably in the business area, and some technical people. Again, I don't think it's going to be the kind of thing where you see anything replacing the Colecos and the Ataris. It's definitely in the higher market area. If it's done right, I mean, it could be the next generation beyond the PC, pretty easily.

What direction will DRI be taking, what market thrusts for the near future?
Primarily we are continuing to build the OEM business that runs system software, and filling the languages out across a broad line of processors and operating systems. So we are trying to build this matrix that makes it very easy to transport programs into any environment.

What else do you have going?
Through the consumer division, we are working on educational software, around the Logo product. Our next major announcements will be in the videodisk area.

Isn't it tricky keeping such a widely diversified effort together?
We've got some real good people. A year ago we were getting defocused a lot, and over the last year we worked on that. Focusing has been a primary goal in the company over the last year—figure out what was giving us a good return on investment, and develop those

areas, and knock those products out that are time-wasters, talent-wasters, and everything else. It's been a good year.

We've done some re-positioning, you know, the AT&T and IBM things, and I think that late 1984 is where we are going to get a really good wrap-up on a lot of products.

Chapter Five

WHAT IT TAKES: THE STORY OF A START-UP

Microsoft, Digital Research, and other pioneering companies staked out their claims in a marketplace that was wide-open, free territory for the taking. Now, thousands of companies are all trying to stand on the same few spots, and conditions are entirely different. What is it like, then, trying to start a software company in today's crowded market?

I met the people from Touchstone Software at the National Software Show and again six weeks later at COMDEX. In between, I had a chance to spend some time at their offices in Seal Beach, California and got an earfull about what it's like to start a software company. They should know, because they were right in the middle of doing it, so their story is about as relevant to recent conditions as one could get. It is also fairly representative of what I heard from other entrepreneurs.

The co-founders of Touchstone are two very dedicated and talented people, Larry Dingus and Carolyn Shannon Jenkins, who were colleagues at MSI Data Corporation. They both have about fifteen years of experience, and both were on a solid, successful career track in the corporate world of

mainframes and minicomputers. But then they began to notice all the action in the micro world: they heard the gossip, saw the fireworks, and finally just packed up and left for the gold fields.

Touchstone intends to be a leader in UNIX compatibility. Their primary product is MIMIX, a program that runs on any of the various UNIX and UNIX-like operating systems, permitting the user to run CP/M programs. They call it an emulator. Their second product, developed with Zilog, is PCworks, a link between IBM PC-compatible micros and any big computer running UNIX. The success of MIMIX depends upon the increasing popularity of UNIX—if UNIX takes off, so will Touchstone.

Larry Dingus and Carolyn Shannon Jenkins, Touchstone Software Corp.

Larry and Shammi (Carolyn Shannon Jenkins' nickname) are big, handsome people. They are outspoken, energetic, and assertive, yet they work very well together because they are old friends, and have a deep mutual regard and respect. I liked the way they bounced off one another, and found them energizing and fun to be around. Larry tends to be in charge of management whereas Shammi's expertise is marketing; but, as you will see, they are both on top of it all.

This was an especially easy interview, because all I had to do was ask, "What's it like, getting started?"

SHAMMI: I don't think we ever knew how long it would take or how hard it would be. The path just keeps on unwinding, and every time you think you're there, they move the finish line. And they keep moving the finish line. You never really get to cash in. You know? The finish line isn't only the cash-in, it's the security, the time when you've got a big enough company, and you've made it somehow.

When I was in sales at Honeywell, I think I made $45,000. Lots of perks, lots of prestige. So why leave? Well, in part it had to do with Honeywell itself—it became a less interesting company to work for and there was less room for individual contributions. But I didn't jump into it right away. I went to work for MSI, then after a little over two years I reached the point where I wanted to test my wings, I guess, and went off to do consulting.

My point is, I still have good friends who either work for Honeywell or who work for other big companies, and I still see, you know, a wistfulness in their eye. These are people who are actually a little older than I was, and were senior to me in the management structure. But today, I'll go to them to seek advice or something, and they just look at me and say, "Well what could I tell you? You've done so much more at this point." I think it's the idea of going for it, making a personal statement. Starting a company like this, it's quite a professional statement.

LARRY: Most entrepreneurs think of an end, a goal. But a business like what we're trying to start here is not an end, it's a process. And it takes time for most entrepreneurs to convert to being businessmen. You really want to cash in, but I think there's a distinction between that pot of gold and something that's long term. That's what we're building here. We may have a product that does very well, and we certainly intend to get rich. There's an entrepreneurial enthusiasm behind all of this. But more importantly, we realize we're building a business. It has to be more than one product. It has to be a reputation that's worked strongly over time that's going to allow us to succeed.

SHAMMI: I think people get turned on by the high-risk, high-reward aspect of it, but in the meantime, it's a lot of hard work. It takes a long time, and it's not just because you had a good idea, or good people around you, or whatever. It takes a whole lot of things over a long time, with a lot of hard work. You know. Lonely hours late at night, getting a proposal done, or . . . everything. You do everything yourself. When you first start out, gosh, you've got to write it yourself, document it yourself, copy it yourself, staple it yourself, address and send out direct mail yourself, bill it yourself, go down to the post office and deliver it yourself. You don't even have a copy machine, you know, and you're a talented person who used to work somewhere and get paid a lot of money.

LARRY: You have to come up with an idea, especially a software idea, that is somewhat unusual, that addresses some kind of a niche. You have to capitalize all of the activities that were described. You have to be able to buy the materials, pay for the phone bills, go to a trade show, and so on. And then you have to establish credibility and reputation. At the same time you are doing all of those things, hanging from the ledge by your fingertips, you have to appear as if you are substantial, like you are going to be around three years from now to support your product and bring new ones out.

SHAMMI: There was a time when we made a crucial decision. It was after we'd gotten the first founders together, and identified our product. We suddenly realized that we were forced to make a decision, which was to either have a little product and run a quarter-inch ad in *BYTE*, and sell a few, and indulge ourselves in some sort of a techie haven where we didn't have to dress or go to work, and never really make any money, and never really be able to attract any capital, but we would have this comfortable little thing where we would own our own spirit and not have to go to work at some factory every day. It was either that, or we had to go for it.

If you're going to go for it, to have a software company that has some potential for being an Ashton-Tate, or a Microsoft or something, then you have to figure out whether your idea is big enough, whether or not it has the kind of appeal that can attract capital. And you have to dress different. Everything is then totally the opposite, but you have to make that decision. I don't think we knew in the beginning that we had to clearly make that decision. When it came time to make it, we made it in the direction of The Big Time.

LARRY: It's awful hard to appear solid, conservative, and business-like with ten dollars in the bank. But we're doing business as if we had a thousand dollars in the bank instead. We're making calls with vice-presidents and general managers at a level of strength, because we know the kinds of products we have are important to those people and are important to us. We really believe in our product, but to go into a vice-president's office with a three button suit on, and appear as if you're a part of an Amalgamated Software with a $100 million bankroll when you really have ten dollars in the bank is a trick. There's no question about that.

SHAMMI: You have to be bold, you know. Some of what we did originally was audacious. I mean the way we developed the product. All of us were sort of high-flyers in terms of having taken on big projects, with big companies in the past. So we weren't afraid of the idea of selling a million dollar thing. For example, I sold large-scale mainframes for Honeywell. So in terms of adjusting one's attitude, the figure of a million dollars didn't make me fall cold into the corner. But if I'd sold ten dollar pencils, I would have been overwhelmed by it.

When we started off, we looked at our resources, and we decided we were going to sell master licenses, we were going to sell to people who would distribute for us. So we marched up, and the first two orders we got were from Hamilton/Avnet and Zilog. That was audacious. We were a brand new company . . .

LARRY: We didn't even know what a master license looked like.

SHAMMI: . . . and the product wasn't done, but when we sold Hamilton/Avnet, we knew that we could do it. We'd done enough testing, we had a kernel of the product done, we were confident, we trusted our technicians. This was in September or August of '82. And what we did, was we sat down for three days and we wrote a very detailed operator's guide. Now we had no product spec, we had no description of the product. But we sat down and we went straight for the operator's guide that showed every key-in, and what the response was, what the menu would look like, and so on.

Then we went to Hamilton, and obviously the thing existed, because we had an operator's guide that usually appears months after the product, right? So we sold the operator's guide. And we knew that by the time we got to COMDEX, the product would work. It was audacious, but see, if you're a marketing-oriented company, or if you're the kind of people that we were at the time, it didn't seem audacious at all.

LARRY: Let me tell you how we got started. Shammi and I both come out of the '60s; the requirement for programmers was really the reason both of us got involved with computers, big mainframe stuff. I'd been in the business for fifteen, eighteen years, Shammi likewise, and then about about two and a half years ago, in 1980, we decided that the micro marketplace was the place to do business. We suddenly realized that there was a whole big market growing out there. Really, because of all the Apple publicity, every company controller I knew was going out and looking at Apple and putting it on his credenza. The marketplace was really changing.

So we got involved with a medical billing product, decided the best thing to do was become experts in a vertical application, and really ended up in changing focus a number of ways. We were interested in micros, we were interested in some kind of a vertical application, and we were interested in doing a product, rather than an hour-by-hour kind of consulting.

SHAMMI: And that's the natural transition from consulting to systems house, where you take software and hardware, and you go and install it, and you involve all your expertise. I think a lot of people do that.

LARRY: Moving from consulting to a product was a business decision. As a consultant, you work one hour, you get paid one hour. When you sell a product, you work one hour, and you may sell 5000 of them. You may sell 500,000 of them if you're VisiCorp. So the payoff's just much better. There are a lot of people who do consulting and are comfortable. But if you want the opportunity for a big hit, well, one of the things that America offers you is the ability to

CHAPTER FIVE

build a mass-production business. And that's really been our intention from the beginning.

SHAMMI: We went to COMDEX in 1981, and we were just blown away. We had spent '80 and early '81 getting interested in micros. None of our friends had anything to do with micros, so we sought to find out about them. We had been futzing around, and seeking out people who we knew had gotten off into this micro world, and talking with them. We discovered CP/M, we discovered UNIX, and then we went to COMDEX. COMDEX was so exciting, there was so much going on there, in COMDEX 1981. And then what really capped it off was all the brightest people that I'd known from Honeywell, who had been senior—really good salesmen, management, and so on—they were there. Here I'd thought in the past year that I'd never see anybody I knew again. Wrong. They all turned up as founders of various micro companies, and V.P.s of marketing and stuff. I mean, they were all over.

LARRY: And it was really funny. There were an awful lot of big companies at that COMDEX show. There were people that we knew in various booths that were just like us, out of the mainframe world, and we were all just standing around scratching our heads, wondering what in the world was going on.

SHAMMI: But a lot was going on.

LARRY: Yeah. An awful lot was going on, an awful lot of business going on at the show. It was a true business show. And that's awfully exciting when you stand next to a guy, and he's shaking hands with another guy, and they just signed a deal. I thought I was going to Las Vegas to have an awful lot of fun and see a trade show, and turned out that all the fun was at the trade show. I didn't spend any time playing Blackjack or the things I normally do in Las Vegas. The fun was right there, eight hours a day, right on that trade show floor. It was just exhilarating.

SHAMMI: And all of the stories that the mainframers had told us about how inept micros were, and stuff—like there's hardware, but

there's no software, blah, blah. Baloney! We were impressed. I mean, there were good looking booths, professional people, good companies, strong software—better software, friendlier. Everything.

LARRY: That's when we really focused on this medical billing package. Shannon's cousin had developed a medical billing package that ran on either UNIX machines or CP/M machines.

SHAMMI: The fellow he had hired, who now works for us, Kurt Welch, he loved UNIX, but they knew they had to sell CP/M systems. They developed this language called Spice, which is a procedural language, more like Pascal, but with the BASIC data type. And it generates an intermediate level code which literally without change can be executed on CP/M or UNIX machines. And it was really a mechanism they used so they could develop software on the UNIX system and go to market with a CP/M product.

As time went on, my cousin decided to go back and be a doctor. We had at that point sold about six of these medical billing systems, and decided that that wasn't a way to get a large business or to make a lot of money, and it had some of the same disadvantages that consulting did, like you could never leave town, or go on vacation. You know, there's six medical offices that want immediate support at any time. So we became frustrated.

LARRY: That's an extremely labor-intensive business, being a systems house supporting customers. Any time you have end users, boy, it's just intense day-in, day-out. All sorts of problems. As the summer of 1982 came around, a bunch of things became clear to us. Number one, the development on the medical product was pretty much wrapped at that point, so the programmers were looking for something to do. It really wasn't our product, and there we were in a business that we weren't very excited about. So in the middle of 1982, we started scratching our heads.

SHAMMI: We had come to really appreciate Kurt Welch's skills as a programmer. He's really an exceptional young man. Kurt was mak-

WHAT IT TAKES 37

ing noises about wanting to do software, UNIX software. Larry and I started meeting and discussing—

LARRY: This is what happened. I'm a product manager, Shammi's a marketer, Kurt's a developer—a true micro developer out of Georgia Tech. I said, "Okay, we've been chewing the fat about a lot of things. Let's have a meeting." This was in early July, 1982. Kurt involved another programmer by the name of Tom Chappell, a good friend.

SHAMMI: These guys are really exceptional. They are extremely technical, the kind of guys that formed computer clubs in Junior High. They gobble up a new chip and write assembler without a manual over lunch. They're incredible. They're also nice gentlemen. They have all the technical blessings of a dirty, unkempt hacker, but they're not.

Anyway, things happened real fast. The idea was, we wanted to run CP/M under UNIX. The Fortune announcement at COMDEX in 1981 is what convinced us there would be a market for UNIX systems, and that's what turned us. Up to that point, we kept asking, "Why are we diddling around with this UNIX system when to be competitive all we can really sell is CP/M systems?" When we saw the Fortune system, and they said they were going to have a UNIX system for $7000, we said, "Whoops! guess what, we've got UNIX, guys." We identified this as being a key part of our ability to enter the market, and have some sort of a leading edge.

It was on the fourth of July, wasn't it? We decided on two things we liked about this idea, and number one was that there were already some UNIX boxes, there was an Onyx, and a Zilog and there would be a Fortune. There were no applications under UNIX to speak of, none. And so the idea of bringing CP/M applications to UNIX had to be a winner.

LARRY: Labor Day weekend we went over to Tom's apartment, and by then he had CP/M running under UNIX on a PDP-1145 minicomputer. So at that point, two things begin to happen simultaneously. We got Ray Norberte involved with the group over the next two

or three weeks, as a founder because of his experience in mainframe software sales. And secondly, Shammi and I sat down and started writing the end user documentation for the product.

We realized that we had the kind of product that was going to need to be extremely friendly. One of the things that UNIX still has a problem with is its presentation of itself to users. CP/M had a history of being much more comfortable than UNIX or other big machine systems, so we had to be at least as simple as CP/M was. We came up with a menu approach to our product, MIMIX, that worked.

Next, we immediately started the sales campaign.

SHAMMI: And immediately means in September, just following this weekend when Tom showed us it could be done. There was a mini-micro show here in Los Angeles, so Ray Norberte and I went down to the show, and found all the people we could, which most notably was Zilog at the time. We said how would you like to run dBASE II on your UNIX system? Or how would you like to run—you know, WordStar or whatever? So what we did was, we got ahold of the people at the booths, and actually managed to meet with an exec from Zilog, briefly. In effect, we test marketed it, and decided that the response that we got was extremely favorable. We decided to go with it.

It was right after that when we formally decided how we would structure the company, and we actually incorporated on September 30. We did it fast, just went down to the attorney and said give us some vanilla incorporation and make it legal.

We didn't have a lot of capital. We capitalized it by contributing funds from each of the founders. It wasn't exactly equal or all cash. For example, Tom Chappell had written this program but he didn't have cash. We had about $25,000 that we started with, originally. It may not be much, but it was our own, and you're talking about people who aren't wealthy. Some of us had assets like real estate, but it wasn't cash, it wasn't liquid. We lived on our savings, used up

CHAPTER FIVE

whatever we had accumulated. Larry and I owned a triplex here in town which we've recently sold. Ray Norberte sold his house.

LARRY: Whoever had assets, we just mortgaged the farm. That's what it amounts to.

SHAMMI: We're driving old cars.

LARRY: We had sold two master licenses. Master licenses involved some limited amount of cash. So we brought in over $130,000 this year, 1983.

SHAMMI: Mostly from courting initial master license fees rather than royalties. It takes us perhaps two weeks to fit our software to a manufacturer's machine. So, we get from the manufacturer a fee—not a very big one—somewhere between $5000 and $15,000, maybe $20,000, it depends on what we're doing. For that fee we agree to adapt it to their machine, and we award them the exclusive distribution rights on their equipment. We provide them with a master distribution program from which they can serialize and reproduce copies of the software, and they pay a royalty.

SHAMMI: The royalty depends on volume, somewhere between 20% and 50%. Of retail. It could go as low as ten. We want them to present us with a marketing plan, to assure ourselves that they have a marketing organization, and so on and so forth. That's one thing you do, but you can't guarantee that it's going to be successful. You get them to commit to some unit volume, and you threaten them with higher royalties or whatever if they don't sell enough, okay? But you can't always make that successful. In the final analysis, they'll sell whatever the market demands. It falls back to us to generate some pull-through so we do that ourselves. We do a lot of direct mail, and we go to trade shows. Just to create a presence.

LARRY: Our first strategy was to announce the product at COMDEX in December, 1982. We had two things in mind. We wanted to announce the product at COMDEX, and we wanted to do it with a major player. We had several possibilities at that point. We were talking fairly seriously with a number of companies, Altos, Hamilton Microsystems, who was a distributor rather than a manufacturer, Zilog we were talking with real seriously, Fortune we were talking with seriously.

So our game plan, between Labor Day in September and the 1982 Fall/COMDEX in November, was to have at least one master license in hand, so when we went to COMDEX we could splash in two places—both in our booth and with some big player. We ended up working very closely with Hamilton Micro, and we signed a master license and arranged for a joint product announcement. Next we concluded the deal with Zilog in January, and at CP/M '83 had the Zilog master license released to the world, and demonstrated in the Zilog booth and at our booth. At Unicom we did the same thing.

You can do a small booth at a show fairly comfortably for about $10,000, but it costs a minimum of $5000. If you decide to do a booth, you better have a $5000 check available. Gosh, with a big booth, you can spend $100,000. Easily.

SHAMMI: We were very successful, I think, in getting a lot of free PR. Now we never had a PR agent, or anything like that, but just by going to the trade shows, and doing a press kit, and just kind of plugging away at it, you know, we have managed to get a fair amount of press. And I think in part it's because we spent a little money wisely. We got ourselves a logo and a good name, and did some things so that people thought we were a real company. We came up with the ideas for the marketing program ourselves.

Coming up with the name, Touchstone, gee, was hard. We thought of a lot of names, but trademarking any sort of computery name in California is almost impossible. They're all used up, and besides, we didn't like them. Touchstone is a real word, and it has a good connotation. We had reached that point where anything was better than a name like Micro Dynamics. Touchstone, it turned out, was available.

LARRY: At that point, I was thinking, okay, in order to really get this product and this company off the ground, we need to capitalize the company. $25,000 ain't gonna do it. We needed to do something to initiate the pull-through advertising, and finance trade show participation, and get our product and name in front of the people who would cause the demand. And we knew we couldn't succeed being a one-product business, so we really needed to finance some R&D, and we needed to finance our sales activity, and that was just going to take money.

We started writing a business plan immediately after we got back from Unicom. This business plan went through about four or five drafts. Trying to put down on paper what you really want to do is very hard. Then it has to be put into a format that the investors are used to reading, because not only do you have to accurately say what your intentions are, but there's a specific way in which they're used to absorbing that kind of information. So you have to tackle two problems simultaneously.

SHAMMI: We probably talked to twenty venture capital outfits. They found what we were doing intriguing and very interesting, but they didn't understand it. On the one hand, they couldn't stay away, they'd come back for a second and third time, but they couldn't measure our potential in any way that they were comfortable with. Secondly, although the five founders all have impeccable personal backgrounds, and reputations, and skills and so on, none of us had ever started a software company before. They would have been comfortable with not knowing what we were doing if they could say, well, jeez, he just started a $200 million company five years ago.

I think they were all generally very much the same, you know, they're nice people, they're all well-bred, and they were helpful. They were trying to explain to us—and that's how we went through four revisions of the business plan—how we should reorganize things into a format that was palatable from their point of view.

Anyway, we concluded that we needed a million and a half dollars. To do it right, to do a fair amount of advertising in the channels we wanted. We didn't reach that determination until about May or June, I think.

I got the impression that they would have wanted, say 60% of the company. And that would have been first round. I mean, when you got all through the whole thing, ultimately what you're going to end up doing is going public, or getting a second round or something. And it seemed as though for openers that was too much. I think they would like to pump up a company, then go public and rake off their profit and still have ownership of a good company.

LARRY: We never got any satisfactory response from a venture firm. We ended up talking to friends in the industry, and realized there was a potential for going public in the Denver marketplace. We have since worked to sign a letter of intent with an underwriter in Denver so we can arrange for bridge financing through a group of businessmen in Denver who do that kind of thing. So we are financing ourselves until the underwriting through this bridge financing.

SHAMMI: We've given away less than 15% of the company on loans. When we go public, we'll sell 40%. After we go public, the five founders will end up with roughly 50% of the company. The net result, by the way, is a far better deal, I think, than we could have got from a venture capitalist.

We turned to the Denver underwriters because, well, we're a development company. We're not profitable yet, no assets. Denver is like a public venture capital source. It's a speculation market. If you have a stock which is highly speculative, that's the marketplace that people go to. They used to do oil and gas, but now there's a lot of high tech stuff coming out of the Denver market. If you were an investor, and you wanted to bet $5000 on a highly speculative, high-tech investment, with a cheap stock price of a dollar or less, you go to Denver.

LARRY: You know, compared with venture capitalists, those guys in Denver are a little wild west. They're terribly sympathetic with en-

CHAPTER FIVE

WHAT IT TAKES

WHAT IT TAKES

trepreneurs. They're looking for products like ours, something high-quality that they can mix in with the other stuff they're doing.

SHAMMI: There are hundreds of underwriters in Denver, okay? We're going to the market with one of the biggest ones, Blinder-Robinson. People tell us that in the worst of markets a strong house can put through deals—at a slower pace, maybe smaller deals, but they get them done. You're in a much riskier position if you're dealing with someone who just formed an underwriter because it was a hot market. They might not be able to pull it off.

Going public is difficult. It costs a *lot* of money. Oh, yeah! You're probably looking at $25,000 in accounting fees. A minimum of $25,000 to $50,000. You're looking at $25,000 to $50,000 in legal fees. Probably looking at $25,000 in printing costs. You're looking at the brokerage fees, which are going to be $10%, probably.

LARRY: Our offering will be for $2 million, and we're going to net somewhere around $1.6 million. Which means it's going to cost us somewhere around $400,000 to go public. That's money at 20%. That's what it's costing.

SHAMMI: There are positives and negatives about going public. It's terribly disruptive. And all the accountants, and lawyers, and the time you spend. But, I'm not convinced that I haven't seen the same thing with outfits that are running with venture capital, or who have investors who drop in once a week, and they drop everything and spend all day courting the investor and explaining how they spent the last $50,000, and so on. It's not a simple matter, no matter how you look at it. Nobody's going to give you a check for a lot of money, then walk away.

We thought about it a lot, and staying small is something that we felt wasn't an option, because of the way the software industry is going. There are very well-capitalized outfits that are going to go out there and throw money at the problem, and just dominate, and preclude there being a healthy market for small companies that do a little business. We felt it was a do-or-die kind of thing.

94

LARRY: We're going to use a lot of our new capital to form a sales effort. So far we've had a hard time letting end users know we have a product. If you can't advertise, it's awful hard to get any pull through going.

SHAMMI: We do what we can. We don't have a lot of money to travel, so we try and maximize our effort. It's interesting, the way we do that is mostly through trade shows. At COMDEX, say, we send our people out on the floor to contact the manufacturers and so on, and bring them back to our booth for a demonstration.

Our only real threat in the immediate future is somebody else who decides to get into the business who is much better capitalized than we are. We're the only company doing what we're doing in the supermicro market. As soon as what we're doing becomes better understood, and appears to be a really attractive business opportunity, Microsoft, or DRI, or somebody could decide to take it over. Would you say that's real?

LARRY: Yes, I would. So we have to capitalize the company in order to be successful, and at that point, we have to bring the product to the marketplace in a way that allows us to ship thousands of units, instead of tens of hundreds of units. And so the most immediate threat is probably not being in the ballgame long enough to play the hand and win.

SHAMMI: So what we're planning is to stay with our people, and staying in business for as long as it takes to complete the stock sale.

There have been two or three times in the last year when Larry and I sat down and said is this it? Really, honest to god, is this it? Is it time to go tell everybody that we can't pull it out this time? We have eight employees. That's our biggest monthly headache. We have two programmers—developers. I wouldn't call them programmers, they do everything, practically. They have bills and rent to pay, and these are guys who could walk out of here tomorrow, and get double the salary.

CHAPTER FIVE

WHAT IT TAKES

95

As you go up the chain of command, you start paying people at the bottom. And you stop when you run out of money closer to the top. And we realize too, you have to deal with people's needs. If somebody is just not in the position to wait, then maybe they get paid, and maybe somebody else doesn't, you see.

Keeping the crew together, that's been I think Larry's single biggest contribution to the organization in many respects. He's built the team, and he's kept the team together under tough times, when for any number of reasons it could have fallen apart.

LARRY: And you can quote her on that. The first time she hasn't yelled at me all week.

SHAMMI: Oh, Larry! But, really, you can't imagine the pressures. We've all got everything at stake here. There are important decisions, and we have to keep together, and we have to be positive about it, keeping that going when it gets real tough.

We all have a lot at stake, and I think all of us have had to face what could happen. We could go bankrupt. We could sell our houses, spend the money, and end up thirty six, forty years old, with no house, no assets, and a sense of failure. We've all looked at it, said, "I can live with that," then we put it away, put it back in the drawer and go on about making it work.

I think it's terribly important to face failure. I think if you hide, if you kid yourself, if you let something ominous out there on the horizon spook you so that you're tense all day, then I think that would be terrible. I think there's a tremendous sense here that even if it all came to nothing, better to have lived our lives and one time gone for it. I don't want to wake up sixty five and say I should have ... I wish I would have ... I could have ... you know, and just be bitter. This way, even if it fails, I will say, you know what? I tried this wonderful thing one time, and I really went for it, you know, just played it all out.

LARRY: There's the other side of it, too, the fun and the enthusiasm. To begin with, all of us like data processing. It's challenging intellectually, it's financially rewarding if you do it right, so there's hundreds of good reasons to be in the field where I am. In addition to that, we have an extremely talented team we're putting together here. They're all bright people. They're fun people to work with. They're fun people to succeed with, and they're reasonable people to address problems with. If you don't have the team put together right, the first problem that comes down the road, you're putting another team together. That's just not the situation here.

SHAMMI: We may get our back to the wall in these early stages, but there's an obvious healthiness. Even our landlord feels it when he walks in here. He doesn't know what we're doing, but it's hard for him to believe that as hard as we work, and as nice as we are, and with the talent he perceives, that it won't work.

LARRY: Every day we're scratching our head. How can we do better from a sales point of view, how can we cut back our cost of doing business? We're continually re-evaluating our strategy. We're trying to expand the way we do business to accommodate our cash squeeze situation. You know, you're writing a book about entrepreneurs, and I think there's a lot of us in the business who are right on the edge of all these things that are going on, but we've never really experienced that entrepreneurial fantasy first person. Or even lived next door to somebody who did, even though we're in the business, in the heart of it. Even though I know tons of people in this business, there are very few out there who are doing one of those big, long-shot successes. You know, fantasies about writing VisiCalc or whatever.

SHAMMI: Don't forget to emphasize the specialness of the people, the synergism. This is one of those companies where it just feels good to be around the place. You can pick it up when you walk in the door. It bounces off the walls and sticks there. You have to have the right people.

WHAT IT TAKES

Postscript

Larry Dingus and Carolyn Shannon Jenkins possess all of the essential entrepreneurial qualities: independence, self-confidence, persistence, drive, hard work, and—hardest of all to come by—total commitment.

Touchstone also has something worth more than money—a talented team that works well together. Many good products have disappeared for lack of teamwork; very few companies have gone far without it. But still, Touchstone is caught in a dilemma: they have to "go for it" to protect a potentially very lucrative market niche, but at the same time they have a product that sells best through OEM licenses (original equipment manufacturers, makers of computer systems) which earns them a far lower rate of return than would sales through distributors and dealers or to end users directly.

Four months later, however, Shammi said that all the work, sweat and sacrifice they had put into the relatively low yielding MIMIX really paid off handsomely when they introduced PCworks. They had already established their reputation and contacts, so the new product was relatively easy to kick off. After the first eight-week blitz, they had exceeded their goals by over 200%. The new product will be sold through the more lucrative channels as well as through OEM licenses.

The evaluation that they had to "go for it" to protect their market niche was astute and correct, but it also has a corollary: in order to be safe, any entrepreneur who prefers to run a peaceful little business had better pick a modest little niche that won't get gobbled up by the sharks and barracudas out there after they have done the groundwork and proved its worth.

Chapter Six

HOW SOFTWARE MOVES: CHANNELS OF DISTRIBUTION

T he products in the microcomputer industry may be on the leading edge of high technology, but business and human relationships are conducted in patterns as old as the human race. The problem of getting distribution, for example, is much the same for a new software company as it was for salt traders in the Land of Kush. You may have a great program, a solution to some real and widespread need, but if you plan to mass-market your product in the tens or hundreds of thousands, then you have to find some way to get it out onto the market in as many places as possible where it can be seen and sold. That is the problem of distribution. To put it simply:

- No microcomputer software company can succeed unless it solves the problem of distribution.
- This is far more easily said than done.

The distribution channels are new and few, and completely over-whelmed by the number of software publishers and their products. Gerald

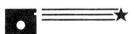

100

Van Diver has been doing market research and collecting data on personal computer software companies for five years. His company, Micro Information, publishes *The Software Guide*, a 1000-page directory of IBM-PC software describing 1165 products from 2950 vendors, and the list grows daily. He says:

"We monitor thousands of products, and 4500 software producers in this industry. Our databank has all the products available, all the companies, and all the people behind the products. We watch the managers move from company to company, watch the companies start from a one man garage, and possibly go to a million dollars, ten million. We just recently did a report on the characteristics of the third party publisher—those are the 4500 companies out there—and we found that 85% of them have been in business for less than one year, have fewer than three employees, and are single product companies. In 1985, I think there's going to be 10,000 programs out there just for IBM. Okay? Now, that's a big business, there's a big potential out there. But it's very expensive to crack that market."

The retail distribution channels for software have only recently been created in this new industry, and so far they are exact duplicates of the channels that exist in any other mass-market business. However, as soon as they opened they became clogged with products. The frenzied and high-cost rush to penetrate the market is greatly intensified by fears of newer or smaller companies that they will be squeezed out of distribution channels. For any entrepreneur trying to break into today's market, distribution is the thorniest problem, the biggest obstacle on the first lap of the Micro Grand-Prix.

To find out what a new software publisher faces in trying to break into an established distribution channel, we are going to hear from a conventional software distributor, a publishing distributor, and finally, a panel discussion by industry leaders on distribution alternatives.

CONVENTIONAL DISTRIBUTION

Scott Hillman, Softsel Computer Products, Inc.

Softsel Computer Products is the biggest microcomputer software distributor in the world, with revenues at least equal to the top superstar software publishers, and growing faster than any of them. The Softsel Hotlist is an industry honor roll, something like the Hit Parade, and getting your product up there is worth fortunes, since retailers use it as a shopping guide. Softsel does what any distributor does, which is to stock products that move, and ship them on order to retailers, taking a percentage in the process. The man who decides which products Softsel will carry is Scott Hillman, Vice-President of Product Services.

SCOTT HILLMAN: My department, Product Services at Softsel, is kind of the supply side of the house. We're the people responsible for getting the product out the door, for servicing the dealers. We're the people responsible for bringing the products into the house. We work in product acquisition, we work in evaluation, and technical support, that sort of thing.

We've got about 180 employees right now in our home office, and about 320 worldwide. Just this last month, October, we had our third birthday. When I started two years ago, there was about twenty-five people. Gosh, a much smaller place. One of the characteristics of the companies in this industry is you always seem to move at least once a year to a building that's about ten times the size of the former building. Well, I would sure like to stay put for a while.

We distribute about 3000 titles. Our mailing list of computer retailers numbers 6000, but I would say roughly 3800 to 4000 are active customers who order on a regular basis.

Wouldn't a new publisher's product be lost in all those titles you carry?

That's a common reaction from vendors. A lot of people that sit in this office ask exactly that question. I think that's due to a lack of understanding about what a distributor does. Especially a mass-marketing distributor as we are.

What we tell the vendors when they come in here, we say it's your responsibility to create pull in the market. We'll provide the distribution, we'll get the product out to the dealers, and we'll handle all the problems, the mechanisms to get the product onto the dealers' shelves. We'll also handle all of the credit problems that go along with selling products to dealers, which is a real big headache for vendors. We're not a marketing organization, but what we have to offer to a vendor is market penetration. And we really support our products vigorously for dealers.

What are your discount rates like?

We vary them, depending on a lot of parameters. Starting with the dealer discount, which is something that is really standard in the industry right now, we sell products to dealers for 40% off suggested list price.

We buy products from the publishers at an average of about 60% discount off list price. Now that 60% can vary in either direction, depending on things like whether we can anticipate that the product will require a high level of support. Some of the more technically-oriented accounting and financial modeling products, things that tend to generate lots of calls, may vary from 60% up through 65% discount. A couple of cases, it's even gone to 75%. But that's as deep a discount as we've ever seen on our product.

What's the top rate you pay to publishers?

Well again, that varies. Probably the best terms that we've ever given to a publisher is right around 50%. It depends on a number of considerations: we might have other conditions to the contract that provide us with a very liberal co-op ad allowance, for example. If it's a recreational product that requires no support, and we are convinced that it will sell at a very high volume, then certainly that's going to make us more comfortable with a lower discount level. And if someone is willing to extend 120 days payment terms, that certainly can be equated to percentage points for discount.

What do you look for when you evaluate new products?
There are basically two major areas for consideration. One is the technical kind of evaluation, the other is a marketing evaluation. It's very important that any new publisher, regardless of size, have the wherewithal to adequately market their new product. And that means, generally, funding to do sufficient advertising and promotion. To get the attention of the marketplace.

We're seeing a real change in the nature of the market. There are tremendous barriers to entry, simply because it is so expensive to bring a product to the attention of the target market. Now, most of the publishing companies are larger organizations with greater financial resources. You see very few companies that are mom and pop shops, or the guy who maybe works at Hughes Aircraft and does programming in his den at night. Now, those people still come up with really good ideas for products, they develop good products, and they still send them to us for evaluation. They come in here and talk to us about them.

The first thing we say is, well, how are you going to market this? How do you plan on advertising this? And they say, oh, well, I've got a little ad once a month in *BYTE* magazine, on page 485. And we usually say, well, look, that'll sell you a few products, but you're not going to generate enough interest in the marketplace to get the level of sales that will justify distribution through a distributor. You know, in that case, you'd probably better function as a little mail order operation through your home, and do it in your spare time.

104

If we don't think something is going to sell in adequate quantities, then it doesn't make sense economically for us to deal with it. And most people understand that. If not initially, then they do after we explain the economics of the business to them. Then maybe we'll suggest they borrow some money, find some capital some place, from a venture capital firm, or from their grandmother, or from the local banker, or from wherever they can get it.

The noise level that exists... If somebody came to me with an integrated software package for IBM right now, like Lotus 1-2-3, well, I happen to know that at COMDEX this year there are going to be six major announcements about integrated software packages. And they're all going up against Lotus and saying we're the next step forward in the integrated software game. If somebody came to me with that kind of software product right now, I'd say, "Hey, you better be prepared to spend a million, a minimum of a quarter of a million dollars this year in advertising. I mean *minimum*."

What else do you look at in evaluating a new product?
The price, and the gross margin, naturally, because that directly affects the profitability. Generally, we look for a volume that is at least fifty a month, and probably more, generally above a hundred copies a month. At that level it tends to pay for itself and covers its fixed costs of handling.

It has to have good documentation. Then there's the packaging, how does it look, is it well-presented to the customer, is it going to attract attention and sell itself when it's sitting on the shelf? Does it look professional? Does it have good documentation?

Price is certainly an important consideration for us. People have come to us with product prices based on, I'm sure, the vendor's fantasies in some cases. We have a pretty good idea now, from our experience with the market, about what price ranges are appropriate for which types of products. So if something falls significantly outside our price range, it's pretty apparent to us that it probably won't sell. And interestingly enough, that can work both ways.

Certainly if something is too expensive to handle with competing products, then it won't sell too well. Sometimes something can be priced too low, especially if it's a business and professional product, because the public still equates price with quality. VisiCorp is famous for that. VisiCalc when it first came out was $99, but they raised the price at several points in its life cycle and the demand simply kept growing.

How accurate have you been at guessing the demand for new products?
Generally we've been real close. I think it's a combination of looking at past experience with similar products and it's also a little crystal balling, just taking a guess. But we can get very scientific here. One of the decisions we made when we opened the doors was to install a data processing system, and we decided to save in our data files virtually every bit of sales information that we had. Consequently, we built a database that goes back to day one, that describes every sale of every product. So we know where our product is sold and to whom, and for how much, and that sort of thing. That has given us a tool that we have used to analyze market trends over the last three years. It's probably the most valuable market research tool that exists for us right now, anywhere.

So we have a fairly clear understanding of, for instance, how a word processor for Apple could be expected to sell. How long it will be popular, how long after introduction it will peak, how long it will remain at the peak, and when it will fall off, and approximately at what percentages. Now, those don't give us an exact portrayal of how a new product will behave, but at least it will give us a baseline to operate from.

106

Did you ever predict a product would go over big and it didn't?
(Laughs) Oh, yeah, that has definitely happened.

PUBLISHING DISTRIBUTORS

The struggle to reach the market may overwhelm some would-be publishers, or be distasteful to others; meanwhile the cost of entering the market puts it beyond the reach of all but the biggest. However, almost the only alternative is for a program's authors/owners to go to an established software publisher and sell it to them, just like a book is sold to a book publisher by any aspiring author who doesn't want to become a businessperson. This well-trod path is the way superstar products VisiCalc and dBASE II reached the market, for example.

But which publisher? The marketplace is still in a froth, full of opportunism and experimentation as entrepreneurs scramble to get in on the rampant growth. Not all publishers are equal in capability, and they are widely divergent in their strategies for breaking into the market. A number of companies, for example, are trying to establish themselves as publishing distributors. These are marketing outfits that are looking for products with one eye and for dealers with the other eye, both hands, and a leg—all the while making confident and reassuring noises at both ends.

A number of publishing distributors—companies like Software Strategies, Softsmith, or The Business Library—are using a brand name marketing concept that features uniformly packaged and documented products that are displayed on their own stylish kiosk that they will install almost wherever they can. In this next conversation, Charles V. Ford speaks for Software Guild, a new company founded by John Martin-Musumici. Charles is a young career executive who worked at product acquisition before leaving the company for parts unknown several months after the interview.

How big is your operation right now?
    CHARLES FORD: We have over 200 dealers currently, and we're signing on an average of a dealer a day. We're looking forward to

3000 dealerships by the fall of next year. Now the company's two and a half years old, and we've been on the shelves since last March. We have upwards of 250 licensed titles and just over 200 on the shelves. In other words, there are more scheduled for production.

Programs go into stores on our own display kiosk, which is our general marketing concept. The mix of product in any particular store is a little bit of what our franchisee pushes, what the end users are demanding, and what the dealer decides on.

When you take on a product, do you want it to be an exclusive deal?

We would prefer an exclusive contract, of course—we feel that we would have a little bit more flexibility in the marketing of that product, and we feel a little more responsible, you know, that it's all on our shoulders to get that thing out there and make it a success. We prefer that arrangement. But we certainly entertain every variant, in terms of an exclusive, or semi-exclusive.

Won't a software author be afraid his program will get lost in the crowd?

Okay. We do have a backlog of 150, 200 programs in our evaluation department that we're not getting to. But once we sign that contract, take it on, it's going to be six or nine months at the outside when we get it on the shelves.

This is a brand name concept marketing effort. We're pushing Softsmith. Now, we do have advertising efforts in terms of specific programs, for example, a bridge game program we'll market through some national bridge periodicals, that sort of thing. We have professional staff who do nothing but analyze the best way to move that product. We also have a "hero" arrangement where we are very excited about one of our products. For example, Smithwriter is proving to be a very successful product right now, and we have recently run a six page ad, with a full-page spread on the Smithwriter by itself. Here's another one. Logomotion. Crossword Magic. These are "hero" programs.

How do you think your company is different from any of the other publishers?
We're working on this complete concept, I mean this complete service idea. Once the programmer has created the work, we take over from there. We reproduce it, and help document it. Actually, we prefer some documentation from the author, but we'll be able to clean it up.

What do you want to see in a new program submission?
We want as complete a product as possible in terms of debugging, you know, a good clean moving system and documentation. We will do Beta testing, but we prefer some testing on their part too. As progressed a product as possible.

What do you pay?
We offer a royalty schedule, the whole works. About 10% of our net proceeds is a good, rough figure. The highest is 20% of sums received, and it's a sliding scale—it's rather a unique feature. It starts at, let's say, 20% of sums received from Softsmith. Now Softsmith is our marketing organ. So sums received by Software Guild from Softsmith, from one dollar to $200,000. Okay? And then it goes down to 15% of sums received by Guild, and so on. Generally, 20% of sums received by Guild usually works out to be about 7% of the retail price.

Those sums are received from your own marketing arm, so that means the sums received go through two stages?
Correct. There's another middleman. We justify that basically through our claim to volume sales. In terms of moving that product in a big way. And we're across the country, in over two hundred locations, signing a dealer a day.

CHAPTER SIX

How many units sold of best moving products?

That's a tough one. We just haven't got any statistics, any sales statistics, because we're new. We've been on since March, and we just don't have any statistics yet. The one thing I'll tell you though, is that we came about a hair's width from our first million dollar month in September, 1983. Our best number yet. I tell you we were thrilled. We were really excited about that. We're making some authors very happy, let's put it that way.

There's that rare individual that we're having trouble moving. There is a step-out clause, where you can just simply move into a non-exclusive arrangement. So much of that is determined on the actual negotiated contract.

What happens to authors with non-exclusive contracts?

Frankly, they're a little less likely to get a hero program rating, and they're not going to get the same royalty schedule that an exclusive contract would get.

PANEL ON INNOVATIONS
IN SOFTWARE DISTRIBUTION

COMDEX presented a splendid assortment of fifty-four panels and round table discussions featuring some of the brightest people in the industry. Most of the programs were slanted toward the retailer, but there was something for everyone, including people who might want to know about Innovations in Software Distribution.

This panel of industry leaders, especially selected for their experience and sagacity, was moderated by Esther Dyson, sharp of mind and tongue, who saved her incisive wrap-up remarks for last. She is a noted industry analyst and President of the prestigious Rosen Research, renamed EDventure now that Esther Dyson has taken it over.

110

David Wagman, Softsel
Computer Products, Inc.

The first panelist is Scott Hillman's boss, David Wagman, founder and Chairman of Softsel Computer Products, the world's biggest and fastest growing software distributor, etc., etc. He wasn't really first, but his overview of software distribution channels is the best place to begin:

DAVID WAGMAN: There are probably eight or ten different ways that software is reaching the consumer today, and they all have a place, they all have meaning, and there's a certain percentage of market share that belongs to each of them.

The first is manufacturer direct to the dealer, and that comes in two flavors, with or without point-of-sale service. That's where the manufacturer/publisher/author, whatever you want to call them, ships directly to a retailer. He may do that sometimes by having his rep call on the guy, introduce new products, tell him what's going on, help him with problems, merchandising. Or he may not, he may act as little more than a mail order operation at the wholesale level, like when the dealer calls him up and says, "Send me a dozen."

Next you have a manufacturer shipping to a distributor, and the distributor ships to the dealer. Typically in that environment, you always have point-of-sale support. The manufacturer is calling on the distributor, and the distributor has someone reaching out to the dealer. The key facet of that kind of arrangement is that a relationship builds, an ongoing relationship between the manufacturer, the distributor, and the dealer.

Then you've got the channel of the dealer to the consumer. This also comes in two flavors, with and without point-of-sale support. With point-of-sale, you have your traditional computer retail store, where a customer walks into a store, they talk things over, and he gets sold a product that hopefully meets his needs. The other

CHAPTER SIX

alternative is dealer to consumer without point-of-sale support, and many mail order operations fall into this category, where it's simply a low-priced, high turnover, volume operation.

And last, but certainly not least, we have manufacturer direct to the consumer, which is getting to be a more and more interesting channel. This also comes with and without point-of-sale. The channel with point-of-sale would most characteristically includes the Fortune 1000 market channel, where many manufacturers are building their own direct sales force to sell their product directly to large corporate consumers. You also have manufacturer direct without point-of-sale, which is where the manufacturers just put ads in the back of *BYTE* magazine and take whatever mail orders come their way.

It's very clear from looking at all these different channels, that many different consumers have many different requirements. So, what I see evolving is a place for all different kinds of distribution to fit those different needs.

Electronic distribution is a big topic, so let's talk a little bit about where that fits in. Well, it actually fits in everywhere, because electronic distributors are proposing schemes that overlap almost all of the different types of things that I just spoke of. But what role does the electronic distributor perform that the manufacturer could not assume himself? We can expect someday to see the manufacturer selling direct to the consumer via electronic distribution. The consumer calls up with a credit card number and down the wire it goes. This is getting more and more practical as we look at the data communications standards that are evolving.

If you don't think that kind of scheme is real or can happen, I only need to point out the success story of Escort Radar Detectors, who are solely mail order advertising. You cannot go into a store anywhere and buy one. There are no discounts available, yet they are the single hottest selling radar detector on the market today. To get one you have to find a phone number, find an ad, call them direct, and pay full retail.

Where are we today with electronic distribution? I don't have any answers, but I have some questions. Where is documentation going to fit in? What about support? Who's going to provide that? Do manufacturers want to provide support or do they want the support to flow down the channel as well? The issue of pricing has been raised. As the consumer becomes more aware of the fact that all he's getting is a diskette with an intangible software product on it, is this going to raise questions in his mind as to the value of what he's purchasing? Finally, there's the issue of technological barriers. As home computers and business computers get larger memories, programs are getting larger, and those will be very difficult to address with electronic distribution.

So I'm leaving you with those questions and no real answers.

—— ● ——

Fred Gibbons, Software Publishing Corporation

Next to speak on the "Innovations in Software Distribution" panel was Fred Gibbons, President of Software Publishing Corporation, publishers of the popular PFS series, including PFS:File, PFS:Report, PFS:Write, and PFS:Graph, all of which are on Softsel's hotlist of best sellers.

FRED GIBBONS: I want to approach distribution from an historical perspective. There was a time in which I used to go down and see Dave Wagman at Softsel, and he'd be in a garage somewhere, and we'd say, gee, would you like to carry our products, and he'd order fifty. Now he's closer to ordering around 5000 a month. But when we look at distribution today, things have gotten awful tricky.

CHAPTER SIX

HOW SOFTWARE MOVES 113

Nothing is ever the same. We thought we had it going pretty good back in 1977 because we had products when there really wasn't much product for the personal computer, and as a result we achieved a certain level of initial success. But, lo and behold, around 1982, as the market started to stretch up into the billion dollar category, we found out that there were competitors, and when you have a competitor you have to start doing a thing called marketing. Marketing means you say what's different about your product, and I think we saw a giant movement starting around 1981/82 to the brand marketing concept. Heavy promotion, heavy advertising, all that.

Well, now we've got lots of competitors, but we seem to be building a lot of similar products doing similar things, and nobody can tell the difference between them all, so now the game is going to shift to distribution. Who's got shelf space? Who can go in and say, Mr. Retailer, I want you to carry my products and not the other guy's? We've gotta start looking at distribution now as the major area for being competitive.

Now, what I'm saying is that the industry will consolidate around those people that have distribution. There's no question about it. And I hate to say it, but most of the software companies that are here today, I don't think are going to have distribution, and I think a lot of them are going to have a very, very difficult time getting their products to the marketplace. They're going to do a lot of deficit spending with the venture money that they've raised, and I'm not exactly sure that it's going to achieve any results, because of a tremendous lack of awareness about distribution by most of the people who are in the business today.

The direct channel is what I think is one of the most interesting channels of distribution. Software Publishing Corporation has decided to develop a direct channel. Now, the vehicle for distributing and the vehicle for delivering may vary. You're going to hear about electronic techniques, as well as physical goods techniques, but direct means a delivery system direct to the consumer.

114

What we did, was we developed a catalog called *Power Up*. Now, the objective here was quite simply to solve a problem. The problem was, we saw lots and lots of good software coming into Software Publishing Corporation, and we couldn't spend the half a million dollars that it was going to take to brand-build around that software. Example: We introduced a product called PFS:Write, a word processing product. The brand PFS was pretty well known, yet we still spent half a million dollars launching that product. I don't know what it would cost to do one from scratch with an unknown brand, but I'd bet it would be in the two to three million dollar class. I think that's the minimum amount of money that I'd want to raise to go out and launch a new brand today.

There's no way you can afford to brand-build around things that might only sell several hundred, at most a thousand units a month. The result is that we have a product that has usable value, but how are we going to deliver these things to the consumer? The answer is, we've got to find a more efficient channel of distribution.

Some of our current dealers are a little disappointed that we're going direct mail. It's a dirty word, direct mail, so we have some concern. The real retailers understand that they are in business to sell hardware, so for them it won't be an issue. But for the software stores, it's clearly a potential threat. I don't know what the answer is, except maybe if the software store becomes truly knowledgeable about the products they carry, if they can answer reasonable questions on software, I think they can continue to be successful. But there's no question that direct distribution is a megatrend, it's going to happen.

Let me just outline the structure. There's really four players associated today with getting software out to the consumer. The author/publisher, the distributor, the retailer, and then of course, the ultimate consumer. Let's talk about the problems that each one of these people has.

From the author/publisher viewpoint, you simply want to get your product out to a customer, a very simple objective. Let's say you've just built a product called Banner Builder, which produces banners, where you type in a line of text and it'll print out sideways out of the printer, CONGRATULATIONS ON THE 4TH QUARTER RESULTS! Nice product, quite useful, but how do you get it out to the consumer? Well, you may want to work through a distributor, someone like Softsel, for example.

Now Softsel wants to carry everything to give the retailer a broad selection, and provide one-stop shopping. But clearly, the benefit of a distributor is saying, Mr. Dealer, you want that, we have it, we recommend it, and it's good.

In the case of the retailer, however, we have an interesting problem, and it's a trend that's continuing. The retailer wants to carry primarily those products which help sell hardware. Now I'm not talking about software stores here, I'm talking about the retailer. We believe that retailers today are starting to standardize on three lines of software as they are starting to standardize on three lines of hardware, a low end, mid-range, and high end set of products. Then they try to get their staff trained and up to speed on those lines, and not screw around with a lot of this other low volume, low profit, accessory software.

If we look at it from the consumer's viewpoint however, the consumer may want this Banner Builder product, okay, but if we look back through that channel, and we look at who's involved, you may see something like this: One author/publisher at the top end, one consumer at the bottom end, but look what's in between—a distributor that might carry up to 4000 products, and a retailer who only wants to select the top twenty-five or fifty products out of that 4000. There's a very, very low probability that the author ever gets his product to the consumer. Now how are we going to solve that problem?

In the *Power Up* catalog, it is our objective to pre-select programs that are good, to make it easier to buy the product, either over the phone or by mail, provide complete customer support. No matter what channel we choose, we absolutely, positively must support the customer. Software without support will sell once, and no more. We want to reduce the cost of introducing products. This is what's really led me along this path, the enormous cost of introducing new products. You've got to find a more efficient way.

We think we're creating a new avenue specifically designed for authors or companies that are R&D as opposed to research and development and Marketing and Distribution companies. Look, we've got to innovate in the channels of distribution, we've got a lot of good product coming downstream, it's too expensive to distribute the way we normally do, we've got to add value here and invent. I think that direct channels are going to be a major, major area.

What percent of your business do you foresee in the accessory category versus the systems software?
We don't know the answer to that. We think, however, that the major opportunity for the independent software companies will probably come in the accessory or the vertical categories. The degree to which that proves true, that the real open market for software companies is in the accessory and vertical area, then I would suspect it could be at least half of our business downstream.

HOW SOFTWARE MOVES 117

Nathaniel Forbes, Gimcrax, Inc.

Finally, we hear from Nat Forbes, President of Gimcrax, a fledgling electronic software distribution enterprise of the most high-tech and experimental nature. Many believe that all a retailer really needs is a special terminal hooked up to an electronic distribution outfit, and then he will have instant access to thousands of programs without having to carry stock. Gimcrax plans to go one step further and by-pass the retailer. Before forming the pioneering Gimcrax, Mr. Forbes had been manager of the Computerland stores in Minnesota, then Director of Sales for THE SOURCE. At the time of the panel, Gimcrax was completing its pre-market stages, and expected to hit the streets in April, 1984. The results will not be at all clear until well into 1985.

NAT FORBES: We are planning the electronic distribution of software directly to consumers, and there are three key features of our business as we see it. The first is that unlike other electronic distribution schemes, we plan to go directly to the consumer, as opposed to going through the retailer. Second, the availability of software from our service will be by membership which we will sell at an extremely reasonable price. Third, we do not expect to use any of the public packet-switch networks, Tymnet, Telenet, Uninet, Autonet. We will be building and operating our own network. Let me explain these three features.

We believe that the inherent advantage of electronic distribution technology is that it provides the ability for a publisher to reach the consumer directly without having to cut in a third party, that is, the retailer or a wholesaler. The schemes for electronic distribution through retailers simply do not take advantage of that feature.

Memberships: In order to guarantee a completely reliable transmission of a product, we must establish a protocol for communications between the consumer's computer and our computer.

118

We are going to put this protocol in a terminal software package that will also allow you to log on to THE SOURCE, CompuServe, Dow Jones, MCI Mail, and so on. That's what you get for the membership fee. It will be marketed under the name Bluebars Software.

Why are we building our own network? It is possible for us to use the public packet-switch networks, but unfortunately, if enough people try to get on the same local access node at the same time, the node can't handle it. We'd be in a position somewhat like THE SOURCE was a couple of years ago, that is, its wild success brought the system to its knees. We investigated the cost of setting up a network and concluded that, indeed, Tymnet and Telenet were both in a terrific business that we ought to be in as well. As Bill McGowan of MCI says, "He who controls his own network controls his own future." So our venture capitalists have agreed that operating our own network is probably the most important feature of our plan.

There are six service considerations in the provision of electronic distribution services. These are, speed of transmission, documentation, security against piracy, price, refunds, and support.

The difficulty is not speed, but time. How long will a person tie up their phone line in order to receive a program? We believe that the limit is about fifteen minutes. The speed issue tells us how much information we can transmit in that period of time. At 1200 baud we can transmit about 92K bytes of code. There aren't a lot of programs out there at the moment that require significantly more than that in their code. At 300 baud the number is more like 27K. That's certainly a limitation, but the future in communications is definitely in the direction of 1200 baud, and I believe next year we will see 2400 baud modems for well under a thousand dollars.

Documentation is the real problem in my view. You simply can't provide it with an electronic distribution system. It's possible if the customer has a printer, but not everyone does. We could send documentation in the mail, but in the three days that it would take, they might just as well go to a computer store and get the code and the documentation all at once. Our solution to this as a marketing-driven company is not to distribute software that requires more than one or two pages of documentation. You won't see Lotus 1-2-3 distributed electronically in the immediate future, at least not at 1200 baud.

Piracy: Electronic distribution is not inherently more prone to theft than any other method. There is no such thing as copy protection for the 5% of the world that views copy protection as a challenge. Our system is at least as secure as any protection mechanism presently used in packaged software.

Price: We believe that the service and support that we will provide, in combination with the speed and convenience of electronic distribution, will permit us to charge at or near retail prices in the short term. In the long term, however, we believe that electronic distribution will accelerate the downward trend in the price of personal computer software. We will be in a position to take advantage of that trend without appearing to be in the lead in discounting software.

Refunds and returns: If the company trusts its customers, the customers will trust it, and that's our approach. We'll simply provide refunds on demand to anyone who requests it, within reason. We'll look closely at customers who abuse this policy.

Support: This is a team effort with software publishers. We do not want to be in the support business for the code, but our responsibility is to support the distribution mechanism. If there is a bug in the program, that is the publisher's responsibility. It is our intention to provide complete support whether we provide it ourselves or whether it's provided by software publishers through us.

How much of the market can you hope to reach?
We believe that personal computer software will be about $12 billion in retail value in 1988, and of that, electronic distribution will be between $1 and $2 billion, so between 10% and 20%. We propose to

120

be in sixty-five major cities, and I think that represents, don't quote me, but maybe 45% of the population of the U.S., so apply to that how many of those will have personal computers.

———— • ————

MODERATOR ESTHER DYSON: The real thing we're talking about here is not products, or distribution channels, or technology—it's money. There's one law of economics that works in the long run even if it gets screwed up a little bit in the short run, and that is this: the guy who provides an investment, if he does so properly, gets a return. So the issue is: who provides it, and who charges for it and therefore gets that return?

There are five distinct pieces to a software product when it finally arrives in a consumer's hand. There's the product itself, and the research and development that goes into it. Number two, there's the product selection. We've just heard that there are 4000 different packages at Softsel. Which is the one you want? There's not a shortage of software, there's a shortage of distribution. On the retail shelf you can only find twenty-five, but which twenty-five? Okay, third is marketing, which is sort of the obverse of selection. How do you get the customer to select your package over another guy's? Fourth, there's the actual physical distribution, whether it's in a truck or down a phone line, by UPS or mail. How do you order it, and how to you get it? Fifth is the support issue, both telephone support, and documentation support.

What we're seeing is a shifting around of who provides these and who charges for them. What we're discussing today is who gets to make the investment in the value added, and therefore gets to charge for it?

CHAPTER SIX

Where is the OEM (Original Equipment Manufacturers) channel going?

FRED GIBBONS: We haven't talked much about that. We need to recognize two very major trends in OEM software, the first of which is typified by the TRS-80 Model 100, the little lap computer with the software inside the machine. That's not the same thing as bundling, it's a dedicated function machine, and it doesn't surprise me to see software become part of the machine, software that we used to consider applications software. A few years ago, the hardware manufacturers made the hardware, and we used to sell compilers, and languages, linkers and loaders. Guess what? Those all go out standard with the system now. We're now starting to see the productivity software set become re-defined as standard system software, so for those classes of software, the OEM channel will come to dominate that market very quickly.

David Wagman, does Fred Gibbons' argument make sense, that the programs in his direct mail catalog are not right for most dealers?

DAVID WAGMAN: Yes, it makes a lot of sense in that regard. Dealers are most interested in best-selling software, and except for the very, very specialized software stores, are not interested in carrying more than a hundred or 150 titles. Where Softsel offers some 3000 different titles, it's easy to understand why there's an opportunity for a non-stocking supplier to have an access channel to get rare or hard-to-find software into the hands of users.

These guys talking about networks and catalogs are small time compared with AT&T, or Sears and American Express, so what makes them think they can compete?

ESTHER DYSON: There's a distinction between American Express, which has a catalogue of, basically, Softsel's hotlist. They've got Visi-Calc and PFS and the well-known products, and Fred Gibbons' catalog that brings stuff that people don't know about. There's a role for lots of people in here, and one advantage is to be first.

FRED GIBBONS: This is software. Basically, what we have to remember is that we understand the software business as well as just about anybody out there, and the nice thing about being early is that the barriers to entry are quite low. Two or three years ago it cost us $50 thousand to introduce the first PFS product, and it was half a million recently for PFS:Write. Two to three years from now the barrier to entry will be in the five to fifteen million dollar category. We are early, and the challenge will be, can we make enough money between now and when it really takes off so that we'll be there when it really happens?

VOICE: AT&T has yet to prove they can market anything to the consumer. It's important to realize that there are some bright people that have left these companies, AT&T and IBM, and gone into these startup companies, and they're the leading force.

RECAP

Five thousand software publishers with nearly 10,000 programs are now clogging the channels and the marketplace. But software has a lot in common with industries that have been around a lot longer, like books and records. The book industry seems to make room for 30-40,000 new titles each and every year, and you can still buy titles that were popular in ancient Greece. It seems unavoidable that the software market will go through more convulsions, and that it will undoubtedly open up. It has to, because the potential is too great to ignore. And each change will create more windows of opportunity.

Future prospects offer little comfort to the software publishers who have to "play it the way it lays" on the day they go to market. For now, clogged channels are the operative reality and the hardest nut to crack. Watching entrepreneurial fireworks go off, and launching your own rocket are two very different experiences.

Chapter Seven

DATABASE SOFTWARE AND THE ROLE OF MARKET POSITIONING

Information management is what computers do best, and what our modern world needs done the most. The amount of information that inundates this society is exploding. Information is power, and information is profit, but information that is neither is called red tape. The world is sinking in a sea of red tape, but one way to stay afloat is to program personal computers to generate replies for the bureaucratic computers, then everyone can get on with something more productive—like working with the kind of information that produces profit.

As seen by David Cole, Chief Executive Officer of Ashton-Tate, the issue is productivity:

"The engine driving this whole microcomputer explosion is the need for increased productivity. The tools have not previously existed for information workers to be productive. An information worker is anybody who collates and manages information—clerks, administrators, marketing people, lawyers, and so forth. In about 1910 or 1920, about 16% of the work force was information workers. By 1980, that became 52% domestically. At the same time, in the post-war period, until 1979, the capital investment per information worker in tools was less than $300 per year, and relatively stable for that period. In 1979, that skyrocketed to $600. Double. In 1980, it went to $800, and that will continue to climb to well over $3000. Compare that to ten to twenty thousand dollars per worker in the manufacturing or agricultural sectors.

"That's the engine.

"We've got a couple of things going on. The percentage of the work force that manages information is increasing, and the level of investment for each one is increasing. And it must happen, it absolutely must happen, because that sector is a brake on productivity for this country."

People or companies who don't deal with their data effectively can get buried by it, or at least they can expect to be surpassed by those who handle it better. From cottage industries and small businesses to governments and conglomerates, and throughout the advanced technologies, information management is at the heart of every enterprise. This is why data management programs are hot properties in a heavily contested market. Of interest here is the way one product came to dominate the field.

There were seventy five microcomputer database software products on the floor at the 1983 Fall COMDEX, all jostling for a piece of the information management market. The biggest and most successful of all the database companies is the software superstar Ashton-Tate, publishers of the famous dBASE II. The story of how they emerged from the pack, and why some other products didn't, is a marvelous object lesson in the meaning of marketing and market position. It's a good story, too.

Wayne Ratliff, Ashton-Tate

By 1978, microcomputers were beginning to get powerful enough, and memory was getting cheap enough, that they could accommodate data management, previously the sole province of the minis and mainframes. That's the year that a very bright man in New York, David Rodman, released FMS-80, the first commercial microcomputer relational database manager.

Meanwhile, across the country in California, Wayne Ratliff, a systems designer at the Jet Propulsion Laboratories (JPL) in Pasadena, was beginning to think about a data system for use in artificial intelligence. This was his hobby, something he worked on at home on his homebrew, kludged-up microcomputer. At about the same time, two other bright men in Michigan, Robert and Malcolm Cohen, were releasing DBM1 as a turnkey microcomputer data system that they installed for their government clients. In 1981 the Cohens took their improved product, renamed Condor, onto the mass market.

It was not until mid-1979 that Wayne Ratliff started putting little ads in the back of *BYTE* magazine for his program, named Vulcan after Spock's home planet. However, he was usually too busy with work at the Jet Propulsion Laboratories to answer inquiries from the ads. Even though *BYTE* magazine columnist Jerry Pournelle raved about Vulcan (and raved at its indecipherable documentation), Wayne never sold more than fifty copies. It wasn't just that his job came first, but mostly he couldn't relate to the myriad problems and the paperwork that comes with running a business, however small. Wayne tried dispiritedly and unsuccessfully to get someone to take over the marketing. He was being threatened with a suit over the Vulcan name, and the whole thing was getting him down to the point that he was thinking of giving it up. At this time, Vulcan had several competitors, including FMS-80, SELECTOR, Analyst, and DataStar from MicroPro.

In mid-1980, one of Vulcan's fans started an anonymous campaign to get a Los Angeles-based distributor, Discount Software, to take an interest in Vulcan. Discount Software, then six months old and coming on strong, was the creation of George Tate, a self-taught microcomputer technician, and his friend Hal Lashlee, an accountant and another early micro enthusiast. As a repairman for Computer Mart, George had watched fellow bench jockeys launch successful companies like Alpha Micro and International Micro Systems. The entrepreneurial bug struck, and George went off in search of his own career. This led to creating Discount Software with Hal Lashlee, and that led to finding Wayne Ratliff's languishing program, Vulcan.

George Tate and Hal Lashlee decided to start a new company to market Vulcan. They brain-stormed with their ad man, Hal Pawluk, and he came up with a new name for the product, dBASE II. There never was a dBASE I. Pawluk had an outrageous ad campaign in mind, and to offset that, he wanted a conservative name for the company. So he invented the name Ashton-Tate. There wasn't anyone named Ashton. (There is now, a parrot who lives in an elegant cage in the employee lounge.) First, Tate and Lashlee went to work on documentation and refinements, and in January, 1981, they released their dBASE II ad campaign with the banner slogan "dBASE II vs. the Bilge Pumps" over a picture of an unwieldy looking piece of industrial equipment. It outraged competitors and insulted the pump maker, but it worked. That ad launched Ashton-Tate's strategy of hard advertising coupled with a high-powered dealer recruitment program that offered good discounts and expert support. Building a strong dealer network really paid off.

In spite of the hefty price, $700, which placed it at the high end of the field, dBASE II took off, and was selling easily 600 a month by the end of 1981. First year revenues of about $4 million grew into second year revenues exceeding $12 million, placing Ashton-Tate firmly in the superstar category, and making author Wayne Ratliff rich on royalties. By the end of 1983, approximately 200,000 units had been sold, and the average number of units shipped per month was running between five and six thousand.

CHAPTER SEVEN

About 35% of sales are through the most lucrative channel, direct to the company's dealer network; perhaps 40-45% move through distributors, which is less remunerative; and only 15-20% move through the low-yield OEM channels. Ashton-Tate employed about 400 temporary and full time people at the end of 1983.

By comparison, Condor has sold approximately 100,000 units, but they say that 60% of those go through the low yield OEM channels, and only 10-20% through their own dealers. That means a big difference in revenues.

So what was the big difference? Why do most people think dBASE II was the first database program? What happened to FMS-80 and Condor? Why did dBASE II race ahead to become the dominant product in the field, kicking dust in the faces of those other good products that were out there ahead of it? This is a lesson on "positioning" which is achieved by aggressively marketing a good product when the situation is still fluid. That's how it's done.

Let's let the entrepreneurs tell their tales:

David Rodman is the author of FMS-80, the first relational database product for the microcomputer, and founder of DJR, the company that markets it. This interview took place late one COMDEX evening in a trashed hospitality suite full of half-eaten sandwiches, crumpled napkins, full ashtrays and exhausted staff members. The party was over, but David Rodman was as immaculately dressed as an East coast banker, only with more flair. He is short, compact, and handsome in a dark, Rudolph Valentino way. He looked done-in, gray in the face and with baggage under the eyes, yet he didn't let on at all—he was smoothly articulate, responsive and very much in focus.

DAVID RODMAN: FMS-80 came out in October of 1978. This was the first product of its kind on the market. We were the first assembly language relational database system. We were the first software or applications development tool.

128

How many people were in your firm back then?
One. Just me.

What happened?
Well, the initial situation was one of taking out a brilliant idea, and trying to put a market together with no knowledge or understanding of what marketing is. At that time, I had a pretty negative attitude toward marketing as such. I was a programmer.

I started writing computer programs when I was ten years old, in 1960. I hung around MIT for a good number of years, and was sort of the mascot of the artificial intelligence group. So my initial exposure to computers and programming was at a very high level, technically.

I worked for some really fascinating projects. I did a couple of jobs for a large consulting company, Science Applications, Inc. We had a contract with the CIA and another contract with the Department of Defense. Boy, that was great stuff! We were right on the leading edge of artificial intelligence, and doing things that no one had ever done before with software. And I loved it a lot, but the only thing was, I couldn't talk about what I was doing. I couldn't really feel relaxed about it; it was very, very high security stuff. I can still not talk about what I was doing. Really fascinating stuff, but I wanted to get out into the private sector. I had always been a capitalist at heart, and . . .

Capitalist? With a negative attitude about marketing? You came out with a great product, way ahead of everybody else, but the world now thinks of dBASE II when they think about database programs.
That's right. It took me too long to get my ego sorted out and realize that there is nothing ignoble about taking on investors. I just had my head in the wrong place about having an investment company come in and giving up pieces of the company. I felt that I didn't

want to get into the high level, high-powered business world. So I didn't.

If I look at what my intention was, and the level of clarity with which I was operating then—or the lack of clarity—you know, really, I can see exactly how my own attitude and my own beliefs completely determined what happened to the product, and what happened to the company. It was really one-to-one mapping of belief to occurrence.

What made you change your mind?
About a year ago, I took a hard look at how I was spending my time and energy. That was the same process I went through in 1975 when I decided to develop FMS-80 in the first place. Last year my company employed about four people, and I was on a trip to England, looking at the English market for the product, seeing how wide open that was. I talked with one of our English distributors who said, you know, you've got the best product on the market. You've *got* to market it.

You must have been disappointed by the notoriety of other products?
Well, not disappointed really. It was more educational than disappointing. It was a bit frustrating, yeah, but that's only my initial reaction to it. If I get past the frustration, I can't blame Ashton-Tate. I created exactly what I have, and I have exactly what I created. Having other products that are technically inferior to ours, nonetheless, taking a bigger market share, if I look simply at what my actions have been, how clear my intention has been, that's exactly what I've created.

So I put a business plan together, and flew around the country talking to venture capitalists. What I discovered was that at that time—and it is probably no longer true—we were in a kind of in-between place, as far as being able to attract capital. On the one hand, we're not a startup, so we didn't fall into the category of startup financing. But on the other hand, our track record, as far as

130

sales versus competition and number of years in business, is terrible. So we don't look too good as an expansion investment, either. And the frustrating thing is trying to hook up with somebody who's got money to invest, who's knowledgeable enough to realize what a great investment this really is. We're still looking.

Do you ever think of scrapping everything and starting a whole new era in microcomputing?
Well, it's conceivable that that's what we'll have to do. Coming out of an artificial intelligence background, of course, that's something I have a great deal of interest in. But I would not simply make a jump from one place to another. There are thousands of people now who are depending on the company and our products.

How many people are in your company now?
There are twelve. Ten here and two in England. In one year we've gone from four to twelve. Our product has gained a tremendous amount of recognition and we've signed on twenty distributors this year. It's because of my clearing my own intentions, getting clear with myself about what it is that I want to create.

It has been very important for me to get out of the way. My expertise lies in creating software and coming up with great ideas. My expertise is definitely not in marketing. So, having recognized that, I've been able to gain the assistance that I've needed and that has made a big difference for us.

——— • ———

DJR staffer Kevin Cook finally explained why the promised photo of David Rodman was never sent. "That got shot down," he said, "when we found out it was for Ashton-Tate—they're competitors." All pleas fell on deaf ears, including the argument of status that David would get from being included in with the industry's leaders. "Look," Kevin said, "David's an

CHAPTER SEVEN

eccentric guy. He doesn't follow the crowd; he goes his own way." So he does, so he does. Good luck, David Rodman, wherever you are headed.

Malcolm Cohen, Condor Computer Corp.

Malcolm Cohen is co-founder and Chairman of the Board of Condor Computer Corporation, publisher of the popular Condor database management program. His face frequently carries the pinched expression of a man with a migraine, but at the time we met he was righteously played out. This was a post-party interview at Condor's COMDEX hospitality suite, and the heavy pace of the expo was clearly taking its toll on everyone.

MALCOLM COHEN: We started in 1977. When we introduced our product in 1978, I don't think there was anything else out there. We were the first to introduce a relational database system for microcomputers.

We got into it because, well, I was a director of research of a labor institute at the University of Michigan, and very frustrated by the lack of software available to analyze large amounts of data. My brother Robert was an electrical engineer for Hughes Aircraft, and he thought that micros were the wave of the future. Because of my experience with database management systems on large mainframes, we thought that putting a data manager on a microcomputer would result in a tremendous new product.

What was it like, trying to launch that product?
We first sold it as a turn key package. Basically, we would sell a Cromemco Computer along with a database software product that we called DBM1. We were charging, like $10,000 for the software, and we were selling it largely to government agencies. We had to charge a lot because it was a very limited market at that time, and equivalent

software on minis and mainframes was costing many times more than that.

Later, in 1979, we began to realize that we should mass market the product. We predicted that CP/M would become a very popular seller, so about the end of 1981 we introduced our CP/M product.

What problems did you face in trying to go into the mass market?
Our biggest mistake was that we didn't really start a mass advertising campaign soon enough. We thought if we had a superior product and took it to OEMs and they selected it, that they would advertise it, and that would bring customers into the stores. That was a mistake, because they didn't advertise our product. What happened was that other firms advertised their products and brought people into the stores, and our product suffered. We should have started sooner for that pull-through advertising.

How many Condors do you ship?
We don't physically ship them all ourselves, but about 5,000 a month if you include all the channels. We sell to distributors, manufacturers, and dealers, and I would guess that maybe 10-20% are through our own dealers, and about 60% through OEM licenses. By the end of 1983 we'll have 100,000 copies sold under CP/M, MS-DOS and PC-DOS.

How did you finance your company's growth?
Up to the time we went into mass marketing, we had financed ourselves from cash flow. At one point it was a choice of not buying my wife a rug she wanted so I could put the money in the business. After we launched the product in 1981, we got advances from manufacturers for tailoring the product for their particular machine, and also we got Commerce Clearing House to invest in us, and we had bank financing. We had to give up about 20% of our company for about half a million. Then we started to really build—we

expanded to around forty people. Then we did a second round of funding with Software Fund. They specialize in investing in software and high-tech companies, and what we did with them was an R&D partnership. Basically, that allows us to give up much less equity for the money. They get part of the royalties and some stock options.

Any problems with managing rapid growth?
It's always a problem. We have eighty people now, and expect a hundred by the end of the year. About three years ago we brought in a President who does the day-to-day operations of the company, and we had a nice situation of thirteen people, all reporting to him. A very nice, happy family. But as we expanded to forty and fifty, we had to develop lines of authority, and this created some unhappiness because some of the original people could no longer report to the president directly. So we had some turnover, and some unhappiness. There are just so many problems that a growing company faces. You can't afford to have a personnel department right away, so you can't address all the issues. We had problems working out the employment contracts.

How are you going to deal with the other seventy five database products?
I don't know that we necessarily have to deal with them.

Don't you have to deal with the fact that dBASE II is more recognized, and has out-positioned you?
First of all, our total number of copies is still very large, so that there are certain segments of the market that we intend to capture. One of our competitors (dBASE II) has positioned itself with the applications programmers, but there are a hell of a lot more end users out there than there are applications programmers. That's the market we intend to capture. And the market is growing so rapidly. In five years it'll be a different game.

134

I'm not sure that the concept that some people are touting, of you get in there and penetrate, and you guarantee that by being there first you'll have the lion's share of the market—IBM has certainly proven that you don't have to come in first. An Apple a day doesn't keep IBM away.

I think one thing that's going to really help Condor is our strong OEM penetration.

What advice would you give to a young friend who wanted to go into software, someone with talent, energy, drive, and motivation, but no track record or financing?
Pick an area which is achievable. Start out and make a mark. For example, I might advise them to write a program and find somebody else to distribute it. Make a name, and let that product be known. The downfall of so many software companies is that they try to do too many things without adequate financing, and as a result, they fail. I don't think that the problem is so much that it costs so much to develop the product as that it costs so much to market it. I question the feasibility of both developing and marketing your own product without adequate financing.

The Lotus phenomenon has essentially changed the whole marketplace for microcomputer software. We're no longer a cottage industry. We've gone into the soap business instead of the computer software business. The average person selling in a store just doesn't have training in all these products, so what basically happens is that the person at the store is selling what's advertised, the products that people hear about.

How do you generate that pull-through?
That remains to be seen. I suspect that whatever I were to say, even if I had the best marketing information today, two years from now it's going to change dramatically. It's brand name identification, mass

marketing. We're positioning ourselves so that we're the data management people.

How about the trade show, is that a good thing for you?
Absolutely. It gives us good visibility. You need two things, you need to have the pull-through, enough advertising, so people come into the stores, but you need to have the product there at the dealers. Trade shows give us a lot of dealer contacts.

Are you expecting much movement in the direction of UNIX?
Oh, yes. Condor is a company that has essentially committed itself to rewrite its product in the C language which will allow full transportability. I think UNIX is going to be a very popular system, but it also depends on what AT&T does. And what the Fortune 1000 companies do. Those companies buy thousands of microcomputers each. Government agencies are addressing UNIX. My prediction is that it will take off, but who knows, maybe some new operating system that we haven't seen yet will replace UNIX?

Looking back, are there things you wish you had done differently?
More marketing earlier!

What keeps you plugging away at it? You've got a company with eighty people, selling thousands of units a month, why don't you retire and put your feet up?
It's too much fun!

SCREEN-ORIENTED PRODUCTS ENTER THE MARKET

Products like dBASE II are high-level languages that have been specially designed to manage data. To use them, you have to learn how to program; to write a sophisticated application, you have to be a sophisticated user. However, because dBASE II was *relatively* easy to learn, especially for simple applications, it was heavily pitched at first as an end user product, something the average computerist could use to solve his or her own data problems. For a time, it was in fact the best available alternative—available meaning a product that masses of potential users can hear about, find in local stores, and have supported by their dealers.

Other companies had different ideas about how end users should be served, and they began to develop products that were screen-oriented. In other words, instead of doing any programming, you merely respond to prompts or fill in forms on the screen, and the program cranks out results. Although simple to use, most of these programs are often slow and usually unable to handle large, intricate, integrated applications. Many end users prefer this solution, despite its limitations, because they don't have to work so hard to get results. However, people with a penchant for programming tend to prefer the greater power and flexibility of the development languages.

Very soon after its release, it was apparent that dBASE II was a phenomenon of a unique kind. It began to win converts in large numbers from the ranks of consultants and applications programmers who used it to develop custom software in a fraction of the time that it took with other languages. Thousands of vertical market software products have been developed with dBASE II, and they created a thriving market for dBASE II add-on products, such as code generators, math and stat packages, graph packs, and so on. Some entrepreneurs have even developed generic mass market products with dBASE II, such as the extremely popular and fast-selling Champion accounting system from Champion Software in Lakewood, Colorado.

Meanwhile, because of aggressive competition from screen-oriented data systems, dBASE II became somewhat repositioned as an applications development system, meaning that it was at least partly nudged off the end user throne. dBASE II was no longer all things to all people. The next two interviews are with entrepreneurs who publish database programs designed for the novice user—products of the kind that repositioned dBASE II.

CHAPTER SEVEN

William R. Stow III, Pearlsoft

William R. Stow, III, is founder and Chairman of Board of Pearlsoft, a company that employed forty six people at the end of 1983. Before opening a micro store in 1977, he had an extensive background in designing computer information systems on minis and mainframes for various branches of government in Oregon. Personal Pearl and its new companion, Accounting Pearl, are expressly designed to allow non-expert computer users to customize for their own business forms and procedures.

When did you first become an entrepreneur?

BILL STOW: I always had that. When I was a kid I started an egg route, delivered eggs to people, and then hired other kids. I had an egg distribution business when I was eleven years old. I had more money than I knew what to do with. But I enjoyed the business, and enjoyed working with people, and setting it up was a lot of fun.

Well, let's get more current. When did you start Pearlsoft?
We formed Relational Systems, now Pearlsoft, in July of 1980. I knew that all of the really advanced work was going to happen on micros in the future. I wanted to move into micros because my concept would give people the capability to quickly create unique applications for their own needs.

We introduced our product, Personal Pearl, in October of 1982 at the West Coast Computer Faire. It took off immediately, and the company became profitable in two months. We had initial contracts with Osborne, and several other manufacturers, and we began selling it on a local basis retail. We market aggressively through OEMs, people like Morrow, Epson, Zenith, Tab, CDI, DEC, and some others.

I would say a lot of the pre-payments from manufacturers funded the company. When it was introduced in October, we had a monthly income of about $100,000 immediately. We have several kinds of OEM relationships. The manufacturer may really be a distributor, where they buy the package from us and re-sell. Or they may be manufacturing it themselves, in which case we get a royalty. Generally, that runs 10-20% of list price from most manufacturers. If we package it and they offer it, then it's normally about a 65% discount, depending on volume. All of it depends on volume.

How many units are out there now?
Of Personal Pearl? Over 70,000.

How did you fund the company?
We started the company with our own money. I talked to venture capitalists initially and learned that I would have to give up 50% of the company. I felt that we needed to spend two years building the software before we could take it to market, and I found the venture people a little bit too short-term oriented and I wanted the time to get the technology right. So we decided to live in a very restricted means for two years while we built the technology. Between the three founders, we put in approximately $100,000. About thirteen people were living on almost no income during that two-year period.

When did you go looking for more capital for the business?
It was in February of 1982 that we took our first outside investments. We raised $300,000 and had to give away 25% of the company. We took in more capital in spring of 1983 from both private sources and venture capitalist sources, just over $600,000, and gave away maybe another 15%.

Our investors have been fantastic. They have helped considerably. We have a very active board that brings a lot of experience to bear on the corporation. The investors also have a lot of contacts around the industry so there's a lot of cooperation between us and other companies. We spent a lot of time with our venture capitalists to make sure we'd work well together before we took the funding.

How much ownership do you now retain?

I'm not sure. I am often asked that, and I never really know. Because it doesn't seem to make any difference, doesn't seem relevant.

We're in the process of acquiring top people in sales and marketing right now, and we're going to have to give up a lot more of the company, but that's nothing compared to the value of the quality of the team we're going to have. You need a good team.

Has COMDEX been worthwhile for you?

It's been outstanding. It cost us about thirty-five or forty thousand dollars, not counting staff time.

What did you get out of it?

We have a telemarketing force that has been talking to retailers on the phone, and they get to develop more personal relationships with the clients they are serving. And we are picking up a lot of new dealers.

What kind of advertising did you go in for?

We wanted to do our initial marketing for OEMs. Personal Pearl is a very advanced product internally, so it's not the story you're going to tell in the retail marketplace. A novice is not going to come into a computer store and have any knowledge of a fifth generation data base system, so it's not something to publish at that point. But it is a story you can take to a manufacturer that has software people who could understand it. During the first year we didn't do any advertising after the introduction of the product. other than what was done through manufacturers. Osborne did quite a bit of advertising, for example. And there were other people who advertised, but we didn't do any at all. And we didn't start until November of this year.

What is your strategy for overcoming the noise in the market?
I don't think you can identify one thing that's going to make you successful, like a particular advertising campaign, or a particular PR campaign. It's like when I first learned how to play chess well. What I found is that most people who play chess, the reason why they don't do well is because they look for the big move. They look for the grand play, and they even study chess books looking for grand plays. Chess masters don't play that way. They only play for very small incremental advantages that altogether lead to overwhelming victory. It's a whole lot of small things.

Richard Certo, ASAP Systems, Inc.

Richard Certo is President of ASAP Systems, Inc., publishers of ASAP FIVE, a brand new and highly sophisticated product that was developed with lightning speed—seven months—and backed by big money and business savvy. His product is based on a new and advanced data technology, and he claims that it is not only the easiest to use of all the data programs, being a simple matter of filling in screens, but also that it is extremely fast and capable of easily building highly sophisticated and integrated applications. If this is true, and if ASAP FIVE is successfully marketed and positioned, his product represents a real threat to the other end user products.

RICHARD CERTO: The technology we use is called Universal Relation. This was a theory proposed by a professor at Stanford University. When we started, I knew that I wanted a better way for people to manage their own information, so one of the first things we did was to hire some people to do a literature search, and we tripped across a new technology in software, Universal Relations, proposed by Professor Jeffrey Ullman. We have taken his theory and commercialized it.

CHAPTER SEVEN

We know now that we are the first people to commercialize that technology. It sits on a relational database and makes it far superior in its mode of operation. It's very easy to use—the user only has to be aware of the names of the data items, and the system takes care of indexing, arranging data items into files, and files into databases. Just fill out a screen, and off you go. A programmer-less system.

We think we have a nine to twelve month lead on anybody out there. We are pretty positive that once people see the interface that the Universal Relation provides, that everybody's going to move to it. It's very friendly, and very different from anything you've seen. We've eliminated 95% of the time and effort it used to take to learn how to use a computer. We are pretty positive that once people see the interface that Universal Relation provides, everybody's going to move to it.

How did you decide to become a software entrepreneur?
I have an extensive background in information systems, designing how information flows in a company and how it's used. I was a CPA, then an auditor, dealing with information systems, and after that I was a financial officer for a military electronics company, and then for Seagate Technology (makers of Shugart drives). After twelve years in finance and information, I decided to try something else. I've always wanted to do something on my own.

I've worked with Peter Yee for years, at other companies and then at Seagate. He has an extensive background in computer science and programming, so I went to Peter and told him what I wanted— which was to find a way for people to manage their own information. We tried to get our employer, Seagate, to do it, but they weren't interested. They're hardware people. In April of '83, we gave notice. We attracted some very talented people—four of the six programmers at Seagate. Peter and I didn't leave Seagate until September/October, 1983, but the programmers left and went to work for us much earlier. We had a product by November.

142

How are you going to market this product?
We're always going to emphasize technology, keep up with the latest advances at the research institutions, work with that. We're going to market the product very differently, too. It's a very different product. We'll go through a pretty independent sales organization, but we're developing that right now, so I can't say much. What I found is that many smaller businesses, say up to a hundred or 200 employees, have an aversion to computers. People are still afraid of them in the work place. We want to deal with that constructively.

This other marketing strategy is a result of COMDEX. One of the things that we've had a great deal of trouble trying to do is set up our product with distributors. They've all paid lip service to it, but they're so overwhelmed with product offerings right now. They don't have the time, energy, or even the insight to recognize whether a product is another me-too or something different that they should distribute. But we found out that we don't need to waste a lot of time trying to convince distributors. We're going to revise our strategy and go right out to the dealers ourselves, and the reason for this is that the dealer response here at COMDEX has been tremendous. The dealers are more willing, because they have to deal with the customers directly, to sit down and take a look at something that they think can help them to sell systems or software. We've signed up almost every single dealer we've sat down with. We're going to go out and hit dealers, but you waste too much time trying to get attention from distributors.

We've brought down nearly everyone in our company, we have a big hospitality suite and we're making a tremendous effort to reach the press. We've easily spent $50,000 coming here, probably more. We've only got a ten by ten booth, but we've done a tremendous amount of work there. We've had both our demo systems busy continuously. After only a few days at COMDEX we've actually signed up about a dozen dealers, maybe thirty five have taken packages, and we have a stack of a hundred to 150 contacts. We're very pleased.

CHAPTER SEVEN

How did you finance the company?

I'm pretty lucky. Since I was one of the early people in Seagate Technology, I owned a nice piece of stock in the company. So my risk wasn't financial, it was more personal. I didn't have to worry about trying to finance the company. I could fund the company all the way, but the reason I'm going after venture capital is to get some outside people involved with the company. To get their contacts and their expertise.

In marketing, we realized at the very beginning—due largely to Lotus 1-2-3—that the software industry is fast becoming market-driven, supported by extensive advertising and product recognition. So we immediately dedicated a major portion of our resources just to marketing the product. We got a little more funding from a guy I used to work for, I twisted his arm, and got $100,000. We negotiated a bank loan, because we ran out of money at the end of November. Don't tell the hotel this. We mortgaged our equipment and furniture and got another $200,000 from the bank. We're talking to venture capitalists right now—looking for a half million at a minimum. That's very little, but we don't need much more in terms of facilities, or equipment or payroll, we need it just for advertising. We'd like a million, so we can bump our advertising to $150,000 a month. That will cover everything we want to do.

The amount we have to give away to get financing gets smaller and smaller as we become more developed. Working this COMDEX thing is going to put another premium on it. I don't want to give up too much because we've got some really strange ideas about the way we're going to approach the market, and things we want the company to do technology-wise, and I don't want a venture capitalist to come in and say, "Hey, I want you to be conservative."

Has starting your own business affected your life in any way?

It helped out tremendously in marital relations. One of the things that happened was my wife came to work on this project, and she's

helping to prepare the manual. Before, when I had to spend some late hours . . . well, now she understands. In fact, I probably get in before she does, now. Now we work together.

Postscript

In April, 1984, Richard Certo reported that ASAP had very little luck getting in with distributors. Worse, they only had about twenty five dealers signed up, in spite of some major advertising efforts to help generate pull-through. It's a tough market to crack. ASAP next decided to go directly after major corporate accounts and are having, according to Certo, "phenomenal success." They fix their targets with lists that show the number of PCs owned by various companies, and have recently been able to score some major accounts that promise orders on a scale of fifty or a hundred units per month. One such customer is a national accounting firm, another is in shipping, and he also said something about the Federal Election Commission. In addition to buying programs, the companies apparently pay ASAP well to set up applications with off-the-shelf ASAP software. Then the companies distribute the customized package internally.

Meanwhile, ASAP has reduced the price of ASAP FIVE to $275 and released ASAP SIX at $395. SIX is a greatly enhanced version of FIVE. ASAP has yet to bring in venture capital, but Certo says they are working on it, and since they will begin to show a profit shortly, are now in a better position to score. Richard Certo says the software market is crazy. Who can disagree?

RECAP ON POSITIONING

In the software industry, "positioning" is almost as popular a buzzword as "integrated" and "user-friendly." The concept was promulgated by admen Al Ries and Jack Trout in 1972, and most recently restated in their book *Positioning: The Battle For Your Mind*. The way they tell it is simplistic, yet it is a very useful notion that contains glittering kernels of truth. It goes like this:

The world is heavily over-communicated. In one year the average mind is exposed to over 200,000 advertising messages alone, a very conservative figure that does not include news and political messages. In self defense, people tend to maintain an oversimplified viewpoint on almost everything, and they respond best to oversimplified messages. The public mind is quickly made up, but once an idea gets fixed it is extremely difficult to change it.

"Positioning" is about getting your name and product fixed in the public mind before it's made up, because once a name is established, it sticks, and millions of dollars of competitors' advertising won't easily dislodge it. The best way to be positioned in the market is to be first. Not necessarily first in fact, but first in the public mind. Winning means to be the "firstest with the mostest," and this means to pour on the marketing money while the situation is still fluid.

If another company is already positioned ahead of you, you can almost never win by going head-to-head with them. They can lose first place, but you can't usually take it away from them if they're at all awake. In fact, all of your advertising tends to help your opponent as much as yourself. There are only two reliable strategies against someone in first position: (1) look for a hole in the market you can crawl into, then establish a distinction which effectively repositions the other company and puts your own first in the newly-defined area—like when Nyquil made millions by being the first *nighttime* cold remedy. Or (2), relate yourself to the first position and run with them instead of against them, as in "Avis is number two so we have to try harder."

MicroPro's WordStar was not the first word processor, and it certainly wasn't the best, but they took first position and have been impossible to dislodge. In spite of the emergence of over 200 other word processors, and in spite of the fact that WordStar has scarcely evolved over the years, it still tops the list with a base of over 600,000 authorized users. That's what positioning means.

In database software, Ashton-Tate's wasn't the first good product, but it was the first good product with a big ad campaign, and first to quickly establish a strong dealer network, and therefore it became first in the public mind. They'll be hard to dislodge. At first, dBASE II advertising was addressed to end users, sophisticated users, and applications programmers, all at the same time. It was for everyone, because there wasn't much else getting a big push at the time, so dBASE II became king of the entire data management mountain. However, when the easy-to-use information systems came to the market in a big way, dBASE II was effectively repositioned, meaning that their first place position was redefined, and they became the leading data base applications development language that a lot of sophisticated end users still like to use.

No menu-driven product has emerged with a commanding position in the public mind, so that market is still fluid, which means that ASAP and dozens of others can still fight for first place in that segment without having to go head-to-head against the repositioned dBASE II. For its own part, Ashton-Tate has just come out with a menu-driven end user product called Friday!, but they will come up against the same positioning lesson that IBM learned when it went into copy machines against Xerox, and when MicroPro went into data management with DataStar and InfoStar—being first in one market position doesn't automatically win the day when you enter another market.

First Position Problems

There are some problems inherent in being in first position, especially in an industry that moves with such dizzying speed as software. Once a software company goes to market, it devotes many of its resources to marketing and distribution, and then the company gets committed to a position and to the technology that it has established. Other companies, however, are using that time and devoting all their energy toward developing new technologies and competing products. That's the main advantage would-be competitors have, the only one they can reliably exploit.

This is what happened when Micro Data Based Systems, Inc. brought out KnowledgeMan in direct competition with dBASE II. That company's first product, a data management system called MDBS, was released in 1979, but it was strictly for the professional user. By concentrating on corporate-level clients, consulting, and custom programming, MDBS, Inc. grew to 120 employees by early 1984, at least twenty-five of whom still develop custom software for major corporations. Their newest product, KnowledgeMan, announced at the 1982 Fall COMDEX and first shipped in May, 1983, is a streamlined data management language based on IBM's SQL language. It sits squarely in the same market niche as dBASE II.

Compared to dBASE II, KnowledgeMan is technologically newer, cleaner and faster, but that's just the technical aspect of the product. It hasn't anything like the dealer network, widespread distribution, or reputation of dBASE II. KnowledgeMan only works on 16-bit machines. Apart from the high quality of its product, almost the only other advantage that MDBS, Inc. has against Ashton-Tate is all the years MDBS, Inc. spent consulting with major corporations, giving them a foothold in the lucrative and growing Fortune 1000 channel.

In mass-market software, widespread distribution and support is just as much a part of the product as the code. This point is well-illustrated by the case of Jon Punnett, an extremely experienced and talented programmer who, after fourteen years of mainframes and international corporations, went in for self-employment and dBASE II. Jon found that with dBASE II he could develop government software on micros instead of minis, and in weeks instead of months. In 1983, he co-founded Blue Chip Software in Victoria, B.C. to make and market products for law offices and property managers. He says that he couldn't practically trade dBASE II for KnowledgeMan even if he wanted to, because dBASE II is so much more widely distributed, supported, and recognized. The clincher is that KnowledgeMan will never run on 8-bit machines. They still account for half of the installed base of micros out there, and he can't possibly turn his back on that large a market. In other words, a great number of his potential customers will want to run his Law Office Management System on CP/M-80 machines, so he hasn't really got any choice in the matter. This is one thing that keeps dBASE II at the top—for the time being.

Ashton-Tate's advanced dBASE III has been eagerly awaited by tens of thousands of applications programmers who have been hoping that it will bring their favorite product at least level with current technology. The competition is hoping too, but not for the same thing, and they are not waiting. The problem faced by Ashton-Tate and the other companies riding a first place horse is to keep their product at the front of the developing technologies in their field. They have major advantages in terms of cash flow and established distribution channels, but they also have certain handicaps in that they must devote energy, attention, and resources to supporting a vast user base, to managing a major corporation, and to keeping up the marketing pressure. Also, they are under great pressure to develop new products that maintain compatibility with their original product, and that can sometimes be a real obstacle to innovation.

This is a fast-paced, turbulent, and aggressive industry, full of surprises. No company can afford to rest on its laurels. Already, there are many companies that have made their mark, then faded away. The first challenge is to get to the top, but the real problem is to stay there.

Chapter Eight

SUCCESS ON THE LOTUS PLAN

Sooner or later the names "Lotus" and "Mitch Kapor" pass the lips of nearly everyone in the micro software business, for those names have become a benchmark, a paradigm for everyone to follow, almost an icon. Lotus Development Corporation is an overnight sensation software superstar and Mitch Kapor is a celebrity, but he is somehow much more than merely rich and more than just famous. Why? Not simply because Mitch's company exhibited perfect professional style, timing and form, and executed a stunning success with unheard-of speed. It's more because they are a modern version of the archetypical rags-to-riches, frog-to-Prince kind of myth, and hero myths are very important, especially in this highly mental, high-tech world.

At the Fall 1981 COMDEX, Lotus did not exist. At the Fall 1982 COMDEX, their product, Lotus 1-2-3, was just being announced, still an unknown. By the Fall 1983 COMDEX, anyone who had not heard of Lotus was certainly not in the business and probably never read any business news. In much less than one year, Lotus had:

- hit the top of the charts,
- reached revenues of $16.5 million per *quarter*,
- signed on over 250 employees,
- completed a $34 million public stock offering,
- been splashed throughout the major media,

and they had everyone in the micro business muttering, "Jeez, who are those guys? They're good!"

It seemed as if Lotus suddenly appeared out of nowhere, but the truth is that founder Mitch Kapor had been making points with micros for several years. He wrote his first product, a statistical graphics package for the Apple II called Tiny Troll, while a student at MIT. That led to a contract with Personal Software (now VisiCorp) to develop VisiTrend and VisiPlot which ultimately made Mitch rich. Having twice designed very successful products, he decided that "the next major challenge had to be to create a major company."

Attention has been focused on the blinding speed of the Lotus success, the unprecedented amounts invested in a new startup company, the millions spent on advertising their new product, or the big numbers at the bottom of their financial reports. But almost overlooked is the crucial first step, that *sine qua non*: an outstanding and timely product. In fact, it took a major commitment of faith, talent and effort, laboriously working through and rejecting many alternative approaches to reach the ultimate refinement of design for the new product.

The idea for Lotus 1-2-3 came in 1981 when Mitch was working on forecasting with VisiCalc and found himself wishing that it was more powerful, thinking how nice it would be if it had related programs, graphics for example, that could be called in as part of the spreadsheet instead of having to be run separately. This thought led eventually to the decision to integrate the three major kinds of business management software in one program—spreadsheet, graphics, and data retrieval. Such a thing had never been done before, but the ambitious design was stimulated and made possible by the announcement of the new IBM-PC, with its larger capacity

CHAPTER EIGHT

and greater speed. Mitch correctly assumed that it would become a new standard in the industry, so he built a program for it. That's what is meant by "windows of opportunity."

Lotus 1-2-3 may have been the first program designed specifically to take full advantage of the IBM's 16-bit potential, and it was aimed straight at the largest segment in the micro marketplace, the business user. As a consequence of its resounding success, the word "Lotus" has now been redefined. Since ancient times, lotus was a fruit eaten by the lotus-eaters to achieve a state of dreamy contentment. Not any more. Now Lotus means "integrated" and "success story" both at the same time. That's what is meant by "positioning."

The development of the company was as ambitious and far-reaching as the product. By early 1982, Mitch had a refined product design that he used to attract $5 million in venture capital from groups led by Sevin Rosen Partners, Ltd., backers of Compaq and many other high tech adventures. This was an extraordinary amount to invest in a new startup, and it was possible only because of Mitch's outstanding track record, and because he presented a coherent and professional business plan that showed that he knew what he was doing. He not only got the money, but some of the best brains in the industry ended up on his board of directors because he went after first-class venturists.

Some people talk as if Lotus invented the top-dollar advertising blitz. It can look that way because Lotus became a media sensation, and because they spent over a million the first three months, and several million the first year just on ads. But buying market share is an old idea in other industries. Venture consultant David Gold said, "What Lotus has accomplished is to set a high water mark for advertising and promotion in this marketplace."

Mitch Kapor has his own perspective:

"The industry as a whole was maturing. People were increasing their advertising and everything was getting more professional. We saw that trend. All Lotus can take credit for is executing a good strategy. It's exactly what the textbooks say to do. The problem is all in the execution—doing ninety two things at once, coordinating people with different skills, and

152

doing it all in a fast moving environment where there's no room for mistakes. Moreover, Lotus had to do it while it was building itself as a company. We needed product to ship and people to answer phones. We had to develop a whole corporate infrastructure.

"There's only one percent magic to this stuff—it's all execution, all perspiration. You've got to have the classic strengths that make a business successful: product, marketing, management, and finance. You have to be good in all those, attract the right management team, be able to translate market needs into a product. I'm just quoting to you from my textbooks!"

Mitchell Kapor, Lotus Development Corporation

Mitch Kapor has a warm, philosophical nature and a natural gregariousness that overcame his initial reluctance to be interviewed. He quickly worked through his reactions: "An Ashton-Tate book? Oh, no, they're competitors, no interview. Oh, well, maybe I should. Okay, I'll do it. Hey, this is interesting!" That took maybe five minutes, and then it was smooth, fluent and effervescent. Competitors? At that time Ashton-Tate's integrated product, Framework, was a closely guarded secret, still many months from market, but somehow Mitch already knew about it. Before he went into business, Mitch was a disk jockey, psychiatric worker, counselor, and self-taught programmer. Now he's the micro-software bright boy, of 1983 at least. This is one very interesting man.

Okay, how did a psychologist end up programming productivity software?

MITCH KAPOR: Well, I was sort of a nerd-manqué in high school. I think the latent potential was always there, but I had to struggle, and it took me a full seven years after I graduated from college to

CHAPTER EIGHT

sort all the stuff out. I mean, I taught myself how to program. I set goals for myself, and worked until I accomplished them. So the potential was there, but I did a lot of work to get there.

I had developed a graphics and statistics package for the Apple that my partner and I were selling in 1979 on a cottage industry basis, and this product was a natural fit with VisiCalc. That led to a contract with Personal Software, which is now VisiCorp, to design and implement two products for them, VisiTrend and VisiPlot, and I got royalties on those. I acted as an independent contractor, and then later sold them the rights—and made my first million.

Did you always want to be in business for yourself?
That was rather late blooming, actually. But I'm the sort of person that finds it very difficult to work for anybody, so in the long run it didn't really leave me much choice. I value autonomy, freedom, achievement. I only got dragged into the publishing business, kicking and screaming, because I realized there was no alternative, i.e., there was no way we could create this software and have somebody else market it. Then that led to Lotus.

I originally just wanted to write software and get paid a lot of money for it.

But when you sold your products to VisiCorp for $1.5 million, you had all the money you could use.
But the reason I sold the products was so that I could do the next thing. I wanted to develop software, more powerful software, something that would require a team of people to develop, beyond what I could do individually. I knew that would take some money.

How has Lotus affected you? Bringing your company to the forefront of the industry, all the effort, making sacrifices, how has that affected your own life?
I have a lot of money now (laughs).

Right. But to make a business succeed, don't you have to live, breathe and eat that particular one thing?
No, that's actually not true. It wasn't a matter of sacrifice. There are people whose life is their business, but I happen not to be one of those. Partly because I'm a little bit older than a lot of entrepreneurs. I'm only thirty-three, but I had fairly broad-based life experience beforehand. I did all sorts of different things that were non-computer related. I live on the East coast, in Cambridge, in part because I have a circle of friends there that are largely not in the business at all. I'm married to a psychiatrist, I just got married again in August.

I have worked fifty to sixty hours a week, independent of where the company was, or how many employees there were. I can't work more than that because I get burned out. And it's not fun. But I don't like to work less than that, either. Now that I'm married, I've started to take vacations again. They're nice. But it's a balance, and people that get so obsessed with their business do that because they're personally driven, not because the business requires it.

What advice would you give to someone wanting to get into the software publishing business?
Oh, god. Well, I would want to have a conversation with them about exactly what they meant by that. Did they want to write software, or did they want to start a company? Most people I know who want to get into the business really want to create programs. They really don't want to be entrepreneurs, and there's a huge difference.

A lot of people have an overly romantic notion of how these things work. I've given interviews where what's come out, the way it was written up, is the idea of one person with a great idea goes into an attic, or a garage or basement for a period of time, and delivers a *magnum opus*, then two weeks later somebody writes a check for a million dollars. It doesn't work like that. I mean, it really doesn't. I would say to anybody that the best thing to do is to disabuse yourself

CHAPTER EIGHT

of this sort of Horatio Alger kind of notion and get down to brass tacks.

What attracts people to this industry is the explosive growth, and the possibility of going from nowhere to a lot in a very brief period of time. What I am saying is that the factors that make it possible are the same factors that make it possible in any other business.

Let me divide things into two categories. First, people that want to write programs and make a million dollars, I think that's really a one in 10,000, or one in a million shot. But in the other case, if they want to start a software business, then the rules that apply are by and large the rules of business, not the rules of software. If you look at what typically makes the difference between failure and success, it has to do with the people first, then the idea second, then the money third.

If somebody came to me for advice, I would respond to him in much the same way a venture capitalist might respond to an initial inquiry. Does the business proposition make sense? Are they proposing to create something that there is a market for? A business has to be based on products which serve markets. So you start out asking what's your market? What value does your product have?

There are a number of people who have been successful doing me-too products, because they have price advantages or other advantages. That's one strategy. Or, you can do a product that is clearly superior and excellent.

Now, think about a business plan. First thing, somebody says, "Well let me see your business plan." Now if they don't have a business plan, they'll have to write one. If they don't know how, there are books that tell you how to write a business plan. Basically, it is systematically thinking through the key issues: what's the market, what's your product, how does the product serve the market? And then it gets down into the details like, what's your distribution, how are you going to make money? What's your management team, how are you going to run a business, how are you going to grow a business? What's the competitive picture? If the market's very competitive, what are you going to do that will distinguish you from the competition?

When a venture capitalist looks at a business proposition, the thing they bet on more than anything else is not the product, it's the person. Part of that means that the founder, or founders, must have management capability. Either themselves, or bring some in. The major reason why the romantic notion fails, is that there is no provision made for managing the growth of an organization. It's just distasteful, or unimportant, or we'll worry about it later. But it is really such an absolutely central issue.

I look at a business plan to see what's the experience, what's the capability, the motivation level, of the founder, and what's the team? Successful companies are not built around an individual, they're built around groups of people. Do they have a team? Can they put one in place? Who are the key people? Does the founder understand the necessity for financial controls for market planning, for operations?

If I could just summarize. Avoid being overly romantic. If you're thinking about the software business, the thing to think about is the business end, as much or more than the software end. Have a business plan. Think through the issues. If you don't have the answers yourself, it's going to be hard to convince anybody else that you do. And when the histories are written, the companies that succeed in the long term are the ones that just apply sound management. The management of creativity, good execution, financial controls, a certain spark of inspiration in creative marketing to distinguish themselves— those are the benchmarks of any successful business in any industry.

People keep saying there's no room anymore in the software industry for a little guy in a small business. First IBM, now Mitch Kapor, and the ante is sky high, so now you need millions. What do you think?

I actually disagree with that. I say that sooner or later you need money. I don't know if it's five million or two million, but money is not the first thing you need. There is still an over-supply of venture capital relative to good opportunities. A lot of second tier opportunities have gotten funded. There are billions in venture capital looking for opportunities, so if everything else is in place, getting money is not the problem. You can start on a relative shoestring, you know, develop your idea, your concepts, a couple of people, do some moonlighting, work some weekends, nights, and get to the point where you can do seed-stage financing, which can be even a couple of hundred thousand dollars from one of many places. Then, take it to the next stage—get the two or three million first round financing that you need. You don't need huge bucks from day one, but you need them sooner or later.

What do you have to give up when you get venture capital?

It's like marriage. There are good marriages, and there are bad marriages. To the extent that you go in with a chip on your shoulder, jealous and paranoid, you are dooming yourself to failure. To the extent that you go in naively, and act imprudently or unselectively in picking a venture capitalist, you are also substantially increasing your risk of failure. To the extent that you go in with your eyes open, from having talked to other entrepreneurs, and having got the goods on various venture capitalists, you're happy to have them as participants. Because they will radically improve the chances of success in your operation, not only from the money they put in, but from the expertise that they provide from having shepherded companies from infancy through launch, and then beyond. They have contacts in the financial community, the press, the industry, they help you hire people, sanity check your plans, and so on. It's not a black and white situation at all.

We've had two rounds of venture capital, and a public offering.

How much of your own company do you own?
Personally? I think it's 18%, but who cares? That's not the issue. People who focus on that are going to lessen their chances. Really. Honestly, I can't tell you that enough, that how much I own is the farthest thing from my mind. The first thing in my mind is, how am I going to build a company that can be successful over the long term?

What about feeling that it's still your company if it really isn't?
Again, to the extent you measure that by the percent you own, versus the respect that you command, and your power, influence and contribution—that's how you ought to measure it. Not by your percentage. It's nuts to do it any other way. It's naive, it's simplistic. That's a personal belief, but one that I hold very strongly.

I've heard you mention "software wars." What do you mean by that?
Software wars. Well, we're in an intensely competitive phase of an intensely competitive industry. Just the sheer number of other integrated products announced at COMDEX—that's what I mean by software wars. A lot of these people are taking direct shots at us to call attention to themselves.

Well, that's what you get for being first, isn't it?
Yeah, sure. But it is a kind of war, because people are shooting at us, and one reason we go to COMDEX is to find out if they're shooting blanks or bullets.

CHAPTER EIGHT

How much did it cost to bring Lotus to the Fall COMDEX this year?

I don't know. But if you're asking what it takes any company to make a major effort at COMDEX, it's a hundred thousand and up.

That's a lot of flash and glitter. You know, it seems like there's so much waste, noise, and distraction out there on the floor and in the marketplace—how much of that is constructive?

Well, look. It's not totally satisfactory with everybody duplicating each other, and re-inventing the wheel, but on the other hand, name something better. If I could think of something better, I would. It's unfortunate, but we go through waves of noise and quiet, and we happen to be in a very noisy wave right now.

Managing your people is a big part of being in business. What advice would you give about how to manage people?

Don't go to business school. That is absolutely critical. Managing people is based on a set of good personal skills. How to listen, how to talk to people, to command respect without being autocratic or dictatorial. If you're not organized yourself, you can't organize other people. These are basic personal skills, life skills, that are the core of management. If you have those, then the little techniques of PERT charts, and how to write an effective memo, and how to run a meeting, can all be learned by experience and working in a company for awhile and latching onto a good mentor, or reading some books and trying some things out.

But it's like playing the piano. You've either got musical abilities, or you don't. If you've got musical abilities, then you develop them by practice and by experience. And if you don't, then you shouldn't be a piano player.

———— ● ————

Ten weeks after this conversation, at SoftCon in New Orleans, Lotus released their new Symphony, the 4-5 to go with 1-2-3. The billboards on the way into town said, "Roses are red, violets are blue, Lotus had one hit, and now we have two." Now they have added word processing and database features, but far more important than that, they have added hooks so other people can adapt Lotus for special applications. This is part of the growing market potential for templates or overlays that allow independent developers to customize a generic product for a specific use. Why develop an entire vertical market package when all you have to do is customize Lotus? So now there's a Lotus software standard, a new kind of compatibility to consider. Clever people.

BREAKTHROUGH SOFTWARE'S TRAKKER/ABC

Mark McDonough, Intelligent Designs, BreakThrough Software

Here's the story of another man who chose the Lotus route to success, but with different results. Mitch Kapor did not invent the strategy of buying your way into a crowded market, but it was becoming increasingly evident that going in big was the preferred way to launch a national software product. This conclusion had already been reached by Mark McDonough when he decided to start his own company, and the experience of Lotus served to strengthen his determination and his belief that he was on the right path.

I met this entrepreneur at the National Software show in October, 1983. There were several new companies making their first public appearance there, but one of them had such an interesting and professional-looking demonstration and display that I was totally surprised to learn that it was their first show. Intelligent Designs of Somerville, Massachusetts was there mainly to get some road experience with Trakker, an innovative combination of word processing and data handling. After watching the demo on their big overhead screen and seeing how you could push data around intuitively with Trakker, I knew I wanted to own that program, and I wanted to find out who was behind the company. I dodged around the young kid that was working the crowd so I could talk to the older guy doing the demo, but I got sent back. The kid was the founder and the company president!

MARK MCDONOUGH: I'm twenty-seven. Everyone in my company is older than I am. I'll tell you my story. I had an alfalfa sprout company in New Hampshire. I sold the company, because produce was not a career business, to get back into high tech. At that time I said to myself, Mark, starting a company is so damned difficult. Murphy's Laws work all the time. It's my philosophy that whenever you strut out into the universe and say, I'm going to do something, it's like all these stumbling blocks are put in your path that you must manoeuver around before you make it. I think that happens in any business, and generally they're only a little bigger in bigger businesses, but the difference is not that great. If you're going to do something, then do something big.

I got into the micro industry about four years ago when I sold for ISA (SpellGuard), then I worked at Corvus Systems, which is the largest maker of computer hard disks. I was their software specialist and looked at all kinds of software to see what was compatible with Corvus. When I had this idea, I couldn't believe that this market gap had been ignored between the easy-to-use card retrieval and the powerful database programming languages. Ashton-Tate has Friday! and they've got dBASE II, but there wasn't anything in between.

All those database programs claim that they're English-like and therefore they're user-friendly, and that's seductive. But they only look user-friendly. If you read a query on the screen—say it's a client list—that says list Name, Title, Zip Code, sort by Zip Code, it reads easily. But when you get the computer prompt, you have to ask it to List, Show, or Display, and you go, "Oh my, what was the name of that command? Did I abbreviate the name of that field, or did I write it out?" No, it's not that easy at all.

Because of my position at Corvus, I was able to check my idea out and yes, indeed, no one else was working on it. So I wanted to start my own company, but first I went out to get business training because you need a sheepskin if you're going to be as young as I am to start a company. I went to MIT, got a business degree, and while I was at MIT I worked on this idea that I had checked out while I was at Corvus Systems.

First I hired a hot shot and had him work on it for a couple of months, build something up. I hired him with my own money. His job for the first two months was to figure whether something as ambitious as this could be done. Yes, it could be done, and it could be done with reasonable cost estimates. Of course all those cost estimates were about a quarter of what they ended up to be.

I had no business plan, I just had a product on hand, going forward. I was still in school, and my thesis at MIT business school was the prototype of my business plan. So I did the marketing research, calling up distributors to ask them if they had something like this, would it sell, how much would it sell? I put it all in a business plan and I'm currently in the process of peddling that plan to individuals who have made it in software.

I'll give you an example of who I mean. One of the top three Fortune 1000 accounting systems suppliers was recently bought out by a huge company. The four principals of that corporation are instant multi-millionaires. They all know software, and they're interested in investing in my company. Those are the types of individuals you want to get if you build the product first and get the management team later—that's the route you have to go. If you do the reverse, if you get the management team together, write the business plan, then you can go out and sell it. If you get all name-brand individuals you can sell the business plan, get some money, then build your prototype.

CHAPTER EIGHT

That's the standard fashion—that's what you do right now to build a business.

I did it the old-fashioned way, which is you get the inventor and then build a product and then go see if you can put something together. Right now, I'm the entire management team. The current round of capital is for the building of the management team. There's about twelve or fifteen of us right now, including lots and lots of consultants. We brought in Price-Waterhouse, we got one of the two top lawyers. That's good advice—get the top level consultants you can get. Get the best PR firm, the best accounting firm. It opens doors like crazy.

When I started, I planned out how much money I would need. I was wrong, I thought I could do the whole thing on $100,000. I'm glad I didn't know. I once saw a whole series of entrepreneurs being interviewed, and they said if they knew ahead of time what it would take, they wouldn't have done it. I think there's a useful blindness that all entrepreneurs have. I found out that it takes a thousand times more money than I ever expected. Now I want to go out into the market with $4 million in equity. I thought I could do it with a hundred thousand. So I raise money. So I sell more of my company.

We're getting a few hundred thousand dollars to build the management section, now we're a good package, now we're what venture capitalists like to look at. Now we look for the four million. We go to the venture capitalists for the $4 million, but first you have to get the name brand managers in. We're getting a few hundred thousand dollars for that, something less than a million dollars just so that we can attract the best people for managers. Then we're a class A product.

We're looking for two crucial managers: the sales and marketing, and the communications manager. We hired the best recruiting firm around because these people are worth their weight in gold, because if they increase the evaluation of my company by half a million dollars, and I pay them $100,000, they've made me $400,000 by hiring on. That's what it takes if you want to get the best, plus equity.

We'll be presenting our package to venturists next month. It's nearly all packaged up. I haven't picked out the venture firms, no. I'm not worried because I've got the name-brand accountants and lawyers that will open the doors for me.

Four months later, by phone

MARK MCDONOUGH: No, we still don't have our venture capital. VC money is really scarce now. You know, it's amazing how much this industry has changed in just one year since Lotus. It's gone from the minor leagues to the major leagues almost overnight. It used to be a young person's game, the booths used to be full of young faces, and a new guy could get started and get somewhere. Not now. The battle has moved from technical to marketing and money, and there's more older guys and women at the top now. You have to be already recognized, have a track record.

Too much time has gone by and my product isn't as unique as it used to be. There's still nothing like it out there, but there's bits and pieces of it here and there.

Venture people are worried about single product companies. They're even complaining about Ashton-Tate being a single product company. And of course we only have one product, and I'm young and I don't have a track record, so they're afraid. People in the ring now are all those who have already gotten themselves established. It's no good for an unknown. You can hear the window of opportunity closing down to a crack and only the cold wind whistling through.

What are you going to do? Do you have a plan now?
I don't know, maybe I'll have to go with a publisher. There's two kinds of publishers, but I've found somebody that doesn't fall into either of those groups. There's book publishers who want to get into

software, but I don't think they'll ever swing it with serious business software, they're more likely to make it in the home market. Then there's software publishers that have a whole lot of products. Like Hayden—they want to be the Sears of the software industry. No way! You'd get lost in a line of products that big. I don't want to be some little part of a VanPack line (Software Strategies' kiosk of uniformly packaged products) or something like that.

I found some people that want to take just three to five good products, you know, be real choosy and publish products that are "break-through" types—packages from people like me who can't afford to bust into the market. And they're going to get venture capital. Call me in a couple of weeks and maybe by that time I can tell you who they are.

Postscript

After another four weeks, Mark McDonough finally concluded that the venture capitalists just weren't very venturesome. He said that they have a fast network and tend to run in a pack; they all seem to run hot or cold at about the same time. Lately it was real cold. He says they've been generally nervous and were avoiding almost all horizontal market products.

Mark decided to strike a deal with BreakThrough Software, a new software publisher in Novato, California. Founder William (Bill) Lohse was Sales Manager at Imsai, Director of Sales at MicroPro, and V.P. of Sales & Marketing at IUS. Bill Lohse and Mark originally met back at the National Software Show in October, 1983. First, Mark interviewed Bill with an eye toward making him president of Mark's Intelligent Designs company, but it was too small for Bill who had dreams of a publishing company with several hit products. Instead, after months of discussion, Mark became V.P. of Corporate Strategy for BreakThrough. BreakThrough will publish Mark's program as one of its three lead products after first upgrading the user interface and changing the name to ABC. Bill Lohse's outstanding record and connections assure BreakThrough of plenty of venture capital to take to market. Meanwhile, Mark is keeping his own company going as an independent product developer.

At the beginning of this interview, Mark McDonough was citing Murphy's Laws and talking about life's obstacles. No one ever said it would be easy, but Mark McDonough hit insurmountable barriers even though he did everything right: he had a good product, some good associates, enough seed money, and lots of creative, persistent energy. It should have worked, so why didn't it? Partly it was unfortunate timing that had Mark hunting for capital in a clogged market and a cautious climate. But if there are any morals to this tale, it is that following in Lotus' footsteps on the road to success is not possible unless you have *all* the ingredients, including a first-class b-i-g new product and an impressive record of past performance to prove you know how to be successful. People don't turn loose of millions that easily. The other moral is the old "where there's a will there's a way." Mark's persistence has finally got his product on the market where he can make more contacts, gain experience, and where he can potentially create a track record that will convince the venture capitalists—next time.

Chapter Nine

MANAGING EXPLOSIVE GROWTH

RealWorld Software entered the microcomputer software business with an accounting program, and that put them up against some big companies in one of the most established and competitive segments of the market. Accounting software may sound uninteresting to those who don't need it, but this is one case where first impressions are misleading.

Accounting and computers are soul mates. After all, the only thing a digital computer can do is manipulate numbers, so it follows naturally that accounting programs have been up and running since the first commercial computers, the UNIVACs, rolled off the assembly line. There are now many hundreds of general accounting products on the microcomputer market, not including the much greater number of vertical market packages, most of which are designed around specially adapted accounting procedures. Perhaps the most common use made of database programs like dBASE II is to build custom-designed accounting applications.

The long-term and widespread dissemination of accounting programs has given us one of the clearest examples of the way software can affect people and society, for software has utterly changed the nature of the accountant's job, and the account too. Accounting programs have taken over much of the drudge work and have freed the accountant to explore the potential of sophisticated spreadsheet and financial modeling programs. As the accounting program cranks out the figures, the accountant massages them with powerful and sophisticated computer tools, asking a lot of significant "What if . . .?" questions that are part of modern software. With the power of the micro, the accountant more easily becomes a thinker, an analyst, and a consultant instead of a pencil pusher and an adding machine jockey. This is one of the many examples of how software can change not just the way people do things, but the way they work and think as well. Power to the people!

RealWorld Corporation is the offspring of a parent company that developed accounting software for minicomputers since way back before there were micros. Like many microcomputer programs, the RealWorld product is a downloaded and reworked version of programs created earlier for the big computers. When RealWorld entered the microcomputer fray, they could count among their assets a lot of good connections, practical business experience, and something that other micro companies have had to get the hard way—a clear sense of what would be required when they won the success they were after.

Struggling for success in microcomputer software is like trying to grab a tiger by the tail—in either case you end up with a whole new set of problems when you get what you wanted. Being on the high end of a growth curve entitles the successful company to high-level headaches in production, financing, cash management, cost controls, and personnel. RealWorld Software is one company that was ready for the challenge—and a very good thing too, because they grew from twelve employees to over 120 in less than eighteen months.

MANAGING EXPLOSIVE GROWTH 169

Larry Byrnes (foreground) and
Larry Wilber, RealWorld Corp.

In the first conversation, Larry Wilber, V.P. for Corporate Communications tells the company's story. Then, President Larry Byrnes explains in detail how his company dealt with explosive growth.

LARRY WILBER: Well, our parent, MCBA—Mini-Computer Business Applications—was founded in Los Angeles by David Gale in 1973. He's one of the first to make a success at packaged software applications for accounting. That was on minicomputers, first on the PDP-8.

Really, the product we're selling for micros is a ninth or tenth generation of that early product. David Gale saw what was going to happen in the micro marketplace, and decided that he could make a micro version of that code and started a new company in about 1980. That was MBSI.

He's a family man, and a man of some principle with some other goals besides business, and he wanted to raise a family in a nicer environment but still stay connected with that same basic business. When David decided to form MBSI, he looked around the U.S. and chose the Concord, New Hampshire area. Beautiful property on 150 acres and subdivided. I'm building a home on a twelve-acre piece of it. So it's really a lifestyle thing as well going on up there. There's no immediate community organized nearby. If you walk out of the city limits of Concord, it's all country. The nearest metropolis is Boston, seventy-some miles away. It's accessible, let's put it that way. And we get a feeling of being together. It's been tremendous for us, I mean, really. I got goose bumps here just talking about it.

What happened was that in 1980, Tandy Corporation came to MCBA. They claimed to have evaluated every available application and found nothing to be adequate to their standards. They asked for a micro version—and who could say no? David had already decided to form a subsidiary to create a micro version, so that became Micro

Business Software, Inc., and MBSI's first customer was Tandy Corporation.

It took quite a while to ease that code into the micro environment. The product was available almost two years ago, but this month (October, '83) we took out our first junior-size page ads. June 30 of this year we changed the name from MBSI to RealWorld. Perhaps the most compelling reason for the name change would be the fact that we do plan a product expansion beyond the business marketplace.

A year and a half ago we had maybe six to eight employees. I think we have 130 or more now. Things really hit the fan about a year ago. At that point everything started to mushroom, profits and all. With a relatively small staff, we were impinging on the market, we were doing well, and we saw that we could make it. And at that point we turned and started investing the profits back into personnel. We hired a lot of people—we hired more than we needed because we wanted to prepare for this day, right about this time when we'd have a strong company in place with well-trained people.

We've never had to look outside the company for funding. We bootstrapped it entirely. What we will do in the future is another question. The market and competition is going to demand larger sums. We are spending millions, but not so much on our marketing efforts. That's been intelligently conceived but modest. Our income in the preceding fiscal year was just under four million, and this year we expect to come in around ten or so.

This all starts with David Gale, the guy that founded the company. David is a fellow who possesses substantial skill. I mean, he's a bright, very capable person in many areas to start with. But what I think is even more unique about him is that he is very purposeful, a man of integrity. He has a high degree of commitment to building the finest product he can, and that's what he does, that's the game he is playing. Profits and success are a result of playing that game. And frankly, I believe that we put together a group of people here that are very consistent with that basic philosophy. You know, that a fellow will tend to bring around him people of like mind.

I guess I'm a little surprised that we look as professional as you say we do. I know most of these people at work, but I also live with them. We're in the same general community up in the woods, back down dirt roads, in Chichester, New Hampshire. Near Concord, the capital city. I'm used to seeing them in jeans, in canoes, and fishing, and in home situations. So I don't think of them as professionals, but I do think of them as individuals.

We have a management technology that we've used in the business which has served us very well—it's the central kernel around which the company is organized. Larry Byrnes should talk about that.

In marketing, we do have distributors, but it's not a simple thing. I'll have to go back and give you some history here. We started out marketing by selling directly to re-sellers, primarily through space advertising and telephone sales. What we were selling during that first full year and a half was source code. We were one of the few companies that actually sold the source code. And of course we were selling those primarily to re-sellers, to dealers, to OEM types, to systems houses, and consultants. However, we had planned in the long run to get into the retail market as well and do it through large display ads.

We sold code the way we did because it's the marketplace that we knew and understood from MCBA minicomputer days. We understood what those folks think, what they need, and we understood the business. We saw the large numbers and the potential profits and everything in the retail, but we didn't want to rush in before we understood it well. And we thought that others might rush in and we could profit by their mistakes. And I think that's happened.

We didn't sell to the end users. So the more they sold, the happier we were because it was on a royalty basis. Every time they sold, we got a royalty, if they're honest. Not all of them are honest, but nevertheless there are royalties. And, well, they could sell to other retailers. I think some of our contracts allowed that. Tandy Corporation sells our software on a royalty basis. So does Televideo, and another big one will be announcing soon. We have a marketing arrangement with DEC for their Rainbow computer.

Now we've entered the retail market, this month. With a pre-packaged, shrink-wrapped product that, you know, you could pull off a shelf. And now we have a contract with software distributors, and I think we will end up signing contracts with three or four of them. So now our hat's in the ring of the retail thing, through the classic distributor, retail store distribution.

In the past, we might have met with more success if we had put more money into marketing earlier. But where would we have got the money, and what portion of the company would we have had to part with? So I'm giving you that as a theory. If things go as it looks like they will, then maybe a year from now I may be able to say that we did everything right.

We have corporate headquarters in Chichester, and that would be about ninety people. And then there's approximately thirty in Florida, which would be the R&D unit. And there's another ten or so out here in the Silicon Valley in the sales office.

We've only been doing four-color ads for a year. Before that we had an extremely modest thing where David and I did the ads in-house, ourselves, and we even took the photographs for them ourselves. We bootstrapped that whole thing. And while we have spent a bit of money on space advertising, I mean our literature is not four-color or glossy, we just haven't poured that much money on it. We've been making profits, and the money has pretty much been poured back into making growth. We've been making around 20% before taxes. And then you have a choice after that, how much profit you want to show after taxes, whether you want to pay bonuses or what, how you handle it. But we've been healthy profit-wise.

The story isn't over yet, that's what I mean. The next episode is coming up. What moves we're going to do and how are we going to be viewed in relation to PeachTree in the next year or two. Our products aren't really identical by any stretch, but, nevertheless, when you ask somebody who has accounting software, there's only one other company that's ever named before us, and that's PeachTree. That's the other story.

MANAGING EXPLOSIVE GROWTH

Success in the software industry entitles you to a new and bigger set of problems, only one of which is the staggering problem of organizing a sudden influx of new people. This is not easy and the way to deal with it is not obvious. Many companies, to their ultimate sorrow, just dealt with things as they came up on an *ad hoc* basis. Experts at the prestigious Touche Ross & Co. delicately moved the responsibility from managers to the managed structure:

"More often than not, the reason for costly mistakes isn't incompetence but the result of poor organizational structure. Or, put simply, no one knows who is responsible for what."

But in blunt terms, mismanagement has endangered or bankrupted a lot of otherwise good companies. That's why venture capital firms look at the qualifications and experience of the management team before they look at anything else.

Larry Byrnes, President of RealWorld Software, explains the highly developed approach used by his company to deal with their explosive growth. As he is the first to admit, there are a variety of ways to deal with the same problems, but one way or another they must be dealt with. You need not adopt his methods in order to appreciate the rich banquet of food for thought.

LARRY BYRNES: In the microcomputer software industry, we are dealing with substantial opportunity. It's a field with explosive growth and all those up-trending curves that resemble hockey sticks. In my company, RealWorld Software, from July of '82 to October of '83, we increased our monthly revenue about 800%. Now, of course, to keep up with that demand, you have to ship software, so you have an equally dramatic growth in terms of the amount of packages that you ship. For us, this has gone up about nine times since July or August of '82. All this growth of course requires people to run the business, and we've increased our personnel from twelve to over 120 in eighteen months.

The key to the success of any business is how well you handle your personnel, how well you organize your production, and how you recruit and train and correct your personnel and keep their morale high and the production high. Keeping the employee loyalty is vital if you want to stick around in this field.

One decision you make as a manufacturer or as an entrepreneur when you get into a high growth business is, do you want to maximize your profits, or do you want to plow your profits back into expansion and growth? We elected to take most of our profits and plow them back into expansion: hiring additional personnel, adding plant equipment, developing new products, putting more money into research, marketing, advertising, and so on.

Now, how do you handle extremely rapid expansion? Typically, in a high-tech business, you start off designing a very good product, a new technical angle, and you assume that because you have a better mousetrap, the world is going to beat a path to your door. But sooner or later competitors come into the marketplace and you have to go through a marketing phase where you start beefing up your sales, your distribution channels, and your marketing. Then you have to go through a financial, administrative, and management phase where you can now control things. You can now put in a sane, sound management system, and procedures that will allow you to control your growth, otherwise you end up violating simple basics like spending more money than you are making.

So it's vital as you mature as a company, that you go through a technical stage, through a marketing stage, to eventually the management, administrative and financial stage where you can actually manage the company as an organization, and not as five men in a garage. You might start off that way, but eventually you have to get into some sort of organizational phase where you assure your future expansion, your future viability, or you won't make it in the business. And that's basically what I want to discuss.

Now, there's probably as many theories about management as there are university business schools, but there's a big difference between theory and the application of that theory. Getting it actually occurring and applying the various management theories, that's a whole other thing.

At RealWorld, we have access to a technology that works for us, it's very successful for us. We're not the source of the technology, we borrowed it from another source, but this technology we feel has a lot of merit. We feel that it has delivered for us. Now I just want to give you a recap, or a sort of a summary of the major points of management that we concentrate on.

A key part of any approach to managing something—to deciding how you're going to organize, how you're going to become a viable enterprise—is to establish exactly what is the Valuable Final Product for your company, and for the departments of your company, all the way down to the individual. Now, the term "Valuable Final Product" has a very specific connotation for us, in the use of this management technology.

Valuable Final Product is something you produce that can be exchanged for something valuable. Typically, people may think of a product as a piece of hardware, a piece of software, something that you can kick, but there's also other things that aren't necessarily seen. For example, a well-established personnel department is something valuable. If you look at the administrative side of an organization chart for a typical organization, you have your finance, your personnel, your recruiting, and so on. Each division could be said to have a product which you can look for from each particular division.

For example, the personnel division is responsible for personnel who are adequately screened, recruited, and trained and they are supplied to the R&D division, or the marketing division, or manufacturing division. That is the product. As far as the administration is concerned, the product in that division is the competent employee. See, you can name a very specific product for that division.

For a finance division, for example, you could say the product is a solvent organization. So the chief financial officer has to look at solvency, and make sure that you have enough operating funds to expand.

Another example would be a research and development division. And the product that we name there, as an example, is quality software and documentation, developed and sent to marketing. Again, you get the idea of an exchange here. A research and development, or software development division, is exchanging a product with another division of the company which they can now use and go out and exchange for something valuable as well. In this case, it goes to marketing and sales, and they exchange it for money.

Another example, let's say the packaging department of a marketing division, would produce attractively designed packaging for software in the hands of manufacturing for reproduction, assembly and shipment. Now that's a very specifically named product. Merchandising tells manufacturing exactly how this product is going to look when it goes to the shelf. It's going to be shrink-wrapped, it's going to contain a user manual, it's going to contain diskettes, it's going to have a label which says which operating system this runs on, and that type of thing. That's the specific product that you name and demand from your merchandising division.

Another example would be a product that you could name for an advertising and promotional unit, or marketing division—the prospects demanding software products. That doesn't mean the amount of mail or how many pieces went out, or trade shows attended. The actual product you are looking for is people calling you up or demanding your software. The advertising and promotion division gets the idea that that's the product that they have to produce. Then they have a much better handle on what their actual function is.

Another example, for a sales division, would be valid orders for software products. So you don't go out, for example, and sell a bunch of software that you're never going to collect on, or just to fill an order. It has to be a valid order, an order that's going to end up in shipment and be exchanged for dollars in revenue and sales. So you name that product very specifically, and you say, Mr. Salesman, or Mr. Vice-President of Sales, the product that I want from your division is valid orders for software products.

For a manufacturing division of a software company, the product could be accurately and speedily filled orders. The idea of accuracy is not to scramble the order and ship the wrong set of diskettes, the wrong set of documentation, or software that runs on the wrong machine. You have to have the idea of accuracy and quality. You also have to have the idea of speed in there. The actual product is filled orders. The order comes in, the manufacturing division has to get it in the hands of the consumer. That's their product. So I tell that division that that's the product that I expect from you.

Another example would be a support and training division that competently trains and supports satisfied users. Now this is a product that anyone who's going to stay viable in this business *has* to produce, and has to produce in abundance. Because if your users aren't satisfied, then eventually your distribution channels are going to dry up, and you're going to get bad word of mouth and so on. But if you have very satisfied users, you get good word of mouth, and you get a demand, and people walk into retail stores and say, "Do you have RealWorld Software?" If the guy says no, the customer will say, "Oh great, so where can I get it?" That's the ideal scene, that's the kind of demand you want. You start by naming that product very specifically from your support division.

From the administrative division, you would want well-managed personnel, finance, plant and equipment. That's their product, and it's the one division that touches all parts of the company.

Okay, now. You add these products up to get an overall product for the company. This is what we have named the Valuable Final Product for our company. It's not necessarily the same for every company, but it gives you an idea of how all these various products that I've named by division add up to the overall company Valuable Final Product which you're exchanging with the industry in general for viability and expansion of your company. A quality software product properly marketed.

Now, that all looks very simple, but let me just say that you can spend an awful lot of time at it, and that time is very well spent, being very specific when you name these products. At RealWorld, we spent maybe a day and a half, you know, sitting around, before we finally worked out all the adjectives, the verbs, and so on and came up with this as the final product. And it's an exercise that I recommend highly to anybody that's going to organize anything.

Now, the way you should start is with your product, which is the overall product that you're trying to produce as a company. And you work backwards from that, to get all of the sub-products that, all in a row, add up to this final product. So you say you want a viable or quality software product properly marketed—well that means you will have to have satisfied users, that means you have to fill the users' requests, the users' orders, that means you have to get the sales, that means you have to advertise, promote, and package the software, that means you have to have a demand for your software, that means you have to develop your software, that means you have to have some kind of an establishment, you have to hire some personnel, you have to have some financing, you have to have a plant and and some equipment.

CHAPTER NINE

Okay? Basic concepts. But time you spend in actually reducing the complexities and getting into the simplicities of this type of an exercise is time well spent.

Okay. Now the next point—and a key point—before organizing and managing anything is to organize it so that it flows. So that you can see the idea of product and exchange between divisions, and so on. From development to marketing, to sales, to manufacturing, to the supported customer, where the overall company exchanges the product with the marketplace.

A key concept in managing anything, if you want to make your life very easy, is the idea of a statistic. A statistic is a number or monitor that can be compared to an earlier number or monitor to show some change. Sales by month, profits by quarter, that type of thing. The exercise of working out a statistic that correlates *directly* with each one of the products that you name for each one of the divisions is highly recommended, a very valuable exercise.

For example, the product of the administration division is the well-managed organization, staffed with trained and competent personnel, properly financed with adequate plant and equipment. One statistic that you could use to measure that would be gross income or profits, divided by staff. It gives you an idea of the efficiency with which you're training and utilizing your staff.

Software development: you require that they graph a statistic weekly, or whatever period you've set, for the number of workable programs and pages of documentation sent to marketing. This is something you can see and measure, or put on your spreadsheets, or the way we do it, the old-fashioned method, is putting it up in graphs on the wall.

Merchandising division: their statistic could be the number of people calling the sales division, asking for data on the products. Sales division: you could use gross sales. The dollars. How much money you actually bring in the front door. The manufacturing division: we use a statistic which we feel measures their product, which is the value of the orders that they ship. So everything that goes out the back door has a value, and you can tell by looking at a graph whether your production is improving or decreasing.

Likewise, with the support division, the number of successful installations could be a statistic that would indicate how well that division is doing on producing competently trained, supported, and satisfied users.

And the overall company, of course, is measured by operating profits, things like percent of the market, company net worth.

Now, one of the benefits of going through the exercise of specifically naming your statistics is that you can take actions in advance. You can predict a slump. For example, if you see in your merchandising division that the number of people calling your sales division is going down, as a statistical graph you can predict that sooner or later your gross sales are going to go down, and sooner or later your shipments are going to go down, and so on. So if you use these statistics properly and review them weekly you can go back and juggle your viewpoint on them, and see what has changed.

For example, if your product starts going down, you might want to look at the number of personnel you've hired recently. We made a conscious decision to add a number of new personnel to beef up our support, marketing, sales, and manufacturing area, and one of the things we noticed was that our profits went down. The reasons for that was that the new personnel are not yet productive because they haven't been trained and put on a job where they can produce the product that you expect of them. So looking at statistics you can say, right, profits have gone down because we have a whole bunch of new personnel, but we better get busy training them and getting them productive. Get the idea?

Okay, another use of statistics is that if you run into difficulty, you can go back to another period of time and see what you were doing then. You say, well, I was getting a lot more calls in, I was sending a lot more promotion out, I was getting a lot more orders. I

EXPLOSIVE GROWTH

was producing a lot more software out of my software development division. So what changed? Ah, well, we stopped producing more new products.

Now you may also run into the situation where you have external factors. Which doesn't let you off the hook, because you have to look at your market research department for example, in the merchandising division. External factors changed, become more competitive, pricing has eroded, or new entries into the marketplace are more competitive. And you look at your market research department, and one of their products should be accurately predicted market changes. So you can go back and find, ah yes, our prediction wasn't that good six months ago, we didn't anticipate that some competitor was going to come in, and there was price erosion, so we have to deal with that now.

So if you're intelligent, and you do a good job of setting up what your products are, and what the statistic is that measures each product, and then if you actually measure each product with those statistics, you'll be ahead of the game.

Now one of the last topics I want to cover here is the importance of personnel. Personnel boil down to three basic topics. First is recruiting the right personnel to begin with. Second is training. The third is correcting that person—or enhancing that staff person—is perhaps a better terminology.

We have a concept that we call a "hat." Which is where you tell this person what he is supposed to be doing. We use "hat" because it comes from the old terminology that's used on the railroad, where the conductor and the engineer each had their distinctive type of hat and it was symbolic of their duties. So when a person comes in and gets a post in our organization, he gets a hat. His hat describes what it is that he's supposed to do. It gives him the purpose of his post, what it is that he is supposed to be accomplishing. The exact duties that the individual is expected to carry out, the exact product that he is supposed to produce, and the exact statistic by which the performance of the post can be measured. The hat should be written.

182

Now there's two advantages of doing it this way. First, if you have personnel turnover and lose a key person, and you have to train somebody new, it's going to be a lot easier if you have specific things written down. Second, if someone goofs on a post, or his statistic is not good, we don't automatically assume that individual is bad, or incompetent. We take the time necessary to figure out what it is that that individual didn't understand about the post. We read the hat and discuss it. Invariably there's something that didn't get across right. Our experience with this has been *very* successful. Our turnover is extremely low. We went from twelve to 120 people and we had maybe two people leave the company in the last year. I like to think it's because we spend a lot of time training the person first so they understand what is expected, and if there is a goof, they know they're not going to get fired, we'll work with them and get them back into a productive mode.

Though they look simple, these basic steps have a terrific degree of power, in that if you understand the basics and reduce them to simplicities, you can organize anything, and get any organization successful, viable, and productive. As I mentioned at the outset, we're an end user of this technology, not the source of it. This technology comes from a gentleman by the name of L. Ron Hubbard, an author, humanitarian, and we think a genius in the field of managing, organizing and production. We've had a high degree of success with it.

Are the principles derived from L. Ron Hubbard imbued in the company?

LARRY WILBER: I suppose they are. We consider that to be a very sane technology, and by actual usage they've really helped us a great deal. I think it's an example of a very workable thing in a pragmatic way. We take an approach to the business not from the view of having fixed ideas or having conclusions going in, but we try to have our eyes open and we try to take a look at what works, and what doesn't.

Quite a number of people in the company are followers of L. Ron Hubbard's ideas. There are quite a few, yes. I'd say maybe a third. But you can rise in the company without regard to that. I think the view is that anybody that can do their job well is deserving in a meritocracy, although I don't think anybody uses that term.

David Gale was a member of scientology. It does make sense when you start a company to find your colleagues in your group, but I don't know whether there's been so much a decision to find them among that group as that it's a matter of close proximity. There's a philosophy there in all of Hubbard's writings that would be consistent with our management technology. It's true that he does say that there would be little sense in living unless you go about it professionally, as you get out of something what you put into it. If you go about it as a professional, that's what you'll get out of it, and if you go about it in a half-baked manner, you'll get a half-baked life out of it.

GUERRILLA MANAGEMENT AT ASHTON-TATE

David Cole, Ashton-Tate

David Cole, President and CEO of Ashton-Tate, developed a strategy for managing high-growth situations that he calls "guerrilla management" which addresses itself to company strategy and even more to stimulating the high levels of morale and enthusiasm necessary to carry a company through the stress and strains of galloping success.

DAVID COLE: Communication is clearly the biggest single problem when you go from fifty people to 350 in eighteen months like we did. That's pretty tough. You're reorganizing all the time, and you've got to have a certain degree of humor, and you've got to brief a lot of people that are affected by it.

Ashton-Tate has grown 900% and 300% back-to-back in the last two years. What we've done is we've taken the existing product, moved it into new markets, and we've established a dominant position. As soon as we announced Framework, and moved into someone else's market we went on the attack. We're engaged in some defensive activities with respect to the database market, but we're in a very aggressive attack mode in the integrated products market, and we're fairly resource rich. So although we used guerrilla management to get to this point, we're no longer in that phase.

What is guerrilla management?
Well, if you look at the resources that a company has and its current position in a particular market, you can get a clue as to what kind of style is needed in order to succeed. An example would be a new startup company trying to enter, say, the accounting software market. Let's say you have low resources, okay, no infrastructure in place,

perhaps the management is not completely in place, you don't have much money, but you have a good product, and you're up against entrenched competition, say six or eight different products that each have around eight to twelve percent share. Basically, in order to gain entry into that market, you've got to take a guerrilla posture, which means you have to strike very, very quickly in key areas. You can't possibly go to all segments or through all channels of distribution simultaneously. You'd be beaten to a pulp. You've got to pick selected areas, and weigh them to determine which is the best area for you to move into.

In high-growth management, it's very important to isolate five or six items which are key success factors for your firm, and you do so knowing that you are deferring other items. For example, at Ashton-Tate back in 1982, for us to focus on controlling cost of goods—you know, in all the technical ways they teach you in business school to efficiently manage production—would have been to focus on absolutely the wrong thing. Other things were far more important. We had a slight lead in the market with dBASE II, and we had to move it from a $1 million product in 1982 to a $10 million product, so we needed to grab share very quickly. That was the primary objective, and we did that by establishing a dealer sales organization. We had a big problem being able to ship product out the door to the people that had agreed to buy it, and we had to deal with that. And then we wanted to expand our efforts in sales and marketing, so we started building a sales force to avoid single-point failure where we were relying on distributors.

Guerrilla management only makes sense in a high-growth environment, an environment which is characterized by very rapid change and a high degree of uncertainty, imperfect communications due to adding a lot of people fast, financial pressure, and organizational stress. You've got to learn to live with uncertainty, and you've got to indoctrinate your organization with the importance of change. Change is very important as an operating principle. You spend a lot of time, when the organization is small, reminding people of the need for change.

Guerrilla management is also a way to keep the team going. I would sum it up by saying that it is a strategy for the morally strong and the materially weak. The way you keep people going is to have a clear vision of where you're headed, and you embody political, social, economic, and psychological factors into the business element. The business element is subordinated to those factors.

It's like a missionary effort. You're engaged in providing a socially important product or service, you're bringing new technology to new socio-economic groups; that's important for us. You bring a very strong moral framework into the business, the idea that we're doing the right thing, and we're doing it in almost a tribal way. You can't do it in memos; you have to do it in groups. Lots of meetings. For the first two years we spent a lot of time out on the floor organizing our people, that was a hallmark of our management. This is clearly a part of guerrilla management—you're all involved, it's a tribal war. You can't do it from a hill sending people into battle, you have to lead them into battle.

You keep reminding people of the basics of the strategy. You have to be open. We published our strategic plan and circulated it. This is what we're doing, this is why. So guerrilla management is effective strategic management for early and mid-stage high growth firms, and can only be done where communication is wide open, nothing withheld.

The number one thing is to have a meaningful mission. If there's no meaningful mission, there's no opportunity for moral strength. You're fighting tremendous odds. People keep saying, "When's the shake-out gonna happen in this business?" Well, the shake-out's been going on for years, but it's affecting bigger businesses now. In the case of Ashton-Tate, the meaningful mission was etched in stone—to shift the balance of power from those who understand how computer technology works to those who are in need of that technology. That's the common mission, and people are often motivated by that to join us.

Chapter Ten

BREAKING AND ENTERING: SUCCESS IN A CROWDED MARKET

The accounting software market is occupied by big, established companies like RealWorld, PeachTree, Structured Systems, BPI, Accounting Plus, Cyma, Open Systems, Star, and several hundred others. This is an aggressive and competitive crowd, all elbowing and jostling for market share. The last thing the world needs, you would think, is another accounting program. But they keep coming.

Is it conceivably possible for a new company to break into this kind of market without millions? Here's the story of two companies that did just that—started in a garage on a shoestring, and broke right into riches. In the last section, the marketing consultant for the second company tells how he accomplished the impossible.

THE CHAMPION'S TALE

The Data Base Research Corporation in Denver, Colorado is a rags-to-riches company that made it with the good old "build a better

mousetrap" method, or in their case, through technological innovation in accounting software design. When they started, no one had any real idea what would happen or where they would end up, and they had nothing to sustain them but their instincts, their faith, and their talent. Like so many other entrepreneurs, they just closed their eyes and jumped into the unknown. Two years later their company employed sixty five people and was soaring.

In 1980, Rusty Fraser and Charlie Hager worked for a minicomputer company in Denver. Rusty was selling minis and developing a passion for programming, and Charlie was an accountant turned ace programmer who was turning out minicomputer accounting applications. It all started when Rusty's friend, Doug Borwick, stopped by one day with a 5 1/4 inch floppy disk. Charlie later said, "I thought it was a toy. None of us had ever seen one before, and we were rolling on the floor laughing about it." But it wasn't long before Rusty and Charlie began to see the handwriting on the wall and they started taking micros seriously.

Doug Borwick was feeling more than a little frustrated with what he saw as inadequacies in the various available microcomputer accounting packages and he kept jabbing at Rusty and Charlie with things like, "Why can't smart guys like you hash up something for micros that acts more like those classy minicomputer programs?"

"Ha, ha!" they said, "You can't get a $2500 micro to act like a $40,000 mini."

Then one day in February, 1981, they saw a *BYTE* magazine ad with a bilge-pump and sent off for one of the earliest copies of dBASE II. Once they got their hands on it, they began to think maybe they could do what Doug wanted after all. In a fit of enthusiasm, they decided to go for it by starting a business to build the better mousetrap accounting system.

In June, 1981, Charlie and Rusty both left secure jobs to chase a dream in a race with starvation. They quickly incorporated and started to work in windowless office the size of a closet. They had no phone, no money, and only a vague idea of what they wanted to do. No one was getting paid, but if

CHAPTER TEN

someone needed something, and if anyone else had a buck, it got shared. These guys gave a new meaning to "under capitalized."

Charles Hager (sitting) and Rusty Fraser, Data Base Research Corp.

Rusty Fraser and Charlie Hager are gregarious and good-natured—so much so that our interview was much more fun than orderly. They were usually both talking excitedly at the same time, saying more or less the same things, echoing and reinforcing one another like twins. That's how you have to imagine it in their story, because they both said it all, ensemble.

RUSTY FRASER AND CHARLIE HAGER: We didn't really know what we were going to do right at first. No idea whatsoever. We just started coding, and right away we ordered a thousand manual covers. We wanted to have them air freight the things out to us because we thought we'd be done right away, not just the software, but the manual too. All in three months. We couldn't afford the air freight, so we just put a rush order on it and paid $40 extra for that. Well, they came in six weeks, and then they just sat in a back room for over a year! (Both cracking up.) It was much more complex than we anticipated.

In October of '81, we sold Doug Borwick some stock and took him in, and that's how we survived. We were just in there coding day and night, seven days a week, and we needed someone to answer the phone—if we ever got a phone—but if we got one, someone would have to answer it. So Doug came in and we had three equal partners. Doug started drumming for investors right away.

Was anyone else in with you two and Doug at the beginning?
Let's see. We got Morris Cohen in late August, and he worked through December for no pay. He even bought a small percentage of

stock. Morris had been a friend of ours for years, a Transcendental Meditation teacher like Rusty. About half the company has been in TM. It's not a requirement or anything, they just heard about us, and we brought in a lot of people through our contacts with TM.

That's interesting. Mitch Kapor taught TM, too. And about a third of RealWorld's people are scientologists. Oh, well. Who else was with you at the beginning?
Rich McConnel. We met Rich at the minicomputer company, when we were all there, before we even started, and Rich was a systems level programmer, doing all those bits and bytes. He was a real quiet, shy guy, young, about nineteen. When we first met him, he would only work at night. He was with a rock band, and after the rock band practice, he would come in and work from midnight to six. He played drums in the rock band, he plays piano, guitar, sings—a one man band.

We got to know Rich pretty well, and we got to be very impressed with his work. When we left the other company, we said, "Rich, come on over with us. We don't have any money, we can't pay you, and we don't even know what you're going to do." That's exactly true. So he would come in every now and then, and just poke around and see what we were doing. That first summer we actually paid him $30, just the first two or three months because he needed gas money and a new pair of tennis shoes. What Rich did was great, he was able to crunch and encrypt our code so we had about a 50% reduction from source code, and he joined all the modules. Fixed it so we can do easy field updates, and that allowed us to develop our concept of custom canned software, where you can upgrade just one aspect of the whole thing for a customer in the field.

How did you survive while you were developing your product?
We just lived out of our pocket. Yeah, we scraped by, whoever had a buck pitched in. After we finished the General Ledger module we sold

that to about a hundred people for $495 and got it polished up with their feedback. Once we had that, Doug started going around raising capital by small stock transactions of one percent here, one percent there. One percent cost $25,000, and we raised about $180,000 over a period of time, a period of about six or eight months. We just showed our first G/L module around the area to doctors and lawyers, relatives and friends, just hustling a buck. We gave away about seven or eight percent for about $180,000, somewhere in that area. Doug says that local investors don't have the big money that venture capitalists do, but they're a whole lot easier to get along with.

Life was fun then, but pretty spartan. There was this tremendous pressure that we put on ourselves and everybody else was putting on us to get the product done. But when you get the product done, the battle just starts. The concept of building a better mousetrap and everybody beating a path to your door doesn't work anymore. You've got to get out there. But we didn't have any plan, we just had to make it all up as we went along.

In the summer of '82 we made up a plan, and we figured out that we could have it made, do everything we wanted to do, for another $100,000 (both crack up). We had it all down, only it's even funnier than those damn binders we ordered. That amount wasn't even a drop in the bucket—it would evaporate before it hit.

When did things really start rolling for you?
When we went to the Fall COMDEX in November, 1982. We had four modules finished by then, and we were all three there, Doug and us, in this very bare bones booth. One of our employees actually financed the booth. Morris Cohen. Actually it was his idea, he insisted that we go.

That show was beyond our expectations. We packed our booth. At times it was three deep in the aisle watching our demonstration. Our product was so innovative, and so new, the truth is—and this is kind of a key point—we didn't really realize what was out there in the microcomputer software accounting products. We had assumed that what was out there was as good as on the minis. That was our only source of reference. We never looked at other packages when we were developing. We did what we thought needed to be done, and we did it the way we thought needed. We didn't look at other packages. If we had, Champion probably would have ended up about half as good as it is.

We were overwhelmed at the show. People were blown away. We saw people's faces turn white when they saw the updating, where you could go in, enter a check, completely change it, reverse it, put it in another month, do anything you want. The system does it all for you. We figured the white faces were the competition. You could see the blood go out of their faces, it was really interesting. That's when we stirred up some interest in the press.

That COMDEX (Fall, '82) was the major turning point in our career. And we almost didn't go. We were still working on venture capital all the time. Some of them came to this show. Initially, they wanted a lot more than we were willing to give up. We dealt with them for about six weeks, and then it broke off. They wanted half the company and more. They wanted a whole bunch. You know, which is typical. So we just dropped it, and it sat for about three months, four months, and then it picked up again after the Atlanta show—the Atlanta COMDEX.

But we had got around 900 leads for dealers out of that Fall COMDEX. We called them all afterward, everybody, and picked up a bunch of dealers. Our sales went up from about $5000, $10,000 at best, in monthly sales in November to $115,000 in December. We picked up about another hundred dealers. Sales dropped a little bit in January. We finished the last module, then raised our price to $795 for each module, and then sales went down to about $80,000. But then they started steadily picking up again and we were doing a little over $100,000 a month, average. In May, 1983, we did about

$120,000. What happened was we really pumped a lot of money into advertising, and steady growth. We started gaining people.

We advertised in *InfoWorld*. We decided we could not cover all 200 publications. So we picked *InfoWorld* because it was well read, and it went to dealers. We did about $140,000 in advertising between December and June. It wasn't exclusively in *InfoWorld*, but most of it was. We got very good results there. Mostly, we're not looking for the end user. We still want to create a dealer network, but we're starting to do combination ads now.

There were probably about twenty new dealers a month. They only had to buy one unit and they got a 50% discount right away, but still, at least half of them were genuine. I think our statistics on re-orders then was probably about 25 or 30%. Most of the business was coming through new dealers. But that's picked up considerably. We're almost at 50%. But we're growing very, very fast. We set up 117 new dealers in October, '83. Just October. And last summer we signed up with Softsel.

How much venture capital did you finally pick up?
$622,500. We gave them 18%. That was September, '83. Between plowing revenues back in, borrowing, and venture capital, we must have way over a million invested in the firm, actually it's closer to two million in total input.

What's your strategy for the future?
There are a lot of software companies that are really products pretending to be companies, i.e., a one-product company. We have made a commitment that we are not going to be a one product company. We're going to have a lot of verticals. We're going to go into hotel management, time and billing, medical, all these verticals. Plus some smaller things like our interface program, Password, will interface with Lotus 1-2-3, WordStar, other programs. We call it our Software Bus.

Okay, you've got sixty-five employees now. What's it like having to live and work in the middle of all those employees?
It's great. We've got a really *great* group of people.

Wasn't growing that fast disorganized or chaotic?
Well it was. Going through the past summer with the fast growth that occurred . . . But we got through that just fine.

You guys make it sound like all fun and games. I haven't heard any horror stories or crises.
    RUSTY: This has been one of the best experiences of my life.
    CHARLIE: It wasn't all smooth, but there wasn't any major crisis.
    RUSTY: Look, the whole thing was a crisis—crisis management—but that all eased off probably around the summertime, with the infusion of that venture capital. But we never had a management crisis.

THE STRATEGY OF THE CLIENT STRATEGIST

Dynamic Business Software, Inc., in Vancouver, B.C., was started by Helen Warn, her brother Don Hawkins, and Mel Wilson, a former Honeywell systems analyst. Helen was a mathematician doing research and programming for the Canadian federal government, and Don was a physicist and accountant with ten years experience at designing accounting systems on minis. By comparison, this startup makes Rusty and Charlie's early days of privation seem fairly comfortable. Helen, who did the major share of the programming, started in the back room of a Vancouver, B.C. computer store. No loans, no investors, no salary. During one period, they didn't even have a printer, so she had to write code out by hand off of the screen.

BREAKING AND ENTERING

Helen Warn, Dynamic Business Software Inc.

Today, DBS is swinging along with nine full-time employees, all hard at work on follow-on products in a casual, cluttered office presided over by Helen's cat, Pascale. Helen and her partners had created an excellent General Ledger product but it was Bill Campbell, a local, self-styled marketing consultant, who created the success.

When Bill signed on as a consultant for DBS, he gave the product a new name, Client Strategist, and a special kind of marketing strategy that paid off. First, he connected with the prestigious Thorne-Riddell, a major national accounting firm, who eventually picked it for their own internal use across Canada. Meanwhile, he was developing a successful dealer network. But the big coup came when Bill sold marketing rights to Reston—a division of Prentice-Hall with major distribution connections—who will be taking the product into the big leagues.

First comes Helen's story about the company and the product, then Bill Campbell explains exactly what he did and why it worked:

Why did you want to start your own enterprise? Money?

HELEN WARN: No, it wasn't that. I was burned out doing what I was doing. I was a civil servant with a clear run to the grave where I could get a good salary and do nothing, like a lot of people in the government. Don't get me wrong, there are lots of people who are active and creative in government, but a lot just put in their time. Anyway, I really wasn't performing to my capacity, so I felt I had to change. Then this idea came up, and it looked like something I wanted to try.

We quit our jobs and moved to Vancouver in early '81 to do it. We were all living on our savings—not a princely sum, just enough to live on. At first we worked in the back of a computer store, but that relationship broke down and we were left for a while without facilities or equipment.

When you started programming, had you examined the other products?
Not really. We never took a close look at any other products, because Don had been designing accounting systems on minis for ten years. I've looked at some since, and we were right, they weren't worth bothering with. None of them are suitable for accountants to do serious client accounting applications. Most of the other products are horizontal packages for businesses, while ours is aimed specifically at accountants.

Did you do any business planning at the beginning?
We didn't have anybody that knew anything about it. We recognized from the first that one person can't really do it all, that to get a product to the market you need so many kinds of expertise. But we didn't realize that we had gaping holes in our own knowledge and experience, we thought we knew more than we actually did.

I made a crucial contact with Bill Campbell late in '81. I met him at the Pacific Coast Computer Fair in Vancouver where he gave a talk. He had been managing a Radio Shack store before that. I made an appointment to see him, and I guess we fit in with some of his plans, so we became his first client. He is really responsible for 90% of our marketing. Bill's second really crucial role was that he was the first person that really had business experience, and he got us started on the right path to running the company in a more professional manner.

So it was very lucky that you met Bill when you did?
Well, it wasn't just fortuitous. I went out looking for someone. Bill was the first one I met, but I talked to several others, too. I personally think that Bill is a very rare bird, and we're very lucky to

have found him. He was head and shoulders above anybody else that we talked to. They all had a sort of snake-in-the-grass aspect that I found unpleasant to deal with, but Bill comes on as a very honest, straight forward guy. He really turned around my ideas about marketers—a great guy. I finally started to appreciate the innovation and creativity, you know, the sheer energy that goes into it.

First he suggested that I show it to people he knew at Thorne-Riddell Riddell (a major Canadian national accounting firm) and they got very excited about it. They tested everything and we were recommended as the best they could find. This was about the middle of '82.

After Bill left Radio Shack in the middle of '81, he was down here at DBS almost every day. He was on the phone trying to drum up a distribution channel, trying to set up a dealer network. He set up presentations with Hewlett-Packard, and got chains of computer stores, and Victor. He was just incredible.

Bill was also trying to help us run in a more business-like manner. When we started this, we had really no conception of it. We all started out with no boss, no employees, everybody was equal. One of the most important things Bill did from a business point of view was to make us separate out the roles of shareholder and employee. Around the office, you have to have a power structure, and that was very important.

Then he got us to package the thing more professionally. You know, binders with our name on it and that kind of thing. He named the product. Before that, we just called it General Ledger. It didn't have a name.

He found us dealers, set up a reasonable discount structure, then he supported them and trained them and stuff. As these people started to be more successful at it, the money started to come in. That worked, and the Computer Innovations retail chain has a good record of selling it. Also, in the accounting business a lot of stuff spreads by word of mouth.

200

It took a long time for word to spread, especially as we were under capitalized and didn't have money to throw at a marketing effort. So far, it's all been shoestring and bootstrap, and that's cost us a lot in terms of opportunity. Bill's retainer became our first big account payable, and we just paid him dribs and drabs as we could. He put a lot of time and energy into us.

Bill's a real go-getter for making contacts. He seems to do it naturally and enjoy it. He created the relationship with Reston. They bought the rights to manufacture and market the product, and they will be responsible for all the advertising, documentation, manufacturing, everything. We get a royalty.

Our contract allowed us to keep on selling it until Reston is all geared up, and that was very important as that gave us a cash flow. They are just now starting to sell it, so now it's all theirs. We're getting four more products in the wings, accounts receivable, accounts payable, and two more general ledgers. Reston gets first opportunity at those last two since they are derivative.

What advice would you give someone that wants to start a company?
First of all, they have to have a source for a good design. I think somebody starting out should go after a vertical market, but they have to know somebody that really knows what the particular group of people they are writing for wants. Then, they'll have to have some marketing contacts. And don't do what we did and start the company naively, without an organization. Go to a lawyer that's familiar with small companies, and get them to help you set things up. You should establish basic principles of operation before you even start. That could save an awful lot of grief beforehand.

CHAPTER TEN

AN END-RUN MARKETING SUCCESS

Bill Campbell left his schooling in chemistry in favor of big computers, and many years after that he left a secure career with Honeywell in favor of little ones. First, he promoted himself into a job as manager of a computer store in Vancouver (getting a degree at the University of Radio Shack, he says) where he earned $80,000 in ten months by dramatically improving profits. Having made his point to himself, he went off on his own to do training seminars on micros for big corporations across Canada but he really wanted to be a marketing consultant for software companies. Helen Warn became his first client and his first big success. Bill has had several more success since—still batting 1000—and he is now doing business in Vancouver, B.C. under the name Soft-Rep Services International Inc.

W.J. (Bill) Campbell, Soft-Rep

BILL CAMPBELL: Basically, in marketing —and particularly in microcomputer marketing—you've got a real major problem, and that's the problem to stand out. To be seen, to be heard. *PC* magazine is now the largest trade magazine in the entire magazine industry. Only eighteen months ago, it was a forty or fifty page magazine, and now it's a 500-page monthly. It is pretty hard to stand out and be seen and be heard if you advertise in that magazine, and the same goes for most of the other magazines.

So let's look at the marketplace. If you do, you'll see that the computer revolution isn't the only revolution going on out there. There's another one called the marketing revolution. Everything we ever knew or learned about marketing, all of our old assumptions, they're not all that relevant today. The methods we need today are quite quite different. We need to invent some new marketing processes to be seen and heard in the marketplace.

Keep in mind that advertising is the last thing you do in a marketing campaign, not the first thing. A lot of stuff goes on before you get there. From the very beginning of your project, there are three things you should think about. These are focus, position, and channels of distribution.

Focus: The first major consideration is focus, and this relates to that marketing revolution that we're in. I truly believe that we need to think through very carefully who our product is for, in as narrow terms as possible. A good example involves my client, Helen Warn, who wrote a general ledger package. Now there were already a lot of general ledger packages on the market, and the last thing the world needed was another one, even if it was outstanding in terms of its coding and all that good stuff. The marketplace can't tell the difference between one general ledger and another, and it's going to cost the person who's trying to buy it an enormous amount of time to try and figure out which one to buy. So how were we supposed to market a product like that?

Well, what we did was to focus the product on a specific target market, and in this case we chose the accounting profession. So we renamed it "Client Strategist." The name was chosen to ring a bell with accountants. All of an accountant's income comes from clients, and he spends most of his time planning financial strategies. But the accountant market in Canada alone is bloody small. We're talking about a total of 50,000 accountants in public practice—a very, very small market. Much smaller than all those who could ever use this general ledger. But if you stop to think about what a lot of those accountants are doing, you find many of them are controllers for various companies. Well, if you're doing the books for five or six or ten companies, that's client accounting. But a controller won't think about buying a client accounting package because he doesn't need client accounting. He does controlling for a whole bunch of

CHAPTER TEN

companies. So we renamed the package again to "Controller Strategist." Now we have two products. It's the same code, but with a different name, and now the end user can absolutely identify with it.

That's the new marketplace—everyone's getting very demanding. They want products designed "just for me."

With two different names we achieved a good position in two different markets, and a free introduction to the accountant's clients. Who recommends to the businessman what to buy? Well, his accountant does. He can't evaluate this product, he can barely keep his own books, so he'll take the accountant's word for it and buy it. If he likes your first product, you have established trust, and there is a two to six times chance he'll buy the next product from you. That's a trust relationship working. You've sold them one and it cost you a hell of a lot to get the order, now they buy the second and third and fourth product you invent.

So for this reason we came up with a third product called "Ledger Strategist." Now the only way that's going to market is through the accountants. They will recommend it, and that's a new distribution channel. And it's all the same software. Different name, and different words in different places in the manual, but three distinct marketplaces, and three distinct names. That's focus.

Positioning: The next major consideration is positioning. Positioning has got a lot to do with what you're going to say, and who you're going to say it to, and when you're going to say it. There's a million people trying to reach your prospective clients, both for software and for everything else. He's got an enormous number of messages coming at him. What you've got to do is establish a statement whereby you connect with benefits and hang onto some hooks that are already in his head.

After you have focused, figured out exactly who your target is, you then write a positioning statement. It's a message to the target that catches them dramatically and clearly connects your product with their needs. For example: "Tylenol—For People Who Can't Take

Aspirin." That's a beautiful positioning statement. You need to go after a niche in the market where you can clearly be number one. You try to identify exactly who your client is and communicate that you're for him, the only one.

There's a little book out called *Positioning—The Battle For Your Mind*, by Trout and Ries. It's worth a fortune. The concept is really quite important.

Young companies have to understand that it's a product you're selling, not your company. Take most of the software in the marketplace today, and look at the binders: you'll usually see the company name biggest, the product name smallest. Even that front cover on your manual is an advertisement. It's a piece of promotional material, and it has a message on it. You spend a bundle of money building up people talking about your product in the marketplace, trying to drive people into retail stores, or any other distribution channel, to buy it. You're not selling your company, at least not yet, not while you're starting out. Hide your company name. Put it on the inside of the cover. Your product is what you have to sell.

Channels of Distribution: The last major consideration is about channels of distribution. Now it's pretty important when you've got a product to try to get it into as many different distribution channels as possible. You shouldn't ignore any of them, but in fact you should be creative and try to invent some new ones. Put on seminars where people come to see your product. There's a lot of people in the education business who travel from city to city doing seminars about microcomputers, and they demonstrate software. And if people have paid to go to an independent talk about what a microcomputer is for and they demonstrate your software, it adds a level of credibility that is unheard of. They are literally running across the country recommending your product. So think about new ways to get your product to market.

Here's another one. Stop and think about who else is calling upon your potential prospect right now with another product, and figure some way you can get them to carry your product at the same time. Because if you can identify that direct sales force, you will really have it made in the software business. We went through this process with Client Strategist. We were running around the States looking for someone to carry it, and we finally found a unique distribution channel. We sold the manufacturing rights and distribution rights for that product to a company called Reston Software.

Reston Software is a wholly-owned subsidiary of Prentice-Hall. If you remember that our Client Strategist product focuses on the accountant marketplace, well, Prentice-Hall had a division that was marketing a tax information service, and they had four hundred salesmen who built up an incredible reputation selling this tax product to every CPA in the United States. They are now running around with Client Strategist under their arms.

Another client of mine has a food and liquor manager for restaurants. We went through the same thought process, and figured out, well, who else was calling on all the restaurants. We identified the cash register salesmen, and now we've got Data Terminal Systems, NCR, and a few others all running around the country selling our product. They've already built up that trust relationship. So direct sales, if you can get them, and if they are already in a relationship with your potential customer, is an enormous thrust in getting your product to the marketplace.

Well, now. If you're like most of my clients, you're broke. They can't afford to spend money inefficiently. The point is to get the most out of your working capital, so it is really key that you do that thinking-through process and that planning to get every bit for the dollar you spend.

After you've thought through your positioning of what to say, and who to say it to, after you've narrowed down your market with that focus, and after you've figured out your channels of distribution so you can tell people where to go to buy the product, now you can advertise effectively.

What's your opinion of the way the software market is developing?
What's exciting is that nobody knows what they're doing, and I would even put myself in that bracket. Nobody's got any experience marketing software. Two years doesn't count, and that's really all we've been in business. Most people are doing things traditionally. They're trying to take software to market the same way you bring refrigerators and stoves to market. You talk about distributors like Softsel, you know, they buy a product from the manufacturer, they stock it in volume, because that's how you sell fridges and stoves, and they move it out to their dealer organization. Well, that's the only way it's working right now, and even that's falling apart. A lot of companies are going directly to dealers because distributors aren't really adding any value. Being their own distributor, that's interesting. It's still traditional, but because we're dealing with electronic media, I believe things are soon going to be done differently. I'm not even sure if it's just the downloading stuff, but at least right now it's the most visible, most highly potential innovation—just downloading software to people.

But I guarantee you that in the next year or two that we're going to find a totally new way to deliver software. And totally new ways to market it. I believe there's going to be a breakthrough in how we market, particularly how we reach vertical markets.

You mean like Amway or Tupperware?
That's an approach, but I'm thinking of networking. You know, maybe as an author, you know other authors from all over America. Or if you're an environmentalist. An obvious example would be the women's type network. You know, if we can get in on that to move product, its magical. Look, a full page ad in *The Wall Street Journal* costs what, fifteen thousand bucks? Or twenty thousand? Thirty thousand? It's crazy. You get into a network, though, and your advertising costs are almost nothing. Okay? Now I don't know how to

do that, yet, but I am working on it. The point is, there's got to be some new ways of doing things. And that's exciting.

I'm pretty sure there's always going to be a huge cottage industry out there. Unique people doing their unique things in their little niche. And they'll either be doing it locally or regionally, but they'll never get wealthy. Alright? And they may not want to, so that's not a problem. However, they may lose their niche if they happen to take a good niche that appeals to a large company. Right? And that's what's crucial. You can't keep a small company in a good niche, because somebody big will come along. In the case of Client Strategist, they were marketing to all the accountants in North America, and they had to get very big, very fast to protect their position.

How much do you think it would cost to start a company just for local or regional vertical markets?
To go into a vertical market, you probably need about a quarter of a million to a half million dollars. Now it really doesn't matter whether you're trying to go to Canada or just one state or province, or whether you're trying to go to all of North America. It's almost the same cost. Because the minute you say, well, I'm only going to do it in one state or region, and therefore I don't need to spend that kind of money, you're fooling yourself, because you're only going to have a crummy looking product, okay? You have to go first class. The cost of going first class is the same whether you do it in one little place or all over North America. Your only major additional costs are for more space advertising and travel.

The other thing is that if you go to five states rather than fifty, you can hit 50% of the microcomputer market. New York, Illinois, Texas, Florida, and California. You add those states up, they have 50% of all the retail outlets, they have 50% of all sales in microcomputers. If you know that, you can cut your advertising costs by hundreds of percentage points, because you're not advertising in Arizona or Idaho.

208

What if someone doesn't have $500,000 to start a company?
I think they've got to go to a publisher and have them publish the product.

But, Bill, what about your Client Strategist? They didn't have anything like that kind of money.
Oh. . . Well, yeah, but they had me.

Chapter Eleven

TEAMWORK

"Successful companies are not built around an individual, they're built around groups of people. Do they have a team? Can they put one in place?"

—Mitch Kapor
Lotus Development Corp.

In order to be successful, a major software enterprise requires more different kinds of talent and experience than any one person can possibly provide. In the first place, the kind of person who can start a company is probably quite different temperamentally from the kind of person who can keep it going. And from start to finish, the successful mass-market software enterprise requires knowledge, skill, experience and contacts in the fields of

technology, production, marketing, sales, finance, and management. It's not that it can't *possibly* be done entirely by one person, but you could just as easily imagine that one genius Harlem Globetrotter might be able to take on another basketball team all by himself. It's not the best way to win in either case.

During an interview with Will Luden, who was once the director of marketing for MicroPro, he was asked why he didn't go into software instead of starting his chain of ComputerEase retail stores. He said:

"In the software business, you have to get married to someone else. You need two people at the head of a company. There would have been myself in marketing and distribution, and someone else with product experience, someone to manage the creative process. I didn't have anyone I know who is a close friend and has product skills. That kind of union is 30% complementary skills and 70% chemistry. What happens when you've been up twenty hours a day five days in a row and you still have a fundamental problem? I didn't want my livelihood to depend on that marriage. If I had had someone, I would have done it."

Michael Griffin, Palantir, Inc.

A winning product in the mass market arena only starts with a first class program. After that, there must be a stable and competent team formed around it to make it go and to keep it growing. An excellent case-in-point of what happens if the team doesn't form is found in the story of my all time favorite word processor, Magic Wand, which was introduced at almost the same time as WordStar, a product that is inferior in every way except in terms of commercial success. Read, then, the compelling tale of Michael Griffin, an extremely capable programmer and designer who has twice had a company fall apart around him and who is now trying for a third time with Palantir, his latest word processor. Once again he has created an excellent product, and once again his product lags behind his struggles to build a good company.

MICHAEL GRIFFIN: Back in 1976 I was working at Ashland Oil doing systems support for an IBM database. I had had a little bit of schooling, enough not to care much for computer science as a discipline, or to think much of it as a professional qualification. Mostly, I had gotten into it by doing it. I started out at IBM at NASA back in 1968, running 360 Model 30s.

My first activity in micros was right after we discovered that this new field was opening up. About November of 1976, my partner brought me this article about micros in *Datamation* magazine. We hit the clubs, started trying to gather information, like sponges. We got an Imsai, a Processor Tech video board, a cassette interface, and kludged together a workable system.

We left Ashland Oil as quickly as we could find any excuse to. We formed a little company called Micro Visions, which is the name he still uses today. We were trying to sell and install systems, although before there was disk or CP/M it was rather frustrating. We were out in the field, sort of floundering, gathering experience, finding out what things you could do, and what you couldn't do. It was late '78, I guess, when I realized that selling and installing wasn't what I really wanted to do.

I started out being a writer, to make my living at a typewriter all day was the way I saw myself going through life. But I wound up programming, so I began to see myself sitting at a console, developing things, applying my own skill and creativity and putting things together. I saw that it was time to do it, and that our first little venture was never going to lead to that. So I found financial backers.

I had written a text editor for a local manufacturer. I had just seen the Electric Pencil for the first time and said, hmmm, you can use micros for word processing? Hell, I can write a better one than that! The investors had known me from my oil and gas days, and so we put together SBA (Small Business Applications, Inc.). They got two-thirds to provide backing, management, and so forth, and I got a third to provide the code and the products. That was probably early in '79. They were getting two thirds of the company for a loan of something like eighty or ninety thousand dollars for the development process, including advertising, which was in the form of loans to be paid back. This was my first experience in setting up a company.

We only had about a four-month development window. For a while it was just me and a machine, and then Bill Radding came on in the second or third month to start doing some advertising, because it was only going to take three or four months to get the product together, right? He had such a feel for it, he even assisted in the design of the product, and he did the documentation. He was the first user, and principal critic, and contributed a great deal to smoothing out the initial design.

We were completed by November, 1979, just before the first COMDEX. Nobody had heard of it, but it was a show that would give us some exposure, and we could meet some people to try to start pumping the product. So at the same time we were doing that, our financial backers, who had been doling out four or five thousand dollars a month to pay the overhead, they told us, basically, that they had lost faith, since three months had become eight months to get the product ready. They thought maybe they had made a wrong turn. December was the last month they were going to carry us. We needed to start carrying ourselves, or they were just going to write off their losses.

So we got into a van, and Bill and I headed out to COMDEX to try to pump this product. We got up there, and set up our little ten foot booth, and we managed to pick up some people, mostly dealers. There were hardly any distributors then, and everything was very small, very one to one. And we managed in the course of those three days to make enough contacts, get enough people interested, that we got back and we could start shipping some product out.

CHAPTER ELEVEN

For three months, it was just Bill and me. And then we took on someone to help handle sales. It was at that point where the financial backers saw that it was going to survive. They had given Bill half of their share, a third of the company, if he could take over as president and save the company. So he did it, he made it survive. He had a flair for selling and talking. He was a terrible manager, but there were only two or three of us to manage, and he was a great idea man, had a lot of flair, a lot of personality, he was able to sell and move the product. And of course the backers immediately started resenting their largesse. It gets very involved and very bitter from then on out, but it carried out through the year when finally there was a fourth man brought in who was supposed to take over the management.

This was still 1980. It finally ended when they tried to use it as a cash cow to get back their little $80,000 investment, while we needed capital to grow.

Based on our first six or nine months experience, I'd come out with the 1.1 release that addressed all the weaknesses. WordStar, while we had been developing Magic Wand, made its first splash. I think the products were completed about the same time. But they started selling theirs at version 0.9 or something, and we didn't start selling ours until it was complete and ready. They also had West coast connections and history and they were there. We were always trailing far back in their shadow. We needed marketing expertise, and capital to do something with it. The financial backers thought they could just sit back and ride it, and collect cash.

And that's the point when I said I'm not going to break my back churning out new products or trying to make this fly while they are doing that. It came to a big schism where I wanted to either run the company or get out of it, and they thought they could run the company without either Bill or me. And that's when it all fell apart, and Bill and I walked out and formed a new company. We actually tried to buy back SBA, made them a better offer than they wound up

214

taking, but their judgement was not at all good. They had no micro sense at all.

What happened was, Magic Wand was sold to PeachTree, and PeachTree and Sorcim did a technology swap. Basically, they traded the Magic Wand source code and the SuperCalc source code so that they could come out with their respective products, SuperWriter and PeachCalc.

We walked out in November, 1980, and formed Designer Software (now Palantir, Inc.) in January, 1981. Bill and I were tired of having traipsed in WordStar's shadow, so we set out to design a full-screen editing program that would take it ahead of WordStar. I had learned a lot from writing Magic Wand. Then we happened into some people who were starting up their own venture with some accounting software, and sort of teamed up with them, and that led to the whole... Their stuff was supposed to be ready within three months, and Bill unfortunately started advertising and hiring staff to develop manuals based on that.

All our money got spent on staff and ads for the accounting program, and it didn't get ready until we ran out of money. Then we were out of salespeople, out of steam and everything else. We've had about a year of almost no movement since the accounting thing, because we had exhausted ourselves. We went through so much cash, and so much energy, psychic and otherwise. There were bad feelings on both sides.

Palantir was ready in early 1982, and we split up from the accounting thing in August, and we've been trying since then to recover momentum. But we had exhausted so much. We've been hanging dead in the water, working through a few loyal distributors. Palantir has continued to sell well through systems integrators. They just need to have a solid product, they don't need promotion to drive the customers to them.

Palantir is getting by through systems integrators, but that's not enough volume. It's kept us alive and treading water, but to make money, and to play the game in this market, to get things you need like toll-free support numbers, we need more sales. That's partly why we've got a new ad campaign starting up, and we've redone the package.

You seem to be a very talented creator who was never able to create a business out of a product. Is that it?
Yeah. My backers ruined SBA, and then with Palantir, like, right now, I am the only person left from the original company. The only one left.

What steps have you taken to reorganize and stabilize Palantir, Inc.?
Bringing in a new president. I had never wanted to be a manager, and Bill had too much flair. Dennis came in the middle of last year to clean up the books, and try to bring some procedures. We brought him in back in March, but we still didn't have a sales department. Everything got much more stable, but we still haven't had the sales department. There was nobody, no legacy of an existing sales network or distribution base. That's where Bob VanIngan comes in, as V.P. of Marketing. That's the other part, the other team to build that sales structure. To generate the cash so that we can actually move ahead instead of doing the dog paddle.

    We're getting new financing. I don't know what we'll end up getting, because they've got a six months figure of about $600,000, and then maybe another couple million. For a mainstream product, you can no longer bootstrap your way up, where you put out a small ad, then with those sales you run a larger campaign, and so forth. The market moves too fast, now.

It seems that as a program writer you have been distracted constantly from programming by having to undertake business tasks that you would rather not do. Is that it?

I find it very frustrating to have the success of what I'm doing depend upon everybody else getting their stuff right. It's just that I have found over the years that I was continually being angry with people I've basically liked and thought a hell of a lot of. And it wasn't that they were incompetent, but it was just style. I'm a good team player in the sense that I can deliver my part on time, or ahead of schedule and help out anybody else who needs it. But if I have to wait, it drives me crazy.

I don't like being in charge of a team. I would rather take orders than give orders, and I don't particularly like to take orders. Tell me what you need, I'll tell you if I can do it, and I'll have it on your desk when you need it. That's the way I'm comfortable working. And I've always wanted to get back around to that. I didn't really want to go into the software publishing game, but when we started, there wasn't anybody in particular that you could rely on to deliver a good enough job of penetrating the market.

What would you like to do if Palantir settles down and starts moving? Would you like to try leading the industry instead of following it?

You hit it on that one. Most of the product ideas that I'm toying with now are the languages, but that would be a long, large-scale project, and I would like to see a shorter term payoff for a while. My personal goal, whatever product strategy we decide on, is to get into a frame where I can work more independently, and work in a design team with other people. I have a very good programmer back home who could be doing his own independent design. We need some management to make sure that the production, the control and the debugging—the day-to-day procedures—are going on in an orderly fashion. So that it doesn't have to weigh on our minds.

What do you think of the Apple Macintosh?
I wouldn't have believed it until I saw it, but I'm in love with the Macintosh. I just got one and I've been in a closet with it for a week. I'm extremely excited—the concepts are right, and it's the kind of machine that people can actually use. Getting a word processor to work efficiently and effectively is going to be tricky, but I'm just very excited about the machine.

Microsoft has even held back the release of their Windows program so they can make it more Mac-like. They're moving strongly in the Mac direction, and they're no dummies. It's the wave of the future.

———— ● ————

The next product is a favorite of the few who were fortunate enough to find it and would probably have been a favorite of yours if the man who wrote it had been able to form a team.

Randy Nielsen, Durant Software Co.

Active micro users are plagued by the problems of file management that are inherent in both CP/M and MS-DOS. Under either operating system, all files have names that are a maximum of eight characters, a dot, then three characters, like FILENAME.TYP. You can use fewer, but you can't use more. When you prowl through your old disks you will find old files with mnemonic names that are indecipherable. What's in them? Who made them? When were they backed up? Should they be backed up or eliminated? There's no way to know and no way to manage those files, other than to laboriously call up each one, read it, and take notes, then take action. Right now there are people going slowly

218

nuts all over the world, especially in businesses, trying to figure out what's on their disks.

Randy Nielsen decided to solve this problem in 1978, but he didn't start to think of his solution as a product until late in 1982. Too bad—for him and for us. His product, Simplifile, displays a date and a line of identifying information along side each file on the disk; it also takes over the operation of most CP/M functions and makes them easy to live with. Simplifile was later marketed under the name AutoDex by someone else, and is now not marketed at all—a great loss to users.

Randy generously shared his experiences and his very well-considered *ad hoc* analysis of the problems of launching a software enterprise:

RANDY NIELSEN: I was a math major at Cal, Berkeley, but I took a lot of computer courses because I was good at it and there was less competition there. I graduated in 1968. Fundamentally, what I am is a crackerjack programmer. In any language. In those days it was PL/I or assembly language. These days it's C. Some activities are just as natural as falling off a log, and programming is like that for me.

In 1977, I was involved with a very young microcomputer company in Oregon. The experience was a total disaster in many ways. I went up there to help run a company that essentially was in the process of self-destructing. Many more companies self-destruct than are destroyed. Real ambitious product plans, no cash flow controls, no sales, a Board of Directors that was mostly doctors. None of us had any real management experience, none of us knew what a marketing plan was, none of us had any idea at all of how to define our product well. What we were good at was going into the back rooms and coming up with things. I was only there because I knew the owner of the company, the president. They needed somebody, and I said sure. It was not a well thought out decision, but I learned a lot from it. Think very carefully before you leap.

I took a job in the fall of '78 as a DP manager for an investment consultant in San Francisco. I thought it would be good management

CHAPTER ELEVEN

experience. Once I had settled in there, regained my sanity, caught up on my sleep, paid off some debts, and got on top of the job, I started to think about what I wanted to do with myself. It kept coming back to ideas. What motivated me then and what motivates me now is not so much money or power as interesting ideas. Also, ideally, I like to work near where I live. And a third thing, I don't relate well to corporate structures.

My job was a trap; in some sense I had a set of golden handcuffs. I was very well paid, but I don't deal well with boredom. I got an Altos, a very early model, because I knew I had to learn more about the microcomputer software business. Then I bought the BDS C Compiler, and in some ways that was a major turning point. It's a damn good system. C is beyond a doubt the best language currently available in fairly wide use for systems work. I mean, you'll get a lot of emotional feelings about this, but C makes Pascal eat it. In fact, Microsoft writes in C. VisiCorp writes in C. The Visi-On series is in C. PerfectWriter is in C. Digital Research is writing all their new stuff in C. BDS C was something I could work with. Before, the thought of doing things in FORTH or assembly language, well, I just had a hard time motivating myself.

I was working with my micro a lot, and in the process, I got thoroughly sick and tired of the way CP/M worked. Also, at work I was evaluating the Xerox 860 system, and the human interface was excellent. Whenever you booted up a disk they displayed a directory with dates, and room for descriptions of your files. And you could select a file just by holding down a cursor key, going to the file, and hitting the function key. I just took these ideas and I started writing a simple little thing to do some of it at home. There was no formal concept, I just thought these were interesting ideas, and I wanted to play with them. At this point I didn't think of it as a product or anything, I was just having fun.

Early versions of it I called Display Manager. It doesn't exactly have a ring to it—it goes "thud." But when I had it sort of complete,

I showed it to a good friend of mine, Tom Ahern, who's somewhat of an entrepreneur, and he fell in love with it at once. He said I could make a million bucks with it, and we sat down and started working out improvements in the way it worked. It took me about four months to code it up in that first version, but it's grown a lot since then.

When it got fairly well along, I thought, now what do I do? I had no sense, or very little, of how to run a business. It was very frustrating, you feel like you have a neat thing and you don't know what to do with it, and it starts to bug the hell out of you. It really irritated me.

About this time, two somewhat similar products hit the streets, Supervyze and CP+. I thought, Oh my god, there are a lot of other people trying to do what I'm doing. I thought I had an untapped niche, so when those products came out I panicked at first. I thought the game was over. But then I looked at them both, and was immensely relieved. They weren't very good. I guess this was late in '81. I checked the products out, but I still didn't know what to do. But then something fairly pivotal happened.

Tom Ahern arranged for me to interview for a job with Taurus Software, the company that did CP+. Their director of software engineering had just quit, so I went and talked to the guy. He had written a business plan and had got over a million to develop a product and go to market. We talked, and I was frankly not impressed. His product was a dog, and he . . . Well, I thought if a bunny like that can do it, why can't I? I was really sort of motivated by that meeting, and I think that's what Tom had in mind.

By July or August of '82, I had decided to do some kind of venture. The more I looked at it, the only way to do it that made sense was to start a company, place some ads, go to shows, and just try to sell it. I'd talked to a few people about software publishers, and the general consensus was that nothing ever really happens with those people.

CHAPTER ELEVEN

I sat down and did some analysis and pretty much concluded that thirty thousand bucks would take me through the first four or five months. Talk about naive thinking. I mean, that is the word: very, very naive. I called up *InfoWorld* and asked them how much for a quarter-page ad, and then I called up some people I knew and asked them how much would they charge me for drawing up an ad. Then I got an estimate to do a brochure, then I thought, god damn, if I could only get into COMDEX. So I put that in my budget and signed up for a booth. I got busy, and in two to three weeks I developed an IBM version. This is one of the marvels about C is that I was able to move over thousands of lines of code. Anyway, I had a very busy time.

I decided to borrow $30,000. I took a deep breath, quit my job, and took out a second mortgage on my house. I didn't need a business plan for that. If had to have a business plan, it would have been hopeless, hopeless, hopeless. I had no concept of how to write one. I simply was not that much of a businessman. I could probably write one now, but I don't want to, I don't like them.

If I had known more of what I was doing, and known more people in the business, I could have assembled a team of people, designed a product line around the whole idea, talked to venture capitalists, raise a million and a half. I could probably have twenty people working for me today. I think there's no doubt a lot of things could have happened. But they didn't.

So anyway, we went to the 1982 Fall COMDEX. Friends of mine helped me get to COMDEX. It was a visible labor of faith, and love and foolishness, and I was really very pleased, and touched. Just before this time, I had major knee surgery, and was on crutches for several months. So not only was I trying to start a business on a shoestring, I also had to deal with daily physical therapy, having a hard time moving around. It was in many ways the roughest winter of my whole life. In fact, I considered abandoning the business, but I had to try.

COMDEX was very exciting, exhilarating. We had a booth, ten by ten, no budget, no expertise. We passed out brochures, showed the product. We sold it at the dealer price of $64 at the show, and sold fifty or sixty of them. We got enormous stimulation from the crowd. Many, many inquiries, also all kinds of feedback about the product, how it could be changed, improved.

The amount of interest shown was outrageously high. We usually had a crowd around our booth, and almost all of them were dealers. And lots of OEMs. Many hints of deals. But a lot of what COMDEX is all about though, is hot air. Any guy who has a business card and wants to act big, walks around, "Well, give me a quote for 5000 of these mothers. Are you seriously interested?" Well, of course I am! But the guy won't even return your phone calls after the show. "Where's your hospitality suite? Any naked women there?" That's a lot of what goes on. You could go to parties every night.

Coming back, I was overwhelmed and scared because it seemed clear that there was this opportunity, but how the hell was I going to capitalize on it? There was an overwhelming amount of planning and work to do. I tried. I returned phone calls, tried to sell it and to respond to people's requests. The biggest requests were to support more formats. I didn't have a staff. I couldn't afford anybody, so I did it myself. I had an answering service.

I put ads in *InfoWorld*, tried to get the product reviewed, started advertising in *PC* magazine. It was pretty hard to get people to actually review it. I don't know how many copies we gave away to "reviewers." But when it did appear in print, it was good. A few times, that's all. Publicity is hard to get, it takes people who know how to do that, who know how to follow up and make calls, nag people, and I almost suspect they write the article for people sometimes.

In the months after COMDEX, life was frankly pretty grim. There were ten-, twelve-, fourteen-hour days. Cash would come in, but it was up and down. Basically, we were still losing more than we were taking in. I was so naive in those days that I expected that it would just take care of itself after a few months. But it didn't.

My OEM efforts failed for two reasons. First, I'm a lousy salesman. Secondly, the product didn't really have a lot of visibility in the marketplace. It's the kind of thing where if I had a million dollar budget and someone who knew how to use it properly a year ago, I suspect Simplifile could be a major product. But I didn't have those things.

The OEMs typically get a license to manufacture it and you get around 10% of the list for each one, if that. People I was talking to seriously would talk six to ten bucks per copy. If they were selling 10,000 units a month, you'd be talking two dollars a copy. Or sometimes people like Morrow would try to cut deals where they would buy rights to a product for a fixed price. What he offered me was under $20,000. I told them to forget it.

In January there was another show, the CP/M-83 show in San Francisco. As a sort of last ditch effort to get some money, I went to that show. The booths were a thousand bucks, and I figured if I sold it for $79 bucks at the show I could at least cover costs, but I did far better than I ever dreamed. I sold $9,000 worth of products in three days. That show saved my ass. That's also where I met the guy who bought the product off of me, Don Hoodes. That's also where I met some people from ITT in Europe who ended up signing an OEM contract with us. It was an incredible show. A fluke, not only for me, for everybody. It was a great show, very exciting, and there hasn't been an end user show since that's worth a damn, except for the West Coast Computer Faire, and I go to all of them.

Anyway, I went from fifty dollars in the checking account to $9,000. I paid off bills, took a deep breath, and tried to figure out how to keep going. Same kind of thing, same process over and over, placing ads, calling people, trying to sell. I was calling the local OEMs and none of it really was going that well. There were occasional dramatic successes, but a dramatic success meant a sale of a few thousand dollars, and the basic expenses of running a business are at least that every month.

Somewhere around March of '83, I was once again almost broke, and the West Coast Computer Faire came along, so I went to that one, and sold five or six thousand dollars worth of product there. I thought, hell, these shows are really pretty nice. But also at that show, I made a deal to sell the product to Don Hoodes.

I'd been talking to Don on the phone for a long time, but I didn't take it too seriously because talk is so cheap. He kept saying I want to do a deal, and I would say, fine, come up and see me sometime, but he never quite did. But at that show he was there, and we wrote up an informal letter of intent and he gave me a check. He bought all rights. What he bought initially was the right to market the product with some changes under the name AutoDex, to test market it, then if he was pleased with the results he would take over the entire product.

What we did next was, we went to COMDEX East in Atlanta, spring '83. He had a huge booth there; the guy is a born promoter. He was very pleased with what he saw, so we struck a deal and he bought the product.

I got a lump sum up front, but the vast majority of the payment is over time, so that will give me about a year to figure out what I want to do next. I get a royalty of 15% of his receipts. I may still make some money from it, but it's hard to say. It depends on how well he markets it. The product is now his. I do not own it at all now.

Frankly, I have my doubts that he'll do a good job of promoting the product. I think he's over his head in the computer business. It moves very, very fast and it has swallowed up lots of people, lots bigger than he is, and I have to question his ability to sell this product. In fact, he and I are having some nasty arguments about that right now.

CHAPTER ELEVEN

Would you like to get the product back?
It may come to that. I hope not. I don't want it back.

Now, let's talk about the business of being in business. It is almost impossible today for a small company to successfully market a general purpose software product. It's too expensive and the competition is too big. Another reason why I am disenchanted with this whole business, is that the way to make it in this game is hype, or mass-market appeal, or consumer merchandising. Hype is perhaps a little judgmental, although it's what I feel about it. I hate that kind of stuff.

I had a product but not a business. If you're to be a successful company, you have to have a product line to market. If you're to bring it to market, you have to have staff, financing, *et cetera.* A business plan is important here, because it at least forces you to address those issues, and I did not. A good plan gives you a set of goals and a time schedule, and you can check yourself against the plan.

The problem for a lot of people is that, until they've been through the ringer once or twice, they don't really appreciate certain things. It's awfully hard to appreciate how tough running a business is until you've tried it. It's sort of like sex, where you can't really learn how to do it right until you've fumbled around a few times.

I think if I'd had two or three other people with me, I would have had a much better chance of success. But I didn't, and it was dying, there was no doubt about that. There were a whole lot of things I could have done, but I am absolutely delighted that I am out of that. It was one of the most rugged things I've done in my life. It was very, very hard.

Sometimes I think about joining other software people to do something as a group. Ideally, it would be with a couple of million behind us. I think if you're going into vertical markets, you don't need a couple million, you can struggle along, although it would sure help. But I think if you're going to develop any kind of reasonable software effort, you need to have partners. And you need to have financing. I won't do it on a shoestring anymore. It's not worth it.

What it comes down to is that I don't have the emotional energy to really try to make it big. I frankly feel it's very unlikely that I will ever develop another general purpose product on my own.

Postscript

The relationship between Don Hoodes and Randy Nielsen broke down not long after the interview and Hoodes stopped making payments. The only relief in an otherwise thoroughly distressing situation is that the contract had an arbitration clause, so the dispute will be resolved within a few months. If not for that clause, the matter could have dragged on through the courts for years and lawyers would be the only ones to benefit.

Randy says that if he ends up having to take the product back, he'll probably turn it into user-supported software the way Andrew Fluegelman and Jim Button have (see Chapter Thirteen).

Chapter Twelve

SMALL CAN BE BEAUTIFUL

The predominant philosophy at COMDEX is "bigger is better." You hear this being discussed and examined about as often as the proposition that breathing is good for you. In other words, it is part of the accepted dogma that everybody wants to either lead their industry or at least dominate some niche in it. If ever the subject does come up, some entrepreneurs will say that "go big or go bust" is a fact of life, that the size of the company is forced by the size of the market it is entering. Others just seem to run at the head of the pack because they prefer it up there. However, not all of the estimated 5000 software companies out there are trying to be superstars. Not everyone wants that kind of life. Size, it turns out, is a matter of both business strategy and personal style.

If there's one thing that all entrepreneurs have in common, it's a compulsion to do things their own way, yet self-awareness is not always part of the formula. The worst mistake an entrepreneur could make would be to design himself into a job for which he has neither the talent nor the inclination. Not everyone with the talent and timing to achieve a big success also has the temperament to enjoy the pressures and demands of the star quality enterprise.

While a small business may be more vulnerable to forces in the market and less tolerant of mistakes in management, it is also less dependent on the talent and investment capital of others. A small business can be more flexible, adapt to changes more easily, and it can even be more profitable in some cases than a mega-business that demands huge infusions of capital, advertising, and big deals to keep it going.

By far, the majority of software enterprises are small and anonymous, but that does not say they are not admirable or viable. Quite the contrary—small business is the American Way of Life.

PROSOFT

Debbie Tesler, Prosoft

Prosoft occupies one unit in a light-industry development in North Hollywood, CA. It is an immaculate and efficiently managed little operation of eight or nine people, meticulously arranged and laid out like a model for a small business, which it is. Founded in 1980 by Chuck and Debbie Tesler, Prosoft offers products for Tandy's TRS-80 line, including the word processor Newscript, and several utilities and games, some of which were written by their son, Glenn Tesler, when he was barely in his teens. He is fifteen now, and quite active in the company. Prosoft is emphatically a family operation and although profitable, it is small because the Teslers want it that way.

How did you get into software?

DEBBIE TESLER: We've always been in software.

CHUCK TESLER: We both graduated from college in 1962, and we joined IBM in Los Angeles three months later. We were married and twenty years old then.

Why did you join IBM?

CHUCK: It beats starving to death.

DEBBIE: A New York State employment agent told us that we had an aptitude for that kind of logic. My cousin worked for IBM in LA, so we got interviews and got hired. They taught us everything. It was very intense.

CHUCK: In the '60's, I loved that company. I liked the people, but I loved the *esprit de corps* and the supportiveness. The people were so bright and capable, a very unusual group of people. IBM is definitely not anything like the press or the public believe it to be. The motives are far less diabolical, far less centralized or intentional than people think. It's 300,000 very individual people. What IBM is like depends upon which of those people you are talking to.

I also loved programming. My real forte is machine language programming, and I can also program well in PL/I and FORTRAN and BASIC not at all in COBOL. But I had a lot of trouble learning how to use a computer. They were conceptually very difficult for me. Years later, when I first got a TRS-80 with the Z-80, which is a different set of instructions, I went through it all over again, and I had sixteen years of programming at that time. It was just as hard and conceptually difficult, and I look at my son who takes this stuff as though he was born with it, and I'm so jealous. It comes hard for me. But, I did very well all through the '70s.

DEBBIE: He was a Consulting Systems Engineer, and that is the highest you can go in IBM in a technical field. Very few can achieve that. It's not a matter of putting in time, but achievement.

CHUCK: I was in the right place at the right time. I worked hard, the projects I was on succeeded, and I had learned from Debbie to ask for rewards instead of sitting quietly hoping they would remember me. I was doing very well in terms of succeeding at projects, in bringing out major products which were well-used, and I was very happy in what I was doing. I had recognition, good money, I enjoyed my work. I never felt like I worked a day in that life. I had great toys to play with.

In 1978, I was working on a project with a friend of mine, and he kept running home after work to play with a microcomputer, and I said to him, "Why are you wasting time with a toy when there are these real computers available?" One time we went over to his house and he showed me this computer that he had built, and it was running Oasis, a very good operating system. So I started thinking, maybe there's something to this.

My brother Larry—he's one of the developers of Smalltalk at Xerox, and of the Lisa at Apple—he brought a Pet down and left it overnight. My son Glenn was ten then and he wrote something on it that surprised Larry, so I thought we should get one for the house. You know, kind of the way people get toys for their kids and the kid never gets a turn? I chose the TRS-80, which was the best of what was available at that time, and bought one at the beginning of '78. I fell so much in love with it that I didn't touch a mainframe computer again for about five months. I didn't expect that to happen.

I was very used to doing whatever I pleased at IBM. There were fifty technicians in that office, and I brought in 10-15% of the revenue all by myself, so they weren't about to mess with success. The attitude of IBM, not just toward me but toward most employees, assumes that you will be self-reliant and self-motivated. There's no such thing as punching a time clock. If you have a problem, yell for help, otherwise give periodic progress reports, that's all. For nine straight years I had one great manager after another, some of the best human beings ever to walk the face of the earth. They could motivate me, handle the politics that I never understood, clear the way so I could charge ahead. They didn't want their senior people like me to program, they wanted us to sell designs and solutions. We were in agreement for once, because I was falling in love with this little microcomputer and finding that it was a lot more powerful and could do far more than people like myself at IBM had thought.

Two weeks after I got the TRS-80, I got a new manager who all by himself balanced out the five supermen that I had worked under for the nine previous years. The only thing we agreed on was that this planet isn't big enough for the two of us, and he set out to get rid of me or destroy me. You have to understand that a manager can do that even though I made more money than he did and was in a higher position and was well thought of. All he had to do was start giving me mediocre ratings, and criticize my work.

DEBBIE: Something else that contributed to the frustration and a bit of bitterness over a period of a couple of years prior to Chuck leaving, is that he actually developed several products that IBM sells. He developed them on his own, after work hours, at home. IBM sells them, and took in $2 million a year then—now $10 million—in profit.

CHUCK: I worked on this thing for three years, a labor of love. I've always worked that way, since 1962. IBM has a program where they will sell software written on your own time, and they will pay you a royalty until a ceiling is reached, then you get nothing, ever. I had to argue and fight to get the ceiling raised to the absolute maximum of $13,000. Wow! There are now 5-10,000 copies out, and each one brings in $2000 a year for IBM. I understood the rules, but I told them the rules were clear but unfair and they had seen the last line of code they would ever get from me as an employee. That meant to them that I had an attitude problem. They're right, I do.

I couldn't find any more motivation in the company. The love of programming was still there, but I wanted to be paid. I was not getting raises any longer. Partly I had topped out, partly my manager didn't support me, partly the company was not structured to compensate someone who could produce something that normally requires teams of fifty or a hundred people to produce. So, I did two things: I started talking to some people at a large bank about

232

consulting or being their employee, and at the same time I started writing a word processor for the TRS-80.

Originally, it was just for myself. I went to buy Scripsit and... yechh! So I went home and started writing my own. And you know, almost none of my programming experience was relevant when I got to micros. I was used to megabytes of memory, never worried about it. This was very different.

Well, by September of 1980 the product was ready to sell, but you can't do that if you work for IBM, so I figured I would have to quit. Then the bank came back and agreed to take me on as a consultant with a guarantee of three days a week for nine months at $750 a day. Now I charge $1200 to $1500 a day and have no trouble getting it, but I didn't know then. I do some consulting even now, but mostly by mail. I don't like driving. The product I developed for IBM that makes them several million a year that they paid me $13,000 for, that was a diagnostic tool that measures what's happening in the computer. I spent three years writing that thing. It produces reports and graphs that show what's wrong. Once I left, IBM didn't keep teaching people how to use it, so everybody's got this thing, but they don't know how to interpret the reports. They come to me for that now.

I quit IBM on Labor day, 1980. From the time I was twenty until I was thirty eight years old, all I knew was IBM, these bright capable people, the protectiveness, the security, and suddenly we're out there on our own.

When did you start thinking of selling your word processor?
I don't know when it changed in my own mind from a program into a product. The word processor had just been growing, and was getting to where it would do things better than anything else on the TRS-80, and although I didn't know it, better than anything else on a micro. But I didn't know, I had never heard of WordStar, I had never heard of CP/M. I have never done market research, never looked at

other products. In September, 1980, I sent a one-sixth page ad off to *BYTE*, but not as a business. I just wanted to see what would happen.

I had no conception about what a business was or meant. I had no business experience. I never had to collect a bill, I never had to close a sale and get a signature for an order, I didn't have to worry about my next paycheck, I had no conception of what it all meant. The ad was mostly just for fun. It turned into a business almost by accident, and I guess I encouraged it just in case the consulting didn't work out.

The first little ad brought in $1400 the first month, and I blush to say that we were charging $35 for that word processor. The response made me think that we could get by on selling that if we had too. We live very modestly. But I didn't realize what it costs to run a business, I only looked at revenues. We figured out later that I was losing a few dollars on each sale. The first year or so it did $1200 to $1500 a month just on some little ads in *80-Micro* and *Basic Computing*. We had a phone put in, Debbie was running the business, and if anything technical came up, I would handle that at night or on the weekend. I was doing the consulting the rest of the time.

From the fall of '80 through the end of '81 the consulting did extraordinarily well. I picked up more clients, and was in fact consulting five days a week, and doing Prosoft evenings and weekends. Debbie was handling things during the day. And my son Glenn had started writing some things we could sell, too.

In April of '81 we came out with a revised version, and Glenn had written a portion of that. The first product was Subscript that we sold for $35, then $40, then we called the revised version Newscript and offered it first for $79 and said it would go to $199 at the end of the summer, which it did. When the price went up we got more sales. A lot more.

In the fall of '81, we were doing very well. By the end of '81 we were still operating out of our house, and the profits were high enough for a family of five to live well. The consulting was bringing in an incredible amount of money. I was getting more than $750 a day at most of the places I went.

January of '82 was interesting. The bank had run out of consulting money, so there went a lot of income. Four months later, the other company I was working for folded their operation also. But it also happened that in January of '82, Prosoft took in twice as much money as in December of '81. And by April of '82 we took in four times as much money as in any month in '81. The business had quadrupled in four months. We hired people, Debbie's mother, my friend Ron, and we came out with release 7 of Newscript, which was more Glenn's work than mine, and Newscript suddenly became the leading word processor on the TRS-80, other than what Radio Shack sells.

DEBBIE: That was when he had to stop consulting. There was no time for him to do both. He was working seven days and nights a week, and I was working a horrendous number of hours, too. I was doing the packaging at night. This was in '81. It was phones and advertising and everything else all day, and at night the packaging. My house was totally taken over. We had no personal life because we had people working at our home; we had people in our kitchen, in our den, we had an office temp. and the only place for her to sit was on the living room floor. We had merchandise in the house, we had packaging material, we had diskettes, cassettes, styrofoam beads, boxes, a thousand manuals. Every room was filled with stuff. When I got up in the morning, there were already people working in my house.

You know, Chuck said when it first started, I don't want an empire, I want to earn a comfortable living for my family. He said we would never, ever, have employees.

CHUCK: Money is important, without question, but this was not being done solely for the objective of making a lot of money. If we had millions of dollars free and clear, what would we do? I'm not going to sit on the beach for the rest of my life. I have to do something with my time, and largely I would still program because I like doing that.

Couldn't you have made more money more easily by continuing to pursue consulting?

CHUCK: Yes, no question about it. That's still possibly true, but more consulting doesn't interest me. I'm not sure Prosoft interests me that much, either, but it's something that happened to us instead of our making it happen.

But why did you choose to concentrate on this little business instead of consulting?

Consulting is labor intensive. If you're honest, you can only bill for the time you spend working, and that puts an upper limit on how much you can make. Now, I can make $1200 a day, or even $1500. That's good money, but if you don't get five days a week of work, it starts falling off. Once the original contracts run out, you have to find other clients, and you're not earning any money for that effort. Another thing with technical consulting is that your skills can become obsolete after a while. The market passes you by, requirements change, and you can't keep up indefinitely.

Why, after all these years, are you still programming for the TRS-80? There's a whole world of CP/M and MS-DOS out there. Aren't you going to end up a buggy whip maker if you stick with TRS-80?

You're only half right. You're right in that the TRS-80 is a buggy whip area, no question about it. The reason we still develop for it is that we have 8000 old customers and a few thousand that have bought our other products. I'm going to offer them a new word processor, Allwrite. It's far better than anything else on the TRS-80, and at better than a 50% discount, a very good price. I expect that several thousand of them will take me up on the offer, all at once. That will bring in a great deal of money. That explains why it still

pays for us to write for TRS-80. Thereafter, we're not going to do any more TRS-80 development, it doesn't pay.

Why don't you go into MS-DOS?
Oh, hell! That's the dumbest thing in the world. Have you seen the latest issue of *PC World*? We have an excellent product, Tallymaster, better than VisiCalc, but why haven't you heard of it? There's too much competition. Now, tell me about word processing competition in that field. I should go compete against Microsoft? PeachTree? MicroPro? Impossible!

Microsoft just put a demo disk of their new word processor in 150,000 copies of *PC World* with sixteen pages of documentation! There's a friend of mine three blocks from here, another ex-IBM software consultant, he came out with a word processor data base manager on the IBM-PC that has been advertised with full-page ads in *PC* and *PC World* for almost two years. Text Plus—and you've never heard of it. I have had this conversation with a lot of people. The companies that are making it on the PC are spending big bucks! Leading Edge spends $50,000 or more a month advertising a product that doesn't even exist yet. How can I compete against that?

The thing to do, you say, is come up with something that nobody else has thought of yet, and get there first. Tallymaster, in a sense, is that. It's an approach to spreadsheet work that human beings can use, but we don't have the resources to promote it.

If I were starting now, I don't know what I would do. If I could identify some nice little protected marketplace, sure, but I haven't been able to come up with one. Tallymaster is the closest I've come, and I don't know how to sell it. I'm not a marketeer.

Do you ever go to trade shows?
Hell, no! I'll tell you what bothers me. I go to these shows and it's like a street with used-car lots on it. Everybody hawking garbage at discounts and cutting each other's throats and saying anything to

make a buck. Here's these people that don't have a product, they don't have documentation, and they're such BS artists that they'll say and promise anything. I can't compete with that kind of individual. I couldn't when I was a kid, and I can't now that I'm in my mid-40s. And I need to. I can't go out and try to sell my products against liars... no, not liars, they're salesmen.

How good are your sales at Prosoft?
We've sold 8000 units, which is nothing by Microsoft or WordStar standards, but there's nothing on the TRS-80 that comes close. Newscript today counts for less than half our revenue. Back then it was probably three quarters. We had FASTER, a speed-up utility for BASIC that Glenn wrote. RPM, that measures the speed of disk drives. And we sold a spelling checker and an operating system from other companies, and a couple of utilities of our own.

Through the spring of '82, we were very profitable, the kind of profits that any of us would like. After that, our sales peaked at four and one-half times anything in '81—and we lost money every month. The reason was, we were spending too much on advertising, on salaries, on promotions that didn't work out. Except for ads in *80-Micro* and occasional direct mailings to customers, nothing's ever worked.

A year or fifteen months ago, we had four or five hundred dealers, of whom one hundred and fifty to two hundred ordered from us every thirty to sixty days. That's pretty good. And 75-80% of our sales were through dealers. Now, I don't think we have twenty strong dealers today.

DEBBIE: The dealers all ran from the TRS-80.

CHUCK: They told us, it's not your product, it's not your service, you're the last TRS-80 company we're still dealing with, but it's a dead market for independent dealers. Now look what happened. When we were doing this out of our living room, it was very profitable and was mostly direct sales with just a few dealers. We moved into other

238

offices, and then we moved here, and we had all these dealers, and never showed a profit—in fact we took a loss. Then the dealers disappeared gradually, and now we're back to the point where over half our revenues are direct mail order, and our revenues are down by one third, and we are profitable again. Because we don't have dealers. No discounts.

In the TRS-80 world, we only give dealers a 40-50% discount. If you want the honor of being allowed to sell CP/M or IBM, you have to give a 70% discount to some distributor. You can't sell to a dealer. I can't get to an IBM dealer. I have to go to a distributor.

DEBBIE: We are kind of inching into other fields. We have Tallymaster and another product on the IBM, but we just haven't promoted it yet, because we haven't figured out quite how to.

Postscript

What would have happened had Chuck Tesler originally decided to take home a CP/M machine or an Apple instead of the TRS-80? Apple actively encouraged third party software publishers, something Tandy has never done, and that marketplace has been far more lucrative. Having hitched his wagon to a recalcitrant star, Chuck Tesler and Prosoft have been led down a dwindling track to a crossroads. The Teslers believe that Tandy may be planning to phase out the TRS-80, but they are sure that one way or another it will surely disappear soon. Meanwhile, the Prosoft story is a serial that ends with, "Stay tuned, folks, for the thrilling resolution of today's drama."

Prosoft has an iron or two in the fire but Chuck hasn't stoked any of them up yet, at least not that he'll talk about. He plays his cards close to the chest, but with all that talent running around in the family, it's hard to get too worried about them. Chuck did say that Glenn is working on a product with another entrepreneur. Glenn has done the software part of a word processing accessory product that will do fancy formatting and spooling of files to be printed and Chuck thinks it could be a winner—if the other guy

CHAPTER TWELVE

would only carry through on the hardware end of the deal, which now seems bogged down on a back burner. Teamwork, anybody?

— ● —

THE T/MAKER COMPANY

Peter Roizen, T/MAKER Company

T/MAKER combines word processing, calculating, and data retrieval functions. In fact, it was probably the first integrated product on the micro market, but apart from a loyal cadre of fans it is little-known. This has been a direct result of the founder's "small is beautiful" philosophy and his non-competitive nature. Founder Peter Roizen lives near Washington, D.C., where he marketed the product, after a fashion, from his home until mid-1982 when his sister Heidi established offices in Mountain View, CA.

T/MAKER is an excellent and useful product that appeared early on the scene. It could easily have been a much bigger deal but that wasn't the boss's style or inclination. Whatever he did, he did well, but he did it *his* way.

PETER ROIZEN: I went to school at the University of California, Berkeley, in mathematics. That was in about '67, I think. I have a very poor memory.

I had the idea for what turned out to be the spreadsheet portion of T/MAKER way back in 1979. I was working with the World Bank, and I could see that there were plenty of people doing simple things for which we had many very complicated tools. I wanted to come up with something that was geared to the person who wasn't attempting anything terribly complicated.

My job was quite dry, so to keep my creative energy going, I started working on this idea. I bought myself a little 48K CP/M micro, and I started programming in the basement. It took about a year. You could call it a part-time effort, but I was at it pretty much every evening until eleven and all day Saturdays and Sundays. My wife was very patient, and fortunately we didn't have children at the time. I think now if I had to start over and try and do it, I wouldn't have the time in my life to devote to it.

I wrote the first version in CBASIC. There weren't that many languages around at the time. Now it's written in C which is much faster, and I think it's a language very well-suited to word processing type applications. Anyway, I worked at it until we had the thing ready to go in August, 1980.

Did you do any business planning at that time?
No, not at all. I thought it was a good idea, I thought one day it might be a basis for something, but it was more like a hobby. It really was. Later I started to realize that it was certainly a useful tool for a number of things, and I thought, well, let's see what we can do to sell it. Other people were selling things. VisiCalc came out about six months before that and when I first saw the name VisiCalc, I was really horrified because our thing is so much a visual calculator that I was worried it was the same idea. As it turned out VisiCalc is a very different approach, and a very different concept. But anyway, I had a full-time job and didn't have the time to set up anything, so I looked for people who were selling programs.

At the time Lifeboat Associates was a name that you saw quite a bit. I probably started talking with them about March of '80 when I had something to demonstrate. To be sure that I could demonstrate it, I drove up there with my machine in the back, carried it up the two flights of stairs, laid the thing out, and showed the guy what T/MAKER does.

SMALL CAN BE BEAUTIFUL

The arrangement I had with them was, eventually, fairly successful. It was a percent of net deal, where they promised to sell the equivalent of about a hundred units a month. At the time, a hundred units a month, like, my god, this is going to be the best-selling kind of program that ever hit the world.

Back then Lifeboat was pretty much the only CP/M distributor there was, but we began to regret to some extent the fact that we had an exclusive arrangement with them. Because as a distributor, you know, they sell a large number of products, many of which compete with our product. And with an exclusive arrangement—well, I mean, their interests and your interests are on somewhat of a divergent plan. I mean, they can stay in business without selling your product, but you can't stay in business without them selling it.

Well, I had quit my job in January of '81, six months after it started to sell. It was making revenues of about four or five thousand dollars a month or something. A bit shaky, you know, the numbers went up one month and down the next month, but I sort of felt that all my life I had wanted a chance to break out and do something on my own, you know, and not get up in the morning and go to some place and follow somebody else's orders.

So I started working on version two, which I guess came out in May of '81. It was written in C, so it was faster, and it had better documentation. I was still exclusively tied to Lifeboat. The initial agreement was for the duration of two years, so I continued enhancing it, trying to add new features, that kind of thing. I didn't really concentrate too much on the marketing.

Sales held for awhile, but with version two I really felt we had a significantly better product. And I could see that other products were having an enormous amount of success, like VisiCalc, who were selling oodles and oodles of copies. So we sort of decided that when the next year came around, we would not continue the exclusivity. Somehow we would try and take over the marketing angle of it ourselves. We figured we had better make sort of a product break of

some kind, so we started working on that, enhancing the word processing stuff, and the documentation.

The contract with Lifeboat ran out about August of '82, but we didn't have anything ready by then, and things sort of dragged on and dragged on. My sister was sort of involved, she was always interested in the company, but she was in school, so we weren't really in all that big a hurry to get going. We finally got the stuff together for COMDEX in November of '82, where we showed with one of our OEMs who was there.

With OEM licenses don't you get just a very small fraction of retail?
Well, I tend to look at these deals in terms of how many are we going to sell to the people that buy those machines if we *don't* have an OEM deal with them. So my own feeling is, I'm very keen on OEM bundling arrangements.

How many OEM deals do you have?
We have one OEM in Japan who evaluated the various spreadsheets and packages and came to the conclusion that T/MAKER was the best. Which is very nice, because I think in a lot of evaluations, they've gone and they've evaluated what has the biggest draw. We're not outrageously priced because we don't have the draw that some of the other packages have. Anyway, they came to Lifeboat and signed an initial agreement for a couple of thousand copies. Actually, I consider those people pretty much our best customers.

Back when your exclusive contract with Lifeboat ended, what was your strategy?
We were just beginning to think about it, as I say, but I really didn't do anything. I assumed that we were going to write distributors and ask them if they wanted to carry our products and stuff. And I had no idea that maybe that was something you ought to start a little bit

sooner. There was no real business organization, just me in my house. After COMDEX, we sort of went on like that a little bit longer, I would say until about April of '83, at which time my sister started trying to line up more distributors for the product, that sort of thing. She was in school, and there wasn't really anybody else that I wanted to set up, we were literally almost forced to sort of continue with no business organization, and just wing it on the basis that the product was known by some people.

She did a few things when she was still in school. She booked us into CP/M-83, and that was the first show we ever did. She got a few signs made up, you know, and hung them in a little ten by ten booth against the curtain. We pretty much had the whole family in the booth, my brother was there, my sister was there, my father was there, my stepmother was there, and my mother even came up one day.

When my sister got out of school, she wanted to set up a more ambitious organization, so we made friends with an advertising agency, and opened up the office in Mountain View. I still live near Washington, D.C., so the separation we have always held is pretty much that I will work on what I want to do, which is to continue with programming and developing, and she will work on marketing, which is actually what she likes to do. It's a pretty good deal. This started in the summer of '83.

Does anyone else work for the company besides you and your sister?
My brother did a lot of work on the documentation last summer, and my father does a lot of travelling for his television consulting business, so he also has a fair amount of experience. He can sell TV people. Since we opened the office, we hired another fellow, a friend of my sister's.

244

Do you take an active role in the day-to-day business?
I mostly talk to my sister on the telephone. I'm Chairman of the Board, so I set policies, like I recently set a policy that we don't do business with the Soviet Union. So I might set a policy like that. I let her pretty much pursue the business, but it's sort of up to me to decide if we're going to take venture capital or not take venture capital.

Did you go out out looking for investors?
Well, we had a business plan that called for venture capital, and when we started to talk to people, it became obvious that when you get money, you get it in exchange for something. We were looking for a couple hundred thousand dollars, but people were saying, well, you know, until we get our money back we need to have a certain controlling interest, or serious interest in the company. Or people would say, well, we need regular reports of income, and balance sheets, and this kind of stuff. In a small company like ours, we just don't have the time to devote to that kind of information presentation.

There's a couple of problems with venture capital from our side. Suppose we get a lot of money, we build ourselves up into a big thing, and then basically for those people to get their money out, you have to go public. I mean, you have to provide some vehicle for them to get their money out. And nobody is interested in earnings. I mean, people want capital gains, and I don't think earnings can generate the kind of gains they want.

I'm talking basically about venture capitalists. We could have looked more towards, you know, the doctors and dentists, but looking for money is a time-consuming task. It can consume time, consume your thoughts, you don't know really what you're doing until you make up your mind about it. Anyway, I went to see a number of these people. I actually made an offer to one person, but he made us a counter offer for about half, and I basically turned it down. And

CHAPTER TWELVE

also, you know, I don't like to have the responsibility of somebody else's money. It's a burden on me. If I take somebody's venture money, I think of it as money in my care, and now it's my responsibility to ensure that he gets all his money back.

So you finally decided not to go for outside capital?
I mean, it just seemed to me that what I want most in this company, is to have fun. I want to enjoy the company. I don't want to go to bed at night worrying about somebody's dollars that they've invested, or worry about payments. We like to pay our bills on time, you know. I want to be in a position where we pay our bills out of money we already have. So we slowed down our initial promotion efforts a little bit to keep in line with what was coming in.

Have you signed up some distributors?
Softsel, Software Wholesalers, yeah. Softsel took a long time, I mean even to get a signed piece of paper took a long time. It took about six months, or even longer. My sister first contacted them about a year ago. Software Wholesalers was very quick, that was no problem at all. Certain of these places seem to, you know, you send them a contract, it gets signed, they buy on your terms, and a few of them they even pay on time. But when you start to deal with bigger places, you send them a contract, they send you a five-page contract that you can't understand, and you kind of make the best of it.

I don't know that it's necessarily fair to name names, but in one case I finally turned over some bills to a collection agency and I just gave up. But now we have a little more leverage, because we're selling a little bit better now, so that means these companies run out of stock, and when they run out of stock, they want to have more. And when they want to have more, they have to pay their bills.

We would rather sell a thousand at a very low price than sell five at a high price, so at first I set the price scale based on the quantity ordered, which seemed very sensible. But the problem is that, say you ship a hundred or even fifty. Okay, then they have a $5,000 bill. They also might have your product in inventory for quite a while, so you've actually created a situation where you actually lose your leverage to collect your money. In a sense I created the reverse of what I actually wanted to have. We've changed it now.

To some extent, this is almost a consignment type business. People don't pay their bills until they've sold the product and collected the money and need more. You can talk to lawyers, and I don't think that there's basically anything that anybody can do. So we try and keep the outstanding balances at reasonable sums considering what they do.

Where does your end-user demand come from?
We have a very loyal user base, I think. We get some letters that are really almost like fan mail. I mean, people will say, gee, I have my word processor, I have my spreadsheet, I have all these things, but I really use T/MAKER every day, and I love it. And so we have a loyal user base who tell their friends, and that generates some sales. We've also had very good reviews in most of the magazines. It's one of the major things we pursue, really, because it's cheap. You watch for an article, say about an integrated package like Lotus, and then you write a personal letter and say, well, did you know that there's been a package around since 1980 that in fact does word processing and spreadsheeting?

Aren't you conducting any kind of an ad campaign?
As soon as the office opened in August of '83, my sister had an ad drawn up, and we started to run a few ads. We had a double-page color ad. She was always thinking, well, we'll get some money to cover this kind of promotion, but it didn't come in. We're currently financing the ad campaign out of pretty much the profit I had made in the previous two years, when I was just drawing royalties and had

nothing going. So we have been running at a pace where we actually are probably spending more than we're earning.

What have your total sales been? And how many do you ship currently?

If you add up everything, our total is like about 10,000. But of those, about 4,000 are in Japan. I would say we're shipping about 300 a month now, excluding all the OEM deals. If you add in OEMs, then our numbers are considerably better. I figure that on about 300 sales a month we can run our company and do a little bit of advertising.

You know, this always gets me—we're always in this transitional period where next month we're either going to make a million or we're going to go broke. And the truth of the matter is that we never make that million next month, and we never go broke either. Somehow we manage, we pay all our bills, everybody gets paid, and the next month now looks the same.

What are your strategies for the future?

Well, we're going to try and do more creative things that are less expensive. We tried some big ads, we got some responses and stuff, but they consume a lot of money in a hurry. And we're sort of trying to think of things we can do that are maybe a little bit more labor intensive, and will produce results. We don't know, we're looking for them.

We attend a lot of shows. We're going to have a mail-out of a demo kit to a bunch of dealers for free. The demonstration disk and a booklet costs us maybe $12, and we could mail that to a thousand dealers for the price of one ad. So we're looking more for strategies like that. We bounce these ideas around, like I've been suggesting maybe we ought to have seminars in the office. You know, take a more regional approach to the Bay area. Maybe we could get ourselves a big company look in the Bay area at a cheaper price than we could get ourselves a big company look across the whole nation.

248

And since lots is going on here, maybe that's a strategy. I mean, really, we're looking.

I say again, maybe in the same vein of naiveté, but I believe there must be ways to do it other than by pouring money on it, what they call "buying your market share." I don't want to do that.

Do you have any advice for budding entrepreneurs?
I'm not the MBA style manager, first of all. I don't have great advice. I just sort of followed my own path and was trying to achieve some reasonable sense of self-fulfillment.

We want to survive, not because we're shrewd at business, but because we have a decent product that we provide at a fair price. I have one son, and I feel that T/MAKER, a little bit, is like another child, like T/MAKER's a certain manifestation of myself. I mean, I feel that this thing, it's a reflection on us and we have to make it in our own way. For better or worse, okay?

Don't you ever get attracted to the flash and dazzle out there and want to try some of that?
I think that one day we may have to try some flash and pizazz and what not. But if you look at our package, you know, we're really not going into pizazz. I mean, we do things that really provide people with a useful, productive tool. Our problem is that we basically like to be honest in our advertising. I mean, if you walk around the floor here, everything is the "ultimate," the "legend before its time," the "total system," the greatest of this, the greatest of that. We like to explain our product pretty much how it is. It's somewhat of a handicap, because if someone walks into our booth, we don't say, hey, this is ten times better than Lotus or something. We say Lotus and T/MAKER are very different products, these are the jobs we feel that Lotus does a better job on, and these are the jobs that we feel T/MAKER does a better job on.

CHAPTER TWELVE

SMALL CAN
BE BEAUTIFUL

I guess I sort of have this basic underlying faith that if—you know, I could be all wrong, but we're still alive, and we're still in business—if you sell a quality product, and if you sell it fairly, and if you do your best to put that on the market, without getting lots of money and lots of pizazz, that you will stay in business. People will find you.

Chapter Thirteen

FREEWARE, CHEAPWARE, AND USER-SUPPORTED SOFTWARE

If small can be beautiful, can smaller be beautifuller? With today's jammed up market, where trying to start up is like throwing yourself against a wall, some people just don't care to go through that form of self-abuse. Until the distribution problem is solved, we will never see or hear about untold numbers of interesting and worthy programs, simply because there isn't room for them on dealer's shelves, or in the crowded and precious pages of industry magazines. *C'est la vie.* Or is it?

Some programmers have begun to look at the idea of user-supported software as a viable alternative for their products. Still in its infancy, the concept was initiated in the spring of 1982 by Andrew Fluegelman, a book maker who later became editor of *PC World* magazine.

Andrew wrote a fine communications program, PC-Talk, but he was resisting the idea of taking it onto the market when he had a brilliant flash of insight. He would give it away, and ask for a modest donation from people who liked it and used it. Guess what—it worked. He calls his concept *Freeware*, a trademarked proprietary name.

Once the program was launched, it spread quickly by word of mouth and even picked up some rave reviews in industry magazines. That's how the idea spread to Jim Button who went the same route in August, 1982, with PC-File, a powerful little database program. These programs compare favorably with expensive commercial products, yet they are either very cheap or free, depending upon whether you get your copy from a friend or from the publisher and whether you make the requested donation.

The collective wisdom in the industry has been that productivity software is not price sensitive. In fact, the biggest sellers tend to be at the high end of the price range, suggesting that buyers think the higher price means higher quality. Price reductions have not helped the sales of sluggish products like DataStar, and price rises have actually improved the sale of other products. However, Douglas Clapp, a regular contributor to computer magazines, thinks that user-supported programs, especially PC-Talk, are taking a toll on sales of commercial programs. As he says, 'If you open the window and lean out, you can almost hear the corporate teeth gnashing.' If he is correct, and if more users become sophisticated enough to take advantage of the concept, it could be that user-supported software will be a contributing pressure in bringing prices down.

The user-supported concept offers a very relaxed and unpressured way to propagate your program. You don't worry about copyrights and protections, and you don't worry about pirates. In fact, pirates are allies who help distribute the program for you. Not satisfied with letting nature take its course, Jim Wallace decided to work a refinement on the user-supported software concept by offering kickbacks to his users. Once you become a registered user of Jim's PC-Write for $75, you will then get $25 for every person who voluntarily registers from a diskette with your registration number. Tuppersoft?

USER-SUPPORTED
SOFTWARE
253

Andrew Fluegelman, Headlands Press

We don't really have to argue whether user-supported software is a community service that pays its own way, or just a different way to be in business, because in either case it provides a much-needed alternative channel of distribution. It may become a popular choice for programmers who don't want to beat their brains out eighteen hours a day to make a go of it in the marketplace. User-supported software just might become an important force in the software world, so let's hear from the guy that created the concept:

ANDREW FLUEGELMAN: I got my PC when they first came out, in October of '81. I think I had one of the first thousand machines. At that time I was working on a book with another author, and one of our visions was that we would write chapters on our individual computers and send them back and forth over the phone. I went and got a Hayes modem and the $40 IBM communications support, hooked it up, and to my dismay discovered that I could not send my files to her. I spent the rest of that first night looking at the program, seeing whether I could modify it, and then the next morning I started writing PC-Talk.

You must have done some programming before?
Actually, I had not. I guess at that point, January of '82, I probably had my computer about three months, but had never touched one before. I enjoyed it a lot, and spent a lot of time, had a lot of fun with it.

What was your background before you got interested in computers?
I was managing editor of the *Whole Earth Catalog*. I was a publisher. I had spent about the last eight years as a writer and an independent book producer. I produced books for national publishers, took them

254

from ideas through to printed books, and did a couple of projects a year. I did subjects that interested me—football, sushi, travel, whatever. The book at the time was about computers.

I'm really impressed that someone who never wrote a program before just up and wrote something that has been reviewed in major magazines as being an excellent product.
Well, I don't know, there are some times when I'm impressed too. I enjoy programming, and I've learned a lot from a lot of people. In writing the code one of my goals was—knowing that I was going to make it available to other people—trying to make it readable, accessible, and logical. You sort of air your dirty laundry when you publish your source code, and that was important to me. I think that helped me to write it well. I know now if I were to go back, I would do it completely differently; you know, your skills get better.

At any rate, I started writing this program just to send my files to my co-author. I got that to work, then I was playing around on networks and bulletin boards, really enjoying it, and kept adding little enhancements to this communications program. Just doing things that I wanted it to do. A couple of months later I passed it out to a few of my friends, and they liked it, and they said I should publish it or do something with it. At the time, there still was no good communications software for the PC other than the IBM program which didn't do very much. This was about March of '82.

Two things led me to the Freeware idea. If I hadn't been in publishing for eight years, I probably would have gone ahead and talked with publishers and made a contract or arranged for distribution and done all the things that I had been doing in the book business. But I had really been through that so many times, and was feeling the joy of this new computer age, so somehow it felt as though I wanted to do something a little different. Beating the same path didn't seem appropriate to me.

CHAPTER THIRTEEN

The other thing was that I had to deal with this issue of copy protection, and I didn't have the foggiest idea how to do that, and I knew that even if I hired someone expensive to do it, it would last about one afternoon.

About that time the local TV station, KQED, was having their annual pledge drive for public-supported television. Somehow that triggered a connection, and in a flash the word 'Freeware' and the user-supported notion popped into my mind. So I thought I would send my program around, and invite people to make copies, and also invite them to make a contribution if they found it worthwhile. It felt right.

So what I did was, I put a notice on *THE SOURCE*, on the IBM-PC bulletin board. At the time, that was a good source of gossip and news, but now it's become hopelessly clogged with advertising, which is what I had done myself. The notice said I had this communications program, what it did, and if you'd like a copy, send me a blank disk and I'll send it to you for free and invite you to make a $25 contribution if you like it. It was about five days later that I got my first two disks in the mail. It was a real shock. It was about a week later that I got my first contribution back. Really, from then on, I think what made the thing catch on was people who got PC-Talk started to put their own notices on *THE SOURCE* saying, hey, this is really good, you should check it out.

I started getting more orders, more contributions, and then the program reviews in some of the national magazines. At the time it was different enough to be newsworthy and to have people take notice. It really spread by word of mouth. I'm rather proud of the fact that I've not invested a single dollar in advertising. I think at this point I'm sort of committed to that just because I like the idea of it.

PC-Talk was out for about three weeks, and although there were no bugs in it, I started hearing about so many enhancements and situations that other people were running under that I hadn't even conceived of that I started making modifications. There was version

256

1.02 then 1.05, and about May of '82, PC-Talk II came out, and that's really the one that most everybody is using. Through the summer I was sending out a lot of programs and getting a lot of suggestions. It was in about March of '83 that I came out with PC-Talk III which mainly included the error-checking protocol, expanded the dialing directory, and had a much better user interface. I totally rewrote the program. I sent a mailing label to all the people who had made contributions, and told them to send me back the label with $10 and I'd send them the new version of the program. And I also raised the suggested contribution to $35. I'm pleased with the way I was able to take care of the people who had supported me earlier.

By this point, the program has become pretty well established. There are a lot of people who just order it by mail, send in their $35 in advance, and we send them back a program. That probably accounts for about 80% of our business now. The other 20% are people who send us disks and have us put the program on them for free. We're kind of discouraging that now, mainly because it takes so long to make a disk copy and deal with everybody's packaging, check the postage and so forth. Our arrangement now is that you send in $35 and get two disks with the program and the documentation on it.

That's not exactly Freeware so much as cheapware, isn't it?
The difference is that I encourage users to make copies and pass them on to other users. Also, I supply the BASIC source code on the disk, and that's another important aspect of the Freeware concept. If you're going to sell someone a program, and if you don't give them the source code, they can't make changes or improvements. I've gotten many suggestions from people who have looked at the code and suggested things that could be done better, and also it lets people adapt it to specialized needs.

The nice thing about it is that when you've offered the program in an open unrestricted way, the suggestions you get never come in the form of angry letters or complaints. People make their remarks in the same spirit in which the program is offered. Working in secret is a very difficult way to be creative.

How many donations do you get from people you've never heard of before?

I would guess maybe about 10% of what I receive is from people sending in voluntary donations. It's very hard to tell. Frankly, I'm happy with this. One of the underlying theories that I had is that when you buy a piece of software, you know, you might have twenty word processors that you try at one time or another, but sooner or later there's the one that you really use. The cost of sampling all those programs really shouldn't be very high to you as a user, but when you have decided on your program of choice, then you're probably happy to pay for it. That's my thought—I think it's making it easy for people to try it, and if in fact they use PC-Talk, they should make the contribution.

The way our business works now is that someone will get a copy of the program from someone else, they'll use it for a while, decide that they do like it, then they'll send us $35 and order their own *bona fide* copy. And one of the things we do is, whenever someone sends us a voluntary contribution, we send them the current version of the program, just as a way of making sure that they do have the real thing and reinforcing contributions.

What kind of income is this making?

I don't know, I don't like to give numbers because it's so variable. It's certainly supporting the person who's running the business for me. I mean, now that I'm the editor at *PC World*, I really can't spend my working time doing it. One of the things I discovered was that distributing programs via the Freeware concept does not alleviate the need to provide user support, and that takes time. Anyway, she makes about $1500 a month, and it pays for the overhead, and it makes enough extra to make me feel as though it's been worth the couple of years of effort getting the thing going. I do think this is a real potential business.

If I have one disappointment about the whole project, it's that I thought this idea would become another force in software, and although it has worked for Jim Button, there aren't that many good user-supported programs that have come to light.

What do you look for in a good user-supported program?
It's just exactly the same as with a commercial program. You have to have a good user interface, good error trapping, good documentation. I haven't seen that many good ones. Doug Clapp speculated that someone might write a good spreadsheet program. I think the opportunity is there. If someone were to come out with a useful, innovative, well-done program and offered it the same way, at this point it might make news again. You know, here's the next good user-supported program. I think a good program would get good press, but you know, it really does have to be a good program.

—— ● ——

The woman that runs Andrew's PC-Talk operation answered the phone one day and sounded more than a little harried. She said they are snowed with work and she can't quite keep up with it. Is that one of the sweet sounds of success?

Jim Button, Button Computer Software

The next person to do well with user-supported software is Jim Button. He says that the real reward for him is seeing his program, PC-File, used and appreciated by so many people. He has a big stack of fan mail to keep him warm on cold Seattle nights. Jim makes a good living from his PC-File program, and will use part of it to send his son to college. In style.

What line of work were you in before you wrote PC-File?

JIM BUTTON: Well, I've been a computer consultant here in the Seattle area for about 16 years, mostly on large mainframes. I'm still doing that, and I do PC-File at home in the evenings.

Why did you go to the user-supported idea?
At first I just sent my program out to friends, and they made suggestions which I would run home and work into it. It went through a great many versions, and then I ended up with a program I called PC-File. My friends were starting to hand it around, and I got more phone calls and correspondence, so I thought I had better do something.

I was encouraged to market it through normal channels, but I wasn't interested in going that route. Some friends had seen Andrew Fluegelman's PC-Talk, and I was kind of encouraged by his Freeware concept, so I thought I'd give that a try, because I thought I had a program that could conceivably get spread around the country that way.

I sent a copy to Andrew and told him I wanted to join up with him. He was delighted and enthralled with the program, and said he had turned down a bunch of others, and that mine was the first good one he had seen that he wanted to be associated with. That's how it got started, but the problem started that people couldn't keep Andrew and me straight. The work was becoming overwhelming, because I'd have to reroute stuff about PC-Talk to Andrew, and I'd get questions about it, and the same was happening to him. Or we'd get one check for double the amount from people who would want both programs.

So we had to solve that by separating ourselves more clearly. Neither of us wanted to take total responsibility for distributing both programs, and we could see then that the sooner we disassociated the better.

How many copies have you sent out?
I would have to guess, because I only keep track of people that send a contribution. But I think that out of our home, we have sent out 5-6000 diskettes. We've had contributions from about 3000 people.

Who works on this besides yourself?
I mainly do the program updates and answer questions and that sort of thing. My son, John, does all the distributing. He gets home from high school and goes right to work, and spends an average of three or four hours a day.

Do you have any plans for the future?
Oh, I have a lot of plans. I really can't drop it because I'm having so much fun with it. I'm going to rename the program at the end of the year to PC-File III, because other programs have come out with the name PC-File and I want a name that won't be confused with them. I never did get a copyright or a trademark. And there will be a lot of major enhancements.

Do you have any other programs in line?
I just started distributing a second program, a communications program. It's like PC-Talk, only it has a considerably different flavor, major differences. It's a program that I developed for my own use

CHAPTER THIRTEEN

and enhanced over time, then I started giving it out to friends, and it just naturally grew into another product. I call it '1-RingyDingy.' Some people have said they wouldn't be caught dead using a program by that name, but the reason I picked it was because I had so much trouble with the PC-File name, and I said, here's a name that no one else will have.

Do you think you might go into it full time?
No. I don't have any plans to stop my other work. My wife is probably spending four or five hours a day on it now—answering the phone, correspondence, backing up John on the distributing. John does pretty much the rest of it, and when I get home, I work on enhancements and things like that.

Is this a good alternative to commercial marketing?
I get a lot of phone calls from programmers asking should they or shouldn't they do it, how to do it, how much can they make. I tell them that if their program is good and of wide general interest, that they can make a lot. Our income on this program averages between $500 to $1000 a day right now, and there aren't many expenses.

The other concern I tell them about is that I got a lot of publicity because the concept was new, and that benefited me greatly. When they come along a year or two later, they may not get so much publicity because it's old news. They have to get it rolling without the advantage that Andrew and I had. Sometimes they want me to handle their program, but I don't have the time for it.

Have you seen Bob Wallace's PC-Write program?
Yeah, but I don't like the way he prostitutionalizes the idea of freeware. He asks $75 for a registered copy, and promises to send you a $25 kickback for every person that voluntarily registers from your registered diskette, Rather than the motivation being honesty and forthrightness, he relies upon greed.

Postscript

Jim Button has since raised his suggested donation (the price to become registered) to $45, and both Andrew Fluegelman and Jim Button are discouraging people from sending in disks to have the programs copied for free. They both now prefer that people send them $10, for which they will provide data and documentation disks by return mail.

User-supported software is definitely a profit-oriented system, but it is also low-key, friendly, benevolent, and not greedy. I only wish that Andrew didn't use the name Freeware, because it seems like a slight misrepresentation, and because it confuses user-supported software with the public domain software which is absolutely free without caveat or conditions. For example, Ward Christensen, a founding father of public domain software and computer bulletin boards, has contributed numerous excellent programs to the public domain, including a CP/M communications program called MODEM that has been so popular that it has become an industry standard protocol.

Chapter Fourteen

NEW FRONTIERS IN MICRO SOFTWARE

All the sound and fury at COMDEX and in the marketplace has really been about relatively minor differences between competing programs in only five basic categories: systems software (includes operating systems, communications, networks, windows), word processing, database management, spreadsheets, and graphics. Make that six if you want to create a different category for programs like Lotus 1-2-3 that integrate applications from the other five groups.

This is not to say that some programs are not better than others; the point is that only rarely has there been a quantum leap forward into a completely unique and different class of commercial software. Word processing, data management, and spreadsheets for the microcomputer were all introduced around 1979, but there was not another categorical innovation in applications software until 1983/4. Now there are two—the first expert system for micros from Human Edge, and the first intelligent information system from Dayflo.

The entrepreneurs in this chapter have broken new ground in microcomputer software design with advanced technology and fresh concepts built into big, innovative programs. These people and their products are setting the pace for the crowds that will soon jump on their bandwagon chanting next year's industry buzzwords. These companies are the hottest new entries in the superstar sweepstakes.

EXPERT SYSTEMS

Possibly the most original and unique of the new software products is an expert system from Human Edge of Palo Alto, CA. In oversimplified terms, an expert system is software that provides the benefit of expert knowledge in some specific area. Ideally, it can be like having your own specialist on constant call.

The Human Edge product line combines the field of applied psychology with hard core expert experience and brings them both to bear on problems of sales, negotiations, and management. For any given problem, the program prompts you to describe yourself, the person you are dealing with, and the goals of the situation—then it prints out several pages of specific, cogent, and insightful advice. The first product released was Sales Edge, then Negotiation Edge and Management Edge.

Sales Edge works on several levels. First, it gives practical advice in voluminous detail. Secondly, even when the advice doesn't seem to fit, it is still thought-provoking. Most important, in order to use the Sales Edge, you have think in a new and different way about the person you are dealing with; the program thoughtfully helps out with words and concepts to stimulate your thinking. Using this product could easily improve the style, sensitivity, and consciousness of many a salesperson. This is a clear example of how software can change the way people think.

James Johnson, Human Edge Software, Inc.

It is refreshing to discover something practical and useful from the field of psychology, and it is a stroke of genius to have made this knowledge widely accessible through the use of software. Both the product and the Human Edge company that publishes it are the creations of Dr. James Johnson.

Did you know what you were getting into when you got started in the software business?

JIM JOHNSON: No. Well, I knew to a certain degree. I had been a sort of an academic entrepreneur, in that I had started at least three different academic departments in psychology and was used to being an administrator within the academic world. I was the chairman of a department of psychology, a vice-chairman of a department of psychiatry, the head of a professional school, and some of these I had built myself. I founded a company in 1977 called Psych Systems, which developed and sold computerized psychological testing systems to psychiatrists and psychologists, an OEM vertical market. Psych Systems does about $8 million a year, and has a hundred employees. But I didn't have a sense of what a consumer marketing company was going to be, and that was very different for me.

Psych Systems grew out of my research in the early '70s on how you use computers to do assessment. As I got more into it, the idea occurred to me that you could not only use computers for psychological assessment, but you could use computers for assessing people's interactions. We did some research and found out that it's fairly easy for someone to assess other people, so then it was a question of figuring out a way to take the interaction between two people to develop a strategic plan for something like sales or management. In 1981, I began doing the literature reviews to see if there was enough research to, say, do a program for negotiation. And in 1983 we incorporated Human Edge. Right now, we have a staff of about twenty.

When did you change your focus from personality assessment and interpersonal relations, to strategies for manipulation of people?
Well, I don't think it's manipulation of people (laughs). It's so you can present yourself in a better way, so that other people will like you better.

It's sort of parallel to the computer industry. Right now everybody is wondering in the computer area, what do you do with computers after you're done with your word processing and spreadsheets? Well, I was thinking about what do you do with assessment. You just describe somebody, and then there's nothing to do afterwards, so I got interested in using concepts related to assessment to actually do something, to make interventions in life in some way.

It's not so easy to take a three dimensional situation where you've got something about a person over here and a person over there, and then their relationship. It's very difficult, so we had to get down to basic concepts, the four or five basic personality constructs that are true—not in a psychopathological sense, but in an everyday sense. How outgoing is a person, how conscientious, how kind, how much do they worry?

The way the program goes together is, first of all, you have to review everything in both the popular and scientific literature on a topic. If it's the sales area, you get every book you can on sales. Then you go and review all the scientific literature on what's related to selling, and find out the rules there. Then you get a group of people—writers, businesspeople, sales experts, and behavioral science people—and they go through everything, and abstract out all the advice. Then it has to be categorized as to where it goes. Some of that advice will be for closing, some will be for how to open a presentation, some will be how to proceed, and so on. Then you take the interactions between types of people and match them to each item of advice.

Each program has thousands of sentences, over 400,000 words of text. In any situation, you have a base level of 144 possibilities for a sentence to come out. We look at and categorize people in twelve major areas. You have twelve on the customer's side and twelve on the seller's side, so that gives you 144. First of all, the behavioral science people have to decide how personality type eleven is apt to get along with personality type nine. So you have that stuff that has to be woven into all the other considerations to select sentences of advice.

How much capital has it taken to get Human Edge started?
It's cost us about half a million dollars to develop our programs, and we have two and three-quarters programs done. The advertising will cost about $2 million next year, so figure $3 to $4 million. Right now it's about a million and a half.

How would you have launched this product without your multi-million dollar Psych Systems company behind you?
Raising the money isn't too hard to do if you have a good idea, and if you're persistent, and you put a business plan together and present it to people. You have to learn how to be turned down a whole lot, but I think if you have a truly good idea, and if you're convinced of it, you'll find people to back it. An idea is worth a hell of a lot. If you're talking about a nothing idea, like let's make a new can of Coke and call it Today Cola, you've got to have a lot of money, and you've got to have dull management people and you've got to have a lot of stuff like that. But if you have a truly good idea like a Xerox machine, or the original VisiCalc, or anything original, then the same drive puts the company together.

Have you got a marketing strategy?
Being involved in the intersect of psychology and computers for a long time, I knew that there would be a tremendous amount of resistance early on. Those experiences forced me to study a scientific discipline called "change technology," and I developed a strategy before we even took our office space. We signed up an advertising firm and a PR firm to work with us in laying out the ideas. When you don't have a product that people intrinsically understand right away, you have a tremendous amount of education to do because they can't even conceive what the product does.

It would be interesting for you to sit in our booth and see people come up, and they say, "Oh, what kind of spreadsheet is this?" It strikes me as crazy that there are 80,000 people here, and acres and acres of equipment, and they only think of three things: spreadsheets, word processing, and data processing. This field has got to fall apart, I mean, it's so boring. You get sick to death hearing about another new word processor. So one underlines, and another one doesn't. Who cares? I really think this industry is boring.

If I was a manufacturer, I would be searching for new types of products, like Human Edge, that offer a chance of the industry growing rather than dying. I walk down these aisles, and what the hell do I care if Fujitsu has another MS-DOS system, or Epson, or whoever? Nothing new has happened. Nobody is announcing a new chip here, or a new operating system that's a major advance.

What do you think it is that drives people to become entrepreneurs?
Well for me, it's like my mother says: I can't hold a job (laughs). No, I think maybe some people like boring things, and some people like exciting things. I can't imagine going to work for General Motors, I can't imagine looking up and saying I've got thirty years to go in this life.

CHAPTER FOURTEEN

Sadly, there are a lot of people who work for money as opposed to personal gratification. I don't do that, I don't work for money. I had more than enough money to live for the rest of my life. I could travel, I could write, I could fool around, anything. So, I mean, why would I risk it all? Because it makes life exciting. I'm not hanging around saying, well, in twenty more years I can retire. I don't even think that. I think what I am doing now is exciting.

A lot of people have romantic notions of what being in business is like, but what kind of person do you think is most likely to succeed at it?

The stereotype of the entrepreneur is pretty well known. I mean, they are sort of hard driving, they believe in ideas a little more than they believe in people, they are self-righteous, they get an idea and they stick to it even though everybody says it won't work. They like the excitement of something that is different and new. They have to be extroverted, they have to be sort of leader type people.

If you take the standard extroverted kind of person who plods along, they can work in large organizations and they can work their way up by working hard, and being liked by their bosses, and so on. But I think the entrepreneurial person, the only way they're really going to get to the top, is by doing it themselves. They are not political enough, actually, to make it in large organizations, is my belief. They have to build their own organization.

What advice would you give someone who wants to be a software entrepreneur?

I think the entrepreneurial aspect of life is fun. I mean, I'm forty-three years old, and I like to get up every morning. My life is exciting, and I do what I want to do. I would certainly encourage anybody to do that. As far as software, for somebody to become a software entrepreneur and do another boring word processing program, or calculation program or database or something like that, I'd say stay home.

My belief is that money isn't nearly as important as making a contribution. If you don't contribute something, if it isn't something interesting and new, then who cares? I wouldn't personally be an entrepreneur to start up another me-too company. I'd be as bored doing that as I would be working on the assembly line at General Motors. I wouldn't do it. Every company I've started has been my own thing, my own invention. Disseminating new ideas, that's what's exciting.

So my advice is to invent something good, then go out and sell it. It's hard, but it's fun. If you don't, if you're just going to start a McDonald's, then who cares? To get a job, start a McDonald's or start a spreadsheet company, to me they're all the same.

Do your employees have participation in the company?
Yes. Everybody has shares in the company.

What else do you do to keep your staff motivated and working as a team?
You have to build a corporate culture that is unique. You do things to make people aware that you are in a startup situation. You have to build a history, first of all, so you take pictures when there was no furniture in the office, and then a month later there is furniture and people say, "Yeah, remember when. . .?" and it's only a month ago. And when you come to COMDEX, you do things like instead of flying down, which would be cheaper, we had everybody drive down so they can remember the old days when we were working on a tight budget. In reality, it ends up costing more to do that. It costs more in terms of money, and tiring people.

The other thing is, you need to work them. The whole organization needs to work all the time. We work until midnight; we work every day. We even worked on Thanksgiving. We have a corporate culture where people who don't work are considered not to have the right stuff. If somebody gets sick, they are considered not to have entrepreneurial abilities if they don't come in anyway. And I tell them, "Okay, you are paying your dues right now. You're learning how to do it, and I'll help you get whatever you want. You give me a couple of years of your life right now, and I'll help you next."

Being in business can be tough. You don't even realize how it's wearing on you, until suddenly it occurs to you that you've been waking up two weeks in a row with a headache because you've been grinding your teeth at night. Anxiety. It's because you never know what's going to happen, and it's *real* hard work. As an entrepreneur, you always have to sort of bob and weave. If something doesn't work, you have to switch directions, and try that. And if that doesn't work, you've got to go back the other direction and try something else until it does work. You know you're right, but you also know it's a tough nut to crack. And so it wears on you, and you see everybody in the organization saying they are suffering from burnout, and they want to talk about being burned out after a few months, but you know that if you are worn down, you have to work harder.

What I do is I work until midnight, and I read until four. I still try and read a book a day, and I have three or four hours of sleep. I mean, that's life, and I know it's going to be that way for a year or so, but you have to live with it. I know that it's going to be hard, I know that I'm going to feel rotten sometimes, get sick, but you don't stop.

Now you're talking about the gnawing, grinding anxiety, but before you were saying it's all so exciting, and how you look forward to waking up everyday? You mean both things are true for you at the same time?

Oh, yes. Sure.

Jim, you're a sick man.
(Laughs.) But the anxiety doesn't last for long. Let's say you're trying to work on something and things aren't going together, it's gnawing at you for days, and then suddenly it goes together, and you feel good, and you get that high period. It's like Aquinus said, you know, there has to be evil so you can know good.

Postscript

Jim Johnson understands that people can be extremely productive and creative under pressure, but it sounds like he institutes pressure intentionally. There is a big difference between being exuberantly driven from enthusiasm or team spirit, and being manipulated and compelled to be enthusiastic. Long term, forced enthusiasm can become counter-productive when it turns into burnout, as is illustrated by Silicon Valley statistics that show an unusually high incidence of divorces and drug, alcohol, and financial problems.

In a phone conversation, Dr. Johnson explained that in order to succeed, any new organization needs to be two or three times more productive than an established outfit of the same size. His management works hard to set an example, and the staff works hard to fit in. He says that those late-hour sessions when everyone has their hair down are very important for developing the sense of cohesiveness and camaraderie which is so essential to any new enterprise. In fact, he thinks a history of hard times is necessary. People have to become aware of their capabilities; not everyone will fit in, he says, and some may find that they would be better off in a low-key operation like General Motors or some government job.

More on Expert Systems

It is interesting to compare Human Edge's second product, Negotiation Edge, with a similar expert system being developed by Roy Nierenberg at Experience in Software in Berkeley, CA. Roy's father, Gerard Nierenberg, is a noted author and authority on negotiation who has led seminars for over 115,000 corporate executives. The Nierenberg software leads you step-by-step on a long and somewhat arduous journey through the Nierenberg training program, avoiding pat answers in favor of teaching you a method. The Human Edge program is a practical productivity tool that gives you an immediate response; it is designed to deliver results quickly, and you might learn something in the process. Nierenberg's program, on the other hand, is really educational software that addresses a very practical problem; it is designed to teach you something about the process of reaching a sound, well-considered, practical result. There's no reason why you couldn't benefit from both approaches. Ladies and gentlemen, cast your ballots with your checkbooks.

There's another expert system product just released called Expert Ease from Scotland. This $2000 program is an empty structure, a framework that will permit any expert to condense his or her knowledge into a sequence of multiple-choice questions for end users.

Purists do not consider any of the current microcomputer products to be true expert systems, but rather a way of merely matching up information. They believe that a real expert system not only contains special information, but it is also capable of manipulating the information, making inferences, and dealing with probabilities. However, the only work that satisfies this strict definition involves advanced artificial intelligence techniques in programmed systems that are presently far too large to fit on the current crop of personal computers. The purists would refer to the Human Edge products as "knowledge-based programs."

It isn't necessary to settle the issue here, because the fact is that "expert system" is an up-and-coming buzzword. The world is about to see a burgeoning new field for micro products, and some new superstar companies will rise on the crest of that wave. It can't be long now until we have Dr. Spock on the family micro. Or maybe Chilton's auto repair guides? Or . . .

IDEA PROCESSING: DAYFLO—THE FIRST INTELLIGENT INFORMATION SYSTEM

Several new products have emerged which combine word processing with a variety of extended capabilities intended to help with the creation and organization of ideas—thought organizers, if you will. The two smaller programs are both designed to help you assemble facts and ideas into a finished written product, but each works on a completely different metaphor or psychology of operation.

The first one out was Think Tank from Living Videotext of Palo Alto. This is an outline manipulation program that allows you to fluidly expand, contract, and shuffle an outline of ideas. You can pour detail into any point whenever an idea occurs, then you can collapse that section of the outline back down to the headers, so that you are left with a clean look at the major structure of your composition. Then there's the Idea Processor from Idea Ware of New York, a computerized cardfile system which allows you to gather, sort and shuffle information, and ultimately to assemble it into a finished report. This is good for a different kind of creative process, another way of working.

Ashton-Tate has recognized the importance of idea processing by making it the basis of their integrated product, Framework. Launched with an $8 million ad campaign, Framework competes directly with Lotus 1-2-3, Symphony, and other integrated products, but adds the power of computerized outlining to help you manage your text file, spreadsheet, graphics and data.

Now for the big news in information processing: Dayflo from Dayflo Software of Irvine, CA, may possibly be the most important new product and the most significant technological accomplishment of 1983. You could think of it as a free-form thought and information catcher, but that sounds too frivolous for what they have actually accomplished. Dayflo could be called a word processing database, but it goes so far beyond data management that it should be called something else entirely—perhaps the first intelligent information system on a micro.

One of Dayflo's biggest problems is that it defies description. Just before the public release of the product, one of the founders said, "We've got the only company in the world that is on schedule with a product that we don't know what it is." Dayflo was designed to work constantly throughout the day at any busy desk and to handle the random in and out flow of any kind or volume of information in an intuitive, free-form manner. It adapts itself to your needs and habits and allows you to work on several things at once. Dayflo is so big in concept that it might be best to let the founders of the company try to explain it.

**Robert Gilchrist (left) and Franz
Zihlmann, Dayflo Software**

Robert Gilchrist took a B.Sc. in Physics at Glasgow. By the time he was twenty-seven, he had 200 people working for him at Honeywell. When he was twenty-nine, he had charge of 3000 people all over the world. He became V.P. of European Operations for Varian Associates, and V.P. of Planning and Development for General Automation. In 1981, at the age of forty-three, he quit in order to start his own enterprise.

Bob is sort of a Scottish leprechaun, with an engaging brogue accent, and a bright twinkle in his eye that implies that he knows the pot of gold is very near. His co-founder is Franz Zihlmann, a bright man of high good humor who speaks with a pronounced Swiss accent. Throughout the long interview, Bob was literally quivering with mirth and excitement, and the two founders were constantly setting each other off. They obviously thought things were going very well down on the COMDEX floor where Dayflo was being introduced for the first time.

ROBERT GILCHRIST: I think for the last ten years I realized that I just had to do my own thing. It was total frustration at not being able to accomplish what I wanted to because I wasn't the top dog.

People viewed me as some sort of visionary, but they never really wanted to put all the muscle behind me to test anything. The only way I was ever going to accomplish anything I really wanted to do was to be the boss.

When I quit, I wanted to create something completely new, I wanted to be a recognized leader, but I had no idea what type of product. I knew it was going to take a lot of time, and I spent six months, as a matter of fact. The big breakthrough came completely unexpectedly. I was in Northern England, in a small cottage about 400 miles north of London. I used to get up every morning about four o'clock, a little bit tongue in cheek, and say, This is it! I'm going to invent the greatest product the world has ever seen! Thursday morning, August 27, 1981, it suddenly just dawned on me. I was so excited! I could hardly contain myself because I really knew that I had stumbled upon something. It just came to me.

The fundamental problem, the way I was looking at it, was, Why do I not use that personal computer more each day? Because it doesn't know enough about me. Why? Because I haven't told it. Why? Because it's too difficult to tell it. If this computer is going to get stuff about me, it's going to have to get what I want to give it, and I want to give it like that! (snaps fingers), like writing a note. I wanted to do something that would make people want to use their computers all day long.

I knew I was onto something big, one of the largest projects ever undertaken in the personal computer industry, and so I went back and started a fund raising process to get half a million dollars to get the thing going, some private funds. I knew I couldn't go to conventional venture capitalists. Nobody would understand what I was trying to do. This was a concept which is very difficult to explain. Even a year later, when we were a lot better organized, we still had trouble explaining it to venture capitalists.

The first thing was getting a director, the vice-president, to manage this whole thing for me. I decided on a man, Franz

CHAPTER FOURTEEN

Zihlmann, who had worked for me twice before. I knew he could handle a large project, a twenty-five man-year job.

When I was talking to Franz Zihlmann, trying to hire him he was being hesitant. So I told him I was going to get a book written, and I said to him, Franz, your name is going to be in this book one way or the other. Now, if you join me, it will say that Franz joined the company, was an entrepreneur, became a millionaire, and you'll be famous. But if you don't join us, I am going to put into the book that we talked to Franz Zihlmann, and the guy turned down the opportunity to become a millionaire. Now you decide what to do.

FRANZ ZIHLMANN: My answer to him was, now I know you are crazy! (Laughs.)

What was your background at that time, Franz?
All my life long, I happened to work for American companies. I started out with IBM in Zurich, Switzerland, worked there for four or five years, then joined Varian Data Machines, which had the European headquarters in Switzerland too, and they offered me the opportunity to move to the United States. That was in January of 1977. That was on a temporary basis, but I liked it so much, being over here, that I just decided to stay here for fixed. I was in Orange County right from the very beginning, with Varian, and then I switched in to General Automation, then Western Digital, then I joined Bob.

What made you decide to give up your security and join this big adventure?
Bob and I have an amazing chemistry together. I think we complement each other so well, that never there needs to be unnecessary discussion about things. Almost by osmosis, we communicate. I joined Bob in October of '81 because I knew we could work together.

How did you like his idea?

At that point, his idea was very unspecific. I quite frankly, at the beginning, didn't understand. He couldn't communicate, really, specifically what he wanted to do. I think his idea was to have something which would be useful all day long. That's where it started.

BOB: I didn't even know how to describe it, that was my problem. At that time, I might have thought of it as the beginning of brainware. I was mortified to find out someone else had trademarked that name. I could have thought of it as an idea processor, and when I saw that that word had been taken, too, I was a little bit upset.

FRANZ: Bob is a visionary, I know him as that, and sometimes it is very difficult to communicate something which is not tangible. But one thing made sense to me was what he was saying, if it's true that everybody got a desk top machine by 1990 on their desk, something must happen. There is no justification having this hardware on the desk with the current type of software. I knew there were opportunities around for a more better utilization, and I knew I could be very influential in what he wanted to do.

BOB: I want you to believe, to understand that this product would not be what it is without Franz Zihlmann. It is Franz Zihlmann who managed to translate my ideas into something. He is an incredible guy. He is very bright, totally bright. He understood right off what I was trying to do, and he was with me.

How did you sharpen up the concept?

FRANZ: This was a very long, frustrating period. At the beginning, we couldn't communicate, Bob and I. I would use a term, and he would use a term, and we would say what do you mean when you say this? Because there were no words, and no terms available for the things. We had to invent the terminologies. It took a lot of discipline, with a lot of patience. When I met Bob, he had about two pages of scribbles, and then for about two months, just Bob and I sat together, and I refined that maybe into a twenty page scribble. A little bit more

CHAPTER FOURTEEN

concrete. All day, everyday, for two months. Then I started going off and bringing in additional people, consultants, which had expertise in certain areas. Again, this is very, very difficult, because now I had to communicate to them what we wanted to do.

BOB: He went out and hired in the structure for the company, which was the project manager, the chief architect, some initial consultants. Within four months we had a team of seven people put together. That was May of 1982. We were able to attract almost anyone we wanted to this project in spite of the fact that it was so difficult to explain. We have, by any accounts, the brightest development team in this industry.

How did you choose the programmers?

First of all, they had to fit in the team. Every person came in because of a personal reference. We were out for the best. One of the guys, Bob Atkins, is well known to be a genius. He was our chief architect. And Wendy Isbell, who is just unbelievable in terms of brightness, the capacity of her mind to grasp the whole, just incredible. She became the project manager.

But I don't think we ever called them programmers. They do program, but they are systems designers, they were with us through the conceptual stage, getting the document done, everything.

When you hired them, did you cut them in for a share?

Every employee of the company is an owner. You couldn't run a business like this otherwise. I didn't want a small project, and when you think a project is going to last two or three years or longer, without revenue and things like that, you better have guys that are going to stay with you. Today, by the way, we have zero attrition. For a software company, that is unbelievable. There are forty people in the company now, and I tell you, I don't expect to see attrition.

How did you finance that first growth to seven people?
I raised $500,000. I formed an R&D partnership because those people are doing it for write-offs as well as for investment, and perhaps they're not so sophisticated. They're not like professional venture capitalists in that they don't ask as many questions. They got about 10% of the company as it then stood, plus a royalty stream with a cap on it. If it weren't for these risk-takers, companies like ours would have a hard time getting started.

So you couldn't explain even to yourselves what you were doing, but somehow you got $500,000. How on earth did you do that?
FRANZ: Yeah, it was crazy. There's a lot of things happen in this world, I think, which sometimes there is no real explanation for it. I mean, once Bob decided what he wanted to do, and I was with it, we were just stubborn, and we said it was going to work. One way or another, it's going to go. I think the other side of that coin, you have to understand that this initial money was not what we call sophisticated money. These are people who are prepared to write it off.

And you both had brilliant credentials in international computer sales and marketing.
That helped a lot. I think what I recognized in people afterwards, is they believed in the team. They saw Bob and they saw me, and they saw this total fusion together, nice complementary backgrounds and capabilities.

After defining the problem and getting the money, what were your next problems?
I would say the next hurdle was to go back into reality and make a product. I call myself an extremely lucky guy in the kind of people I've been able to get in. They were people that I knew, friends of mine. But even so, we went through a dramatic challenge then. Once we had the functional requirements definition down, we had to define

CHAPTER FOURTEEN

the user interface. We went through a lot—gosh, for another four months—to finally come up with the metaphor you now see.

When we finally got the metaphor, now we could go and do the architecture. And then the design. It had tremendous challenges in it, because we put ourselves into requirements which we barely could meet. A lot of the venture capitalists who we in the meantime wanted to invest in the second round, came in and said if you guys could do this, it would probably be doggone slow. *If* you can do it. A lot of people said you can't do it, but we did. We were able to solve all these problems.

BOB: In March of 1982, I started going out to raise the next round of money, to keep the team going. That was probably the funniest round. We were just literally thrown out of every respectable venture capital office in the business. One guy after half an hour, he said, "Let's stop, let's just stop. I have not understood a single thing you've said since you started, and even if I did, I don't think you could do it." That was probably one of the most despondent days of our life. We could not communicate what we were trying to do to people who were supposed to be in the business. We were so depressed!

FRANZ: Bob and I started finding out how the venture capitalists tick in March of 1982. It was very discouraging. First of all, most of them said we're not investing in software, we don't even understand software, it's kind of intangible and who needs it anyway? So when we went to the first three, we tried to understand what they know about software, and how they tick, and what they want to see from us, and then we could write the business plan.

Time worked for us then. Software suddenly got popular, very fast. Very, very fast. Because IBM had announced their PC, a lot of people jumped on that bandwagon, started writing software, and things suddenly became really obvious to the venture capitalists. But even so, it was a big, big challenge and very discouraging. We were just persistent. We approached it like sales, and said one out of ten is going to be interested.

As discouraged as we were from the initial experience, when we really hit the field to go and actively search for money, we didn't have to see that many. We probably saw twenty to get the money. What they did, they sent in their industry experts to analyze it. In August, it really started coming together, and we had at least ten industry analysts turning the place inside and out. We learned a lot from them. They were all nice guys, and they all came back enthusiastic. They loved the people, they loved what we were doing.

BOB: At that time I almost died, I had a heart attack. I was in the hospital for two months, not expected to live. They did a bypass operation, then my health just came back up. But think of the venture capitalist community. People that had wanted to do deals were gone. However, I'd already raised enough to keep the team going. Two or three days after I got out, I knew I was on a winner when venture capitalist people started coming to my house. I was frail and feeble, but our lead investor kept coming around.

FRANZ: That was our biggest challenge, when in August Bob had his heart attack—I was on my own then. Basically, I was trying to keep the company afloat. I came up with new prospects, and I tried to attract as much as I could. It was almost an impossible task, you know, the founder in the hospital, and they didn't even know if he would survive.

They must have been impressed that the team was functioning anyway?
I think that was what did it for them. I think they all saw the professionalism, they saw us hanging together.

BOB: They didn't just give us the money, they made conditions. I would have to bring in a president pretty fast, but I had always want-ed to bring a president into the company, you know. I don't believe that the founder should be president. Entrepreneurship is different from management. Absolutely. And I've been in management, that's where I made my name.

Well, the money came in and we've been roaring since that time. We went up to forty people, with thirty on development. I think we'll be considered the most professionally managed startup company in the industry, without any doubt. I don't think there's a top guy in management without an MBA except me.

How much capital have you raised all together, and what did you give for it?
We raised $3.5 million for 62.5% of the company. We're in the process of going for more right now.

What's it like, trying to keep all those investors happy and quiet?
FRANZ: That is one of the concerns I had, how would that feel? How you are going to run the thing? It turns out, it's not a problem. Once they invest in you, they're part of your team. At least our investors are like that. They want the best. They know we want really hard to get this thing going, we know they want it to go. And I really was positively surprised how that works out, that these people are helping you more than they hinder you.

First of all, they don't mingle much into the business. They appear on the board level, and we have our monthly board meeting, and we explain to them what we do. And sometimes we bring problems up to that level, and I say, can you help? What do you think you would do? Strategic problems: marketing, distribution. They had some contacts, and they have business expertise.

What's your marketing strategy?
BOB: I think we're doing the classical strategy which the best of the software companies have done, which is to line up some wholesalers like Softsel, and others I'm sure, and large chains, dealers, and so on. Then we'll do heavy advertising, both at the user level—you'll see

us in *Business Week* and the *Wall Street Journal*—and heavy advertising aimed at the dealers. We'll have dealer training seminars in each city, free running demos for their shops, and so forth.

When Franz and I were at COMDEX last year and saw all the exhibitors, all those new companies, we came away depressed. A year ago we were worrying—even if we're the best in the world, how'll we get anybody to find out that we're good? What you see on the floor, the big booth, the musical presentation, the professionalism, that is the result of intense worrying from last year. We've put over $100,000 into this expo.

How will you generate pull through?
FRANZ: We have talked an awful lot about that. It's not one solution to the problem, it's multiple solutions. One thing, we have is heavy advertisement in all media, but that really isn't enough. I think equally important is to spread the word through the influential community, the key industry leaders, and we have talked to some of them. They are excited about it, and they have little newsletters that go to the Fortune 500 companies, and people read about it and say, hey, that looks good. And these things come up in staff meetings, and they say, hey, Dayflo's a neat product. The grassroot development. That is a secondary strategy, which I think already works here. Until four weeks ago, we had absolute quietness, didn't talk to anybody about Dayflo. Within four weeks, everybody talks about Dayflo. No advertising, none whatsoever. We have been totally mouth closed, but we already started to get the industry gurus to spread the word. See, that's the way it goes.

Do you think Dayflo will have an effect on people who use it?
I think there's a very good comparison with the new spreadsheet technologies now, you know, the effect on the accountants. I think it will even appeal to the ego of these people. You know the term, "Information is power?" Dayflo will really turn that into practicality. It

CHAPTER FOURTEEN

makes the user a new person, because he feels good, he's always up to date, always on top of it. He looks organized, he is really on the ball, and he's more efficient, you know, he's really feeling good. I think Dayflo will allow him to do that.

What advice would you give someone who wants to get into software?

Last year I would have said it's a money problem. I'm now totally switched. It's only an idea problem. Now that I have gone through this thing here, I think that you must have something which people need, solves a problem, and has a marketplace out there. After that, you have to go and get the money you need.

If you talk about the young and bright person with no business experience, then that's a challenge. It really is. I still believe he needs business and marketing experience. One of the biggest things is going to be how you market. That noise level down here is so incredible. My god, here I got this little gadget, right? Who knows that I have that? How do I communicate that? A lot of people have noise and no gadget, that's where you get all the noise.

Maybe he should be teaming up with someone. It looks like one person can't do it. A business takes different backgrounds, and experiences, and capabilities. I would say you need to team up.

I have interviewed people who had a very good and early start, but they ended up with a bad team.

This is one of the biggest concerns I have in general about this industry. Software business is a people business like no other thing I know. It is worthless if you don't have this talent, if you lose the talent. Because you have to grow. This is not something which stays put, it's not like once you've got this piece of hardware gadget and it's going to always stay like it is. Software grows, it's something alive.

If you lose that talent . . . I could name software companies where that's happening. The initial talent is no longer there. The company

took off, and it's still growing, but, you know, it's already dying. Why? Because the people are no longer there. I feel this is going to be the challenge for companies, software companies. I cannot underline more, I am so convinced that this software business is such a people business, like nothing else.

Well, Bob, you've been described as a visionary, and your company certainly started with a grand vision, almost a megalomania. There you were, out pondering on the heath like Macbeth when the grand idea suddenly struck.

I don't think I ever had visions of grandeur. But I tell you, I wanted to change something, make a significant change to society. When I was a kid, my hero was Winston Churchill. I thought I should go into politics and really shake this place up, but I found I didn't have the talent. Right now what I would like to do is make America aware of the importance of personal computers.

I'll tell you my burning dream. I've been an international guy, and worked in so many countries it's just unbelievable, I think thirty. I know the world, and I think America does not understand at this moment what it must do to reclaim its worldwide leadership. And it's all to do with the fact that America, unlike Germany and Japan, is really not good at long-term planning and organizing. We just can't do it.

But America has one thing that no other country has got. There are a lot of people who want to be their own little entrepreneurs who can afford to buy a personal computer. I believe America should turn itself into sort of the think tank for the world. And we have got every advantage there. We use the common language of the world, we have more personal computers than anybody else, we have already shown we are the best people at writing software for personal computers. I mean, you don't see Japanese software here at COMDEX, and you won't for some time.

CHAPTER FOURTEEN

Having spent most of my time abroad, I can see this in America far better than most. We are the world's best entrepreneurs and marketers. There's no doubt about it.

Postscript

As of Spring, 1984, Dayflo employed fifty five people and they had only begun to ship their product. By the way, forty-five of the staff have IBM-PC XTs on their desks running Dayflo—they use what they sell. Dayflo had just brought in another six million dollars in new venture capital, which makes ten million dollars in total. This doubles the old industry record for investment in a new startup company that was set by Lotus just last year. Bob said they were about to miss their first payroll when the money came in with only two hours to spare.

Because of the advanced quality of the product, the heavy capital commitment, and the managerial expertise of the founders, it seems a good bet that Dayflo will be one of our next microcomputer software superstars.

Meanwhile, four employees of Lotus Development—their entire artificial intelligence department—have just split off to form Prelude Development with the intention of developing AI products of their own. In addition to some intelligent interfaces for Lotus products, the group is planning to develop "what could be called intelligent databases, wherein the user doesn't have to worry nearly so much about the structure of information." Had they seen Dayflo?

The new wave of data and information products, led this year by the giant Dayflo and the fast little ASAP FIVE, are greatly expanding the usefulness and accessiblity of the personal computer. In 1984, the computer has become more than ever a tool for all the people.

Chapter Fifteen

PRICE WARS, PRODUCT DEVELOPMENT, AND THE SHAKEOUT

The entrepreneurs in this book are a highly selected sampling of who's out there stomping around in the software industry. With few exceptions, you have heard from people and about companies that attended COMDEX or some other major trade show. All but a token few are aggressive business people hacking away at the big success, fighting for room at the top. The big winners are probably not entirely representative of the several thousand smaller companies out there who do not attend national trade shows and who do business in a smaller, quieter way.

Fred Gibbons, president of Software Publishing, was quoted as saying "well over half of the companies in this industry aren't profitable." Perhaps not according to his definition of profitable. However, most software entrepreneurs earn a good living, although only a few are getting rich. *List* magazine developed data from a thousand software firms showing that only a third of the software entrepreneurs earned over $50,000 per year, while the other two-thirds got by on $20-50,000. That may not sound lucrative to Gibbons, but tax accounting being what it is, that income undoubtedly represents much more spending power than an equivalent amount in wages. *List* reported that the typical company generates annual revenues ranging from $100,000 to one million dollars, and employs two to twenty-five employees. And what's wrong with $20-50,000 a year, especially if you are independent and happy?

However much the entrepreneurs may earn, the big question is whether there is room at the top for the hundreds or thousands of firms that are fighting for a piece of the high ground. This raises the "shakeout" issue. It is very appealing and very common to compare the software industry today with the auto industry of the early '20's. That was a time when there were a lot of different auto makers, a lot of experimenters, not many roads, and most people didn't have a car. The world knew it was on the verge of a revolution, but no one could possibly predict its size or significance. No one could tell which or how many of the multitude of companies would survive in the long haul. Industry analysts point sagely to the fact that the auto industry shook itself out so that there are now only three major auto makers left in North America. Many people in the microcomputer industry are certain that the same fate awaits the crowd of software companies that are jostling for market space.

In one way or another, nearly everyone in the industry believes in shake-out, although few mean exactly the same thing by it. Shake-out is some vague kind of economic Darwinism; people "just know" that it is the natural order of things for big companies to get bigger at the expense of smaller ones. Shake-out is also a matter of common sense, because any fool can see that not all of the 200 or so word processor publishers can grow into industry giants, nor can seventy five mass-market database systems all hit the hot list.

PRICING POLICIES

The shake-out boogeyman adds special poignancy to a related major debate—the issue of pricing and the fear of price wars. Severe competition creates a constant pressure and temptation to cut prices; it could suddenly flare up at any time to become a major factor in the shakeout process. No one ever forgets that mass-market software costs almost nothing to produce once the idea is perfected. A dollar or less for a disk, and a few dollars for manuals and a wrapper—that's the total materials cost for products that sell for hundreds of dollars. You can see why price wars are constantly anticipated, but whether with glee or dread is at the heart of a raging debate on this issue.

BYTE magazine columnist and science fiction writer Jerry Pournelle belongs to the contingent that thinks software costs too much. In his view, writing good software is fairly equivalent to writing a good novel, and he makes his living on books that sell for $4.95, or $19.95 in hardback. Others in the price cutting camp think that because software becomes obsolete after a few months or years, it would be fair to compare it to disposable products, like razor blades, or phonograph records. Even videodisks of multi-million dollar movies can be purchased outright for far less than most software. So why should we have to pay $395 or $595 for a program? The carrot at the end of this stick is the notion that publishers would sell a lot more software (and lose a lot less to piracy) if their products cost less.

The opposite point of view is well represented by Bob Lydon, the editor and publisher of *Personal Computing* magazine. Bob made a strong case for keeping prices high when he gave his keynote address to members of the software industry at the 1983 National Software Show. It went like this:

Don't Give Away The Store

"Don't be lulled into believing that we're in a constantly expanding marketplace. Sooner or later this unbridled growth will slow down. It's a complex marketplace that is very specialized and with many subtleties. In order to succeed, the software company must clearly identify its customer base, and avoid the waste in trying to reach out to all segments of the market.

"The market for your specific product is not a fraction of the total market, but a fraction of only that specific market fragment to whom your product is addressed. You must clearly define exactly who it is that might buy your software, and find out exactly what the motivations are for buying that particular package at that time. You have to identify your universe. There are a total of seven to eight million computer users in the U.S. today. But are they all realistic targets for each product? Are they all prospects for, say, a communications package? No, because only about 23% own a modem to begin with. Once you know how many potential customers there are for a specific product, you have to determine how much it will cost to get a message to a potential buyer. Say there's three million of them. Your marketing approach should begin by determining how much it will cost per hit to talk to each of those three million prospects. If you don't build in the gross margins to reach the potential market, you're committing commercial suicide.

"Price is not the sole, determining factor in the decision to purchase a product. You can reach Joe Sixpack with your message, but chances are he won't buy your product at any price. I believe that our job becomes one of realistically determining your potential customers, then figuring out the most efficient way to reach those target prospects. Most of us should be focusing on our customers more accurately. Our resources are being dissipated trying to reach a mass audience, a great part of which isn't at all interested in your software product.

"I think we're giving away the store. I believe we're charging prices below what's necessary to do an effective job of marketing and new product development. If we keep marketing by cutting prices, I believe we'll soon find ourselves in the same situation as our cousins out there selling calculators, or semi-conductors, or digital watches. Sales will climb for a while, then level off while profit margins sink below the acceptable line, or worse yet, become losses. Unfortunately, many of us are now heading down this path. Others of us, I believe wisely, are taking the profit path. They establish a realistic price for their software that allows a substantial gross margin, then they plow back a healthy percentage of that margin to stimulate sales of existing products, and to develop new products and new markets. The true consumer companies have been using this approach for

PRICE WARS AND THE SHAKEOUT

many, many years. Profitably. Right now it's an industry decision, and you're the people that can make that decision. You can either give away your gross margins, or use them to keep this industry alive, healthy, and growing.

"Proper pricing—building in enough profit to permit you to adequately market your software and your company—is as important as the product itself. If you don't protect yourself at the cash-register, the industry and ultimately the customer, will be the loser. I'll give you an example. Several years back, I bought an excellent communications software package. I paid about $85 for it, and it's one of the best, most useful software packages I've ever seen. Today, there are people with much lesser products, marketing their products at over $200, and they're outselling the software I bought by plenty. We know that it costs under $10 to produce, package, and ship a typical software product, yet I see the $200 products in computer stores everywhere, and I rarely see the one that I bought for $85. Who's the loser? The company that sold me that $85 one for sure, but how about the consumers who could have benefited from the superior features of that product. The consumers are the losers, too.

"By contrast, a company like Lotus—a lot of people in our business criticized Lotus at the beginning. I heard criticism from marketing people and software entrepreneurs that Lotus was out of their gourd for spending as much as they did at the launch for advertising and commercials. They spent their promotion up front in the tradition of Ford and Kellog. Lotus 1-2-3 is a good product, but is it the best? I'm not sure, but the last time I looked, it was clearly selling at the top of the charts. And selling at a price of around $350. The margins are there for Lotus to reinvest and develop new products, and to continue as a leader in our industry.

"For most new software products, the window is very short, and timing is all important. Like Lotus, your best bet is to enter the market full-bore, rather than trying to tiptoe in and expect to make an impact. The people who might want to buy your product probably won't hear about it if you take the tiptoe approach.

"The point I'm making is simply this: it doesn't pay to give away the store, either by low initial pricing, or by price cutting. Know what your margins have to be to successfully distribute and market your product, and then stick with them. As I've said, we're fortunate at this time to be at the crossroads in a young industry. We can take the profit path, and maintain our modules and have money to grow, or we can go the high-tech path and literally kill the industry by taking the easy way out. If we're going to become a $20 billion industry, as some have predicted, I think the choice is only too clear, and it's up to you."

— ● —

Randy Nielsen (Chapter Eleven) had originally wanted to set the price for his product at $89, but he came under a lot of pressure from retailers and distributors to bring it up to at least $129 so that distributors and retailers would have enough margin to make carrying the product worthwhile. Even $129 is a bargain compared to the price of many leading products, but not low enough to encourage people to take something home and try it on impulse the way they would a record or a book. Many entrepreneurs have said that pricing their product is one of the toughest decisions they have to make because there are no reliable guidelines. Price is not related to what it costs to produce and sell the product, so publishers have set prices by their gut reactions. Pricing is known as "the black art."

One factor that keeps the cost of software high is the need to support users of what is, after all, a complicated kind of product. In this particular regard, software is quite different from any other published product. It may be very much to the consumer's advantage to tolerate somewhat higher prices in exchange for high-quality support. Eventually, however one of the dominant companies will figure out that while a slimmer profit margin may force them to operate more efficiently, it will also make life far more difficult for competitors trying to gain a foothold in their niche. In other words, established companies may be able to keep a competitive advantage by setting prices low. For the time being, however, higher prices prevail.

CHAPTER FIFTEEN

PRODUCT DEVELOPMENT

Another ingredient in "shake-out fever" is the fact that very few software publishers have been able to develop more than one star quality product. Typically, a company rides some rocket to the top, but their subsequent products are ho-hum yawners that do well only because of the company's established market strength. MicroPro, for example, is tops in revenue right now, but although they have made a lot of money, they have never made any other kind of waves in the industry—they are neither innovators nor leaders in anything but market share. How long can they ride on WordStar?

It is becoming clear that in order to stay at the forefront of the industry, a publisher absolutely must be able to develop high-quality new products at the leading edge of the industry. This is especially important in an industry where products have a notably short lifespan. Yet only Microsoft can so far be said to have a proven program and a record for software development. Some have not yet tried, others have tried and failed. Digital Research, however, has begun to develop products outside of its narrow area of expertise, so we may see some major products from that company.

Software companies seem to be discovering that product development is an entrepreneurial kind of activity that works best in small, independent groups. Microsoft, for example, tends to use small design teams of three or four people per product. Following the same logic to a different conclusion, Ashton-Tate has devised a unique development strategy that may become popular in the industry. President and CEO David Cole tells how they do it:

"Back in 1982, we started developing sources for new products. We wanted to combine product design and development—which takes place best in a small, discrete, fairly intimate, non-chaotic environment—with the power of centralized distribution and marketing. The two environments do not mix well. For example with the Forefront operation that developed Framework, we have a 15% convertible preferred position in that company. We basically were involved in creating that company, and when you boil it down, it's one of the most exotic stock option programs in the business. We have ongoing responsibility for the operation of the company, and we have a call on the balance of their stock a couple of years hence, so we can turn it into a wholly-owned subsidiary downstream."

Forefront Corporation is only one of the various software development companies that Ashton-Tate has created or bought into. In a parallel development that may have been a chance coincidence, Lotus Development took similar steps in order to salvage relations with a group of four designers who split off to do things their own way. Lotus decided to fund at least part of the new Prelude Development company. This way, instead of just disappearing, the departing talent will be closely allied with Lotus, and both will benefit. Perhaps this will be the wave of the future for industry leaders, because so far the in-house product development efforts around the industry have not been very impressive. Buying into small, outside development groups may be the best way for star companies to develop innovative, high-quality products, and to stave off the shakeout that nearly everyone says is coming.

Sheldon G. Adelson, The Interface Group

However, one captain of the microcomputer industry bristles and snorts when he hears the chickens running around cackling, "Shakeout! Shakeout! The market is falling!" That's what it sounds like to Sheldon Adelson, who was voted one of the twenty-five most influential executives by *Computer Retail News*. He is in a position to know what he is talking about, because he is President and founder of The Interface Group that puts on the Interface Show, the Federal DP Expo, COMDEX/Fall, COMDEX/Spring, COMDEX/Europe, COMDEX/Winter, COMDEX/Japan, twenty-eight regional Computer Showcase Expos, and four *BYTE* Computer Shows. These will earn his company an anticipated $175-200 million in 1984. In addition, he has personally invested in over seventy-five microcomputer companies. He says, "They're like ice cream to me; I just see one and I want it."

Sheldon Adelson's remarks on shakeout were made at the keynote address to COMDEX/Fall '83:

"COMDEX today is more than a trade show. I think it is fair to say that it is both a reflection of the state of the industry, and at the same time, it is a catalyst for the industry's growth. Because of this, I am utterly amazed when I read reports that the computer industry is in trouble, that the shake-out is at hand. I've been reading this stuff for a long time. To all those prognosticators of doom and gloom, to all those Chicken Littles who cry, 'The shakeout is coming!' I simply say, 'Thank you, but the computer industry is alive and well at COMDEX.' Let them see that no one will miss in the remotest sense the small handful of companies often cited as representing the shakeout. Let them see that at COMDEX there are five to ten better financed and better managed companies building on the mistakes of each company that couldn't make it. Let them come to COMDEX and walk the eleven miles of aisles. Let them come to COMDEX and talk with the more than 1400 exhibitors representing every facet of the computer industry, increasing in all product categories from last year. Let them interview the industry giants and the over 400 new companies, here at COMDEX for the first time. Let them come to COMDEX and join the 80,000 computer resellers who are anxious to bring these products to market. Let them examine our plans for the 1984 Fall show with more than 7500 booth units. And if, after all that, they still want to say that a shake-out is under way, all they are really saying is, 'Don't bother me with the facts, I've already made up my mind.'

"COMDEX has become the pulse of the computer industry. You know that, that's why you're all here. The show's spectacular growth is easily understood, as it parallels the spectacular growth of the industry. It's all here. The new products, the new companies, the new hardware, the new software, the new ideas—all at COMDEX. Here's some of what I see that's new at COMDEX: exciting software integration products, micro to mini and mainframe links, personal computers becoming tomorrow's workstations, combined voice and data systems, local area networks, compatibility, portability, windowing, speech input and output systems, and scores of determined new companies in every area. What I don't see at COMDEX is a shake-out.

"But what about the bottom line, getting those products to market, to the end user? We have first-hand experience that the product you see at COMDEX does not stop here. We at the Interface Group see them go on into our end user shows. We see them at Interface, our twelfth annual show that reaches large-scale data communications and information processing buyers in the top 2000 companies. We see them at our Federal DP Expo, a ten year-old show where we target the largest of end users, the United States Federal Government. And most important of all, we see them at our Computer Showcase Expos, the more than twenty regional shows we produced in 1983 for the small computer end user market. We are so encouraged by what we see, with the vitality of this marketplace, that we are now planning thirty-five of our Showcase shows for the exploding end user market for 1985.

"If shows are any reflection of the state of the industry, then the pessimism that we hear about the health of the computer industry is truly unwarranted. That does not mean that we can sit on our successes, not by a long shot. We operate in a fiercely competitive marketplace where it's survival of the smartest, the most aggressive, the fittest. But I offer this caution: if we choose to believe the rumor that times are tough and that shakeout is upon us, then that mistaken belief will surely bring these rumors to reality. We must guard against becoming part of a self-fulfilling prophecy. If each of us faces the challenge of adjusting to the spectacular industry growth, I believe that we will prove the naysayers wrong for a long time to come."

Like other entrepreneurs, Sheldon Adelson works twelve to fourteen hours a day simply because he loves what he is doing. He has long since stopped counting his money because to him it is just another tool of being in business. He keeps at it because "it's fun and a lot of satisfaction," and he stays on top of every detail in his company because "that's how an entrepreneur gets his jollies." Adelson is convinced that there is a world of room for more companies. Although he cautions that entrepreneurs are born, not made, he offers this advice to newcomers:

"Nothing in the book says you have to invade the entire United States all at once. The most successful consumer product companies do one metro area at a time. There are forty metro markets, so just establish yourself really well in one of them, create a track record, and grow."

It was a surprise to find how frequently COMDEX cropped up in almost every entrepreneur's story. COMDEX has been a vital forum and a nurturing environment for virtually every company that has risen to prominence in the microcomputer software industry. As Adelson says, COMDEX offers new companies "an instant dealer network." All things considered, it only seemed fair that Sheldon Adelson, founder of COM-DEX, should have the last word in this book about the microcomputer software industry. And with the exception of the author—who always gets the last word in every book—that's exactly how it worked out.

Epilogue

HOW TO BE A SUCCESSFUL ENTREPRENEUR

"American is a nation of shopkeepers."

—Adam Smith, 1776

"The chief business of the American people is Business."

—Calvin Coolidge, 1925

"We are the world's best entrepreneurs and marketeers. There's no doubt about it."

—Dayflo founder
Robert Gilchrist, 1984

302

Entrepreneurial enterprise has a long history in North America. It's what we do best, and the way we do almost everything that gets done. It's like a mania; whatever happens in America is almost immediately turned into some kind of product or enterprise. If, for example, some psychologist thinks one apt thought, then right away there's a book, then a center or an institute gearing up to do business. Even our religions are run like enterprises, and we only wish our governments would run as well as a good corporation.

The best-selling book *Search for Excellence* describes how America's best-managed corporations get results by encouraging small teams in autonomous entrepreneurial efforts within the company. That's what works; that is exactly how the IBM-PC was developed. The best of what gets done in this country is accomplished—in spite of governments and economies—through entrepreneurial effort. More than apple pie, better than "the can-do spirit," the entrepreneurial ethic represents our national character.

We have a national flower, a national bird, and a national everything-else. Why not a national model entrepreneur? The entrepreneurs interviewed for this book are all uniquely different individuals, yet they have a great deal in common. Enough, at any rate, to justify some generalizations that can be combined into a composite sketch of the ideal entrepreneur.

QUALITIES OF THE SUCCESSFUL ENTREPRENEUR

Independence: At the next Fall COMDEX, someone should put on a show featuring all the software entrepreneurs in a grand chorus singing "I did it my way." Entrepreneurs tend to be gregarious extroverts, yet the sentiment of the song explains why the show will probably never go on: they couldn't all do it their own way. Fiercely independent, most successful entrepreneurs left good jobs because they had enough of doing someone else's thing someone else's way.

Self-confidence: Entrepreneurs, like entertainers, need a high degree of self-confidence. Some have a giant ego that gives them the conviction that they are right, that they know what they are doing and have something that the world needs and that is worthwhile. They might even think of themselves as being on a bit of a mission or crusade. For others, the self-confidence seems less a matter of ego and more a kind of functional naiveté: they are enamored with their idea and constructively blind to the obstacles involved. You often hear some entrepreneur say, "If I had known what I was getting into, I would never, never have started in the first place."

Dogged determination: However it is come by, the entrepreneur's self-confidence requires a thick skin because an entrepreneur cannot fold up in the face of failure, nor be deterred by being told "no!" almost endlessly. Most successful entrepreneurs have cut their teeth on some past failures, but they didn't quit; they learned. In order to succeed, an entrepreneur needs a virtually unlimited reservoir of persistence and tenacity, also known as dogged determination. As Woody Allen said, 80% of success is just showing up. Make that 95%, and add an appetite for hard work and long hours.

Motivation: Even if a person is independent, self-confident, thick-skinned, hard-working, and determined, that's still not enough to make a first class entrepreneur. The critical missing element is motivation. Like the gas for your car or the electricity for your micro, it takes lots of motivation to drive all those other entrepreneurial qualities, to make them work.

What motivates entrepreneurs? When asked, most of them say in one way or another that it's the money. That's the easy answer, the least contentious and most superficial answer, the one that everyone understands without question or argument. But I don't believe it. It is certainly a part of the truth, but only people who have never had money could possibly think of it as their primary goal, and not many of them will stay deceived. I was at a seminar attended by over 300 would-be software entrepreneurs where one speaker began by saying, "I assume that we are all here for the same reason: to make the most money in the least time for the least effort." It didn't go over. The woman next to me leaned over and whispered, "What a creep!" and nearly everyone I asked said they thought it was a crass remark and not necessarily true. It seems they all had money as a goal, but primarily as a means to some other end. Some of the biggest and most successful entrepreneurs said that they don't even care much about what percentage of their companies they own so long as they get to do what they want, their way.

Enthusiasm: I don't know of any software entrepreneur who has made a bundle and then quit in favor of fun, frolic, or anything else. They always keep at it long after making their fortunes, so it becomes quite clear that money is not what keeps them pumping. They are hooked on what they are doing; they like it. They use words like "personal satisfaction," "a personal statement," "it's creative," or more commonly, "it's fun!" They have, in other words, a great deal of enthusiasm for what they are doing, and that is the healthiest form of motivation there is.

An attraction to action: Entrepreneurs tend to prefer action to reflection. Introspection is not absent, but it isn't generally a top priority. They love playing in the big action, very much like champion surfers or downhill skiers—because it's thrilling. They like risk because it adds spice and ups the ante. Most of the new stars are entrepreneurial high rollers, and they're good because you have to be good just to get in the game.

The entrepreneur plays for the action, for the personal involvement, for the adventure. There it is: *the true entrepreneur is an adventurer*. This is a person who thrives on the process rather than the attainment of any particular goal of money or power. In fact, letting money become the primary focus is an insidious pitfall that can knock someone right off of the entrepreneurial high road. Without those loftier goals and a sense of adventure, an entrepreneur is just another merchant. In its finest expression, an entrepreneurial enterprise is imaginative, risky, and far-reaching. It is a business adventure in the truest meaning of that term.

ACHIEVING SUCCESS

We have seen over and over again that being a good entrepreneur is not enough to guarantee success in software. A capable team is usually required, by the nature of the software business, and an experienced team is always required by venture capitalists. A good software company needs an entrepreneurial team with expertise in technology, product development, production, marketing, and management—at least. The essential role of teamwork in the software industry may be a harbinger of the world to come.

The personal computer is one of the driving forces carrying us into a New Renaissance where the operative entity will be the team, not the individual. Historically, the term "Renaissance Man" was used to describe an individual with wide-ranging enthusiasms and expertise in several areas. But the individualism of the past has run rampant and run its course; it no longer serves the needs of the modern world. Just as in the software industry today, most efforts in the future world will succeed only where people get together cooperatively to work in collective enterprise. People will come together to create the New Renaissance Teams that will build our future.

Maybe.

We may be the world's best entrepreneurs, but we haven't done so well at working together harmoniously, with the result that our growth in productivity is among the lowest in the world. Our peculiar adversary system of management where everyone is out for what he can get takes the life out of work, the pride out of product, and turns jobs into sentences; and the company song goes "I can't get no (bam, bam) satis-fak-shun!" The software entrepreneurs are proud that their industry is not afflicted with these kinds of problems, yet they don't seem to realize that for most of them it is only a matter of time. A new company is just naturally full of excitement, optimism and vigor, but what will keep things humming and morale high after the thrill is gone, when there are hundreds instead of dozens on the staff? Only a few software companies seem to understand that they dare not reproduce the same kind of management environment that has led older industries into premature paralysis.

The astonishing success of the Japanese has created an intense interest in their management methods as we struggle to find out what makes our competitors so effective. There are books on the subject full of a great variety of different Japanese management techniques, and many American companies are trying out various eclectic assortments of neo-Nipponese

306

methods. Unfortunately, the problem is not one of method but substance. No method can work without an essential, underlying and often unstated factor: sincere mutual commitment.

The one thing that the Japanese have that we don't (apart from a stronger sense of national identity) is mutual commitment. From the top to the bottom, every person knows they are in it together and for life; everyone works for the good of the family, the company, the country. Any great company will recognize that people are its greatest resource and will do everything possible to sustain them, to help them grow, and to deserve their loyalty. The company is completely committed to the staff, and that is a necessary precondition to demanding commitment in return. It is always give and take, not demand and take.

Now for the final step in the success story. Being an entrepreneur is a game where you can constantly revise your definition of what it means to succeed, just as in the game of life. This is very tricky, because you can get everything you want and still come up empty. Worse, by succeeding at goals that are personally ill-fitting, you could gain a burdensome responsibility or design yourself into a job you don't like. If you get stuck in a rut, what difference does it make that it's lined with thousand dollar bills or that you made it yourself?

It turns out that success is not found in achieving any particular goal so much as in the quality of your day-to-day involvement in the process. The person who takes satisfaction from working in a small way may lead a more successful life than some smash-hit superstar with ulcers and a broken family. What does success mean, anyway? It isn't money, it isn't fame, it isn't power. Success is not getting what you want, but rather thriving on your life's adventure most of the time. You are a success if you wake up eager to go to work most mornings.

EPILOGUE

ACKNOWLEDGMENTS

I owe a great deal to Susan Hykin who rolled up her sleeves and spent many hours polishing away rough spots and to Teri Kuchenthal for her creative suggestions. These talented and busy people were especially generous with time taken from their own busy lives and spent freely in the name of friendship. Their care and support really mattered.

Thanks are due, too, to Peter Grant for his *tour de force* critique, and to Robert Dill for thoughtful suggestions. Suanne Morgan deserves special mention for having heroically transcribed mountains of interviews—perhaps ten times the quantity that eventually appeared here.

It is every author's dream to be blessed with supportive, amiable editors and my dreams came true when I met up with Jane Mellin and Bill Jordan.

Thanks, Adrienne; always.

Appendix B

Addresses of Companies

Apple Computer, Inc.
Mike Murray
20525 Mariani Ave.
Cupertino, CA 95014

ASAP Systems, Inc.
Richard Certo
2425 Porter Street #14
Soquel, CA 95073

Ashton-Tate
David Cole, President
10150 W. Jefferson Blvd.
Culver City, CA 90230

Blue Chip Software
Jon Punnett
1835 Fort St.
Victoria BC V8R 1J6
Canada

BreakThrough Software
William Lohse, President
Mark McDonough, V.P.
505 Marin Drive
Novato, CA 94947

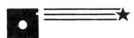

Button Computer Software
Jim Button
Box 5786
Bellevue, WA 98006

Condor Computer Corp.
Malcolm S. Cohen
2051 South State Street
Ann Arbor, MI 48104

DJR Associates, Inc.
David J. Rodman
303 South Broadway
Tarrytown, NY 10591

Data Base Research Corp.
Rusty Fraser
Charles Hager
66 South Van Gordon #155
Lakewood, CO 80228

Dayflo Software, Inc.
Robert Gilchrist
Franz X. Zihlmann
2500 Michelson Dr. Bldg. 400
Irvine, CA 92715

Digital Research, Inc.
Gary Kildall
Box 579
Pacific Grove, CA 93950

Durant Software
Randy Nielsen
1780 Franklin St.
Berkeley, CA

Dynamic Business Software, Inc.
Helen Warn
1221 Bidwell
Vancouver BC V6G 2K7
Canada

EDventure (was Rosen Research)
Esther Dyson
375 Park Avenue
New York, NY 10022

Gimcrax Inc.
Nathaniel Forbes
Box 6250
McLean, VA 22106

Headlands Press
Andrew Fluegelman
Box 862
Tiburon, CA 94920

Human Edge Software Corp.
Dr. James H. Johnson
2445 Faber Place
Palo Alto, CA 94303

InfoWorld
Stewart Alsop II
1060 Marsh Road
Menlo Park, CA 94025

Intelligent Designs
Mark McDonough
380 Broadway #212
Somerville, MA 02145

The Interface Group, Inc.
Sheldon G. Adelson
300 First Avenue
Needham, MA 02194

Lotus Development Corp.
Mitchell Kapor
161 First Street
Cambridge, MA 02142

Micro-Information
Gerald Van Diver
15420 Eagle Creek Ave.
Prior Lake, MN 55372

Microsoft Corporation
William H. Gates
10700 Northrup Road
Bellevue, WA 98004

Palantir, Inc.
Michael Griffin
3400 Montrose Blvd. #718
Houston, TX 77006

Pearlsoft
William R. Stow, III
SW Parkway
Wilsonville, OR 97070

Personal Computing
Robert J. Lydon
1625 The Alameda #600
San Jose, CA 95126

Prosoft
Chuck, Debbie & Glenn Tesler
Box 560
North Hollywood, CA 91603

RealWorld Corporation
Larry Byrnes
Larry Wilber
Dover Road
Chichester, NH 03263

Soft-Rep Services
International, Inc.
W.J. (Bill) Campbell
2317 Oak Street
Vancouver BC V6H 2J8
Canada

Softsel Computer Products, Inc
David Wagman
546 North Oak Street
Inglewood, CA 90302

Software Strategies
Gerald Van Diver
7412 Washington Ave. So.
Eden Prairie, MN 55344

Softsmith
Charles V. Ford
2935 Whipple Road
San Leandro, CA 94587

T/MAKER Company
Peter Roizen
2115 Landings Drive
Mountain View, CA 94043

Software Publishing Corp.
Fred Gibbons
1901 Landings Drive
Mountain View, CA 94043

TouchStone Software Corporation
Larry Dingus
Carolyn Shannon Jenkins
909 Electric Avenue
Seal Beach, CA 90740

SURVEY

Thank you for purchasing an Ashton-Tate book.
Our readers are important to us. Please take a few moments to provide us with some information, so we can better serve you.
Once we receive your reader card, your name will be kept on file for information regarding program disks to accompany the book.

Name: _____

Company Name: _____

Address: _____

City/State: _____ Zip: _____

Country: _____ Date: _____

1) How did you first learn about this publication?
21-1 ( ) Someone who saw or bought it
 -2 ( ) Software dealer or salesperson
 -3 ( ) Hardware dealer or salesperson
 -4 ( ) Advertising
 -5 ( ) Published review
 -6 ( ) Computer store display
 -7 ( ) Computer show
 -8 ( ) Book store
 -9 ( ) Directly from Ashton-Tate

2) Where did you purchase this publication?
22-1 ( ) Directly from Ashton-Tate™
 -2 ( ) From my dBASE II® Dealer
 -3 ( ) Computer show
 -4 ( ) Book store

3) Have you purchased other Ashton-Tate books and publications?
23-1 ( ) Yes 23-2 ( ) No
 If Yes, please check which ones:
23-3 ( ) dBASE II for the First-Time User
 -4 ( ) Data Management for Professionals
 -5 ( ) System Design Guide
 -6 ( ) dNEWS™
 -7 ( ) Through the MicroMaze
 -8 ( ) Everyman's Database Primer
 -9 ( ) Reference Encyclopedia for the IBM® Personal Computer
 -10 ( ) IBM PC Public Domain Software, Vol. I

4) What type of software programs are you using now?
24-1 ( ) Accounting
 -2 ( ) Spreadsheet
 -3 ( ) Word Processing
 -4 ( ) Other (Please specify) _____
_____

5) What type of software programs are you interested in?
25-1 ( ) Academic/Scientific
 -2 ( ) Agriculture
 -3 ( ) Building
 -4 ( ) Business
 -5 ( ) Financial
 -6 ( ) Health Care
 -7 ( ) Home/Hobby
 -8 ( ) Insurance
 -9 ( ) Membership/Registry
 -10 ( ) Professional
 -11 ( ) Real Property
 -12 ( ) Software Utilities
 -13 ( ) Spreadsheet
 -14 ( ) Integrated

6) Whom are you purchasing the book for?
27-1 ( ) Business
 -2 ( ) Self

7a) Who will be the actual reader?
28-1 ( ) I will be
 -2 ( ) Someone else will be
  Title: _____

7b) What make and model computer do you use?
28-3 _____

8) Do you expect to purchase other software programs during the next 12 months? If so, what type?
29-1 ( ) Accounting
 -2 ( ) Sales
 -3 ( ) Inventory
 -4 ( ) Other (Please specify)_____
_____

9) What subjects would you like to see discussed?
30-1 _____
_____
_____

10) How can we improve this book?
31-1 _____
_____
_____

11) What is your primary business?
  A. Computer Industry
32-1 ( ) Manufacturing
 -2 ( ) Systems house
 -3 ( ) DP supply house
 -4 ( ) Software
 -5 ( ) Retailing
 -6 ( ) Other _____
  B. Non-Computer Business
33-1 ( ) Manufacturing
 -2 ( ) Retail trade
 -3 ( ) Wholesale trade
 -4 ( ) Financial, banking
 -5 ( ) Real estate, insurance
 -6 ( ) Engineering
 -7 ( ) Government
 -8 ( ) Education

34-1 ( ) Military
 -2 ( ) Health services
 -3 ( ) Legal services
 -4 ( ) Transportation
 -5 ( ) Utilities
 -6 ( ) Communications
 -7 ( ) Arts, music, film
 -8 ( ) Other _____

12) What is your position and title? Please check one in each list
POSITION
35-1 ( ) Data processing
 -2 ( ) Engineering
 -3 ( ) Marketing/Advertising
 -4 ( ) Sales
 -5 ( ) Financial
 -6 ( ) Legal
 -7 ( ) Administration
 -8 ( ) Research
 -9 ( ) Operations/production
 -10 ( ) Distribution
 -11 ( ) Education
 -12 ( ) Other _____
TITLE
35-13 ( ) Owner
 -14 ( ) Chairperson
 -15 ( ) President
 -16 ( ) Vice President
 -17 ( ) Director
 -18 ( ) Manager
 -19 ( ) Dept. head
 -20 ( ) Independent contractor
 -21 ( ) Scientist
 -22 ( ) Programmer
 -23 ( ) Assistant
 -24 ( ) Other _____

13) How many employees are in your company?
36-1 ( ) Less than 10
 -2 ( ) 10 to 25
 -3 ( ) 26 to 100
 -4 ( ) 101 to 300
 -5 ( ) 301 to 1,000
 -6 ( ) over 1,000

14) I would like to remain on your mailing list.
37-1 ( ) Yes 37-2 ( ) No

38-1 I'd like to purchase additional copies of the current edition of this book at $16.95 plus $1.50 handling.
 ☐ My check is enclosed.
 My MasterCard/Visa card number is:

_____

Expiration date _____

Signature _____

ENTREP

BUSINESS REPLY MAIL

FIRST CLASS   PERMIT NO. 959   CULVER CITY, CA

POSTAGE WILL BE PAID BY ADDRESSEE

ASHTON·TATE ■.™

10150 WEST JEFFERSON BOULEVARD
CULVER CITY, CALIFORNIA 90230